# Classical Rome Comes Alive

# Classical Rome Comes Alive

Hildegarde Wulfing Roberts

Illustrated by
*Benita Campbell*
and
*Hildegarde Wulfing Roberts*

1992
Teacher Ideas Press
A Division of
Libraries Unlimited, Inc.
Englewood, Colorado

*meo amanti viro*

TEACHER IDEAS PRESS
A Division of
Libraries Unlimited, Inc.
P.O. Box 6633
Englewood, CO 80155-6633

---

**Library of Congress Cataloging-in-Publication Data**

Classical Rome comes alive / [edited by] Hildegarde Wulfing Roberts ;
   illustrated by Benita Campbell and Hildegarde Wulfing Roberts.
     ix, 208 p. 22x28 cm.
     Includes bibliographical references and index.
     ISBN 0-87287-915-1
     1. Rome--History--Study and teaching.     I. Roberts, Hildegarde
Wulfing.     II. Campbell, Benita and Hildegarde Wulfing Roberts.
DG206.5.C55     1992
937--dc20                                                    92-13233
                                                             CIP

# Contents

# Preface

This anthology is a collection of historical accounts translated from six Roman writers: Livy, Julius Caesar, Tacitus, Petronius, Pliny the Elder, and Pliny the Younger, and two accounts are from the Greek writer Plutarch, who lived in Rome for a short time. It can be used as a companion to any secondary level Latin or social studies class that includes reference to ancient Rome. These two disciplines are not, however, the only ones to benefit from these enjoyable tales. The Teacher Ideas section that follows each chapter presents activities and exercises suitable for language arts, history, and philosophy classes. It is not necessary for the teacher to be classically educated, because all essential information is provided. Answer keys are provided at the back of the book for all Teacher Ideas activities. A list of resources follows each chapter, and a glossary of terms can also be found in the back of the book.

Each chapter describes either a historical event in Roman history or a social aspect of ancient Roman culture. For example, chapter 8 describes Julius Caesar's defeat of the Gauls in 51 B.C. Examples of chapters that describe ancient Roman culture include chapter 12, which discusses pharmaceutical cures of the first century A.D., and chapter 16, which discusses slavery.

All chapters are preceded by an introduction that furnishes important information for the lay pupil of classical Rome. For example, the introduction to chapter 5 gives information on the wars between Rome and Carthage, which helps the student understand the political rivalry between these two powers.

The Teacher Ideas section in each chapter contains five activity categories. The first category—Discussion Questions—can be used for all disciplines. Two types of discussion questions are provided. Eight questions are meant to assess reading comprehension. The student should be able to find the answers directly in the text. Two subsequent questions require students to analyze the information and draw on their own experiences and knowledge. The second of these questions is more difficult than the first, and the teacher may choose to use one or both questions depending on the class's expertise.

The second category—History Lesson—presents a short essay on a particular aspect of Roman political history that relates to the story in the chapter. For example, in chapter 2, this section details the difference between the *patrician* and *plebeian* classes in Roman society. Also included are several suggested topics for further research that might interest the student who wishes to delve more deeply into Roman history.

The third category—Language Arts—is geared primarily to English and philosophy teachers. Vocabulary Building is designed to help students increase their understanding of words with Greek and Latin roots. Next come literature lessons, critical-thinking exercises, creative writing assignments, dramatic readings, and movie-watching suggestions.

The fourth category—Cultural Lesson—is suitable for all disciplines. A short essay either describes a modern custom inherited from the Romans or a custom enjoyed by the ancient Romans themselves. For example, this section in chapter 4 discusses how the modern calendar is really a Roman creation. Chapter 15 discusses ancient Roman bathing rituals. Activities are provided at the end of this category.

The fifth category—*Et Alia* (And Other Things)—offers fun activities for everyone. Occurring only in odd-numbered chapters, these activities include making maps, a word search, and making a timeline.

Each story is described briefly in the table of contents. Please note that it is not necessary to follow the chapters in order. However, they are listed chronologically, moving from the story of Romulus and Remus and the founding of Rome in 753 B.C. to the invasion of the Huns in A.D. 410. A schema for coordinating each story with history lessons, language arts, culture, and other information is provided in the appendix.

# I Romulus and Remus
## *(753 B.C.)*

### INTRODUCTION

Surrounded by the Mediterranean Sea, the Italian peninsula enjoys a mild climate and fertile volcanic soil, which enticed settlers from various locations. There is archaeological evidence that as early as 3000 to 2500 B.C., small agricultural communities existed in Italy, and the continued migrations of other peoples helped shape the character of this peninsula. Out of central Europe (1600 B.C.) came bronze-using settlers, and in about 1200 B.C., other Indo-Europeans (including the Latins of central Italy) migrated to Italy. Between the eighth and sixth centuries B.C., seafaring peoples came to colonize: the Phoenicians settled in Sicily, the Etruscans in northern and central Italy,[1] and the Greeks established small cities in southern Italy from Tarentum to the bay of Naples. This mixture of cultures (Greek, Latin, Etruscan) heavily influenced the character of ancient Rome.

There are no written records of these early inhabitants. Ancient Romans relied upon oral tradition and legends to learn about their ancestors. The Roman historian Titus Livius, more commonly known as Livy (59 B.C.-A.D. 17), spent 40 years writing the entire history of Rome from its beginning to the time of Tiberius (emperor A.D. 14-37). His work, entitled *Ab Urbe Condita* (meaning "From the City's Founding"), contained 142 books. Only 35 books remain, however; 107 are lost.

Livy begins his work with a general introduction that reveals his attitude toward his role as a historian. He sees himself as a moralist and hopes to inspire his readers to act like the heroes of history. His actual account begins with the premise that Italy was originally colonized by Aeneas, son of the goddess Venus, and his followers who escaped the annihilation of Troy. This legend, of course, must be considered fictitious, but it endowed the Romans with an illustrious ancestor and a glorious past. Aeneas's direct descendants, according to Livy, were the twins Romulus and Remus, fathered by the god Mars. It was they who built a new city called *Rome* (named after *Romulus*).

There is some historical truth to this tale. Livy reveals that Romulus and Remus chose the Palatine Hill as the location for their city, and archaeological evidence supports an early settlement on this spot. It was an advantageous site because the seven hills upon which the city was built were a natural fortress, and the Tiber River lay to the west, encircling an island. Whoever controlled these hills and the island dominated the trade along the river to central Italy. Romulus and Remus may be legend, but the city itself was not.

---

[1]Some scholars believe the Etruscans were native Italians. See Donald J. Crump, *Mysteries of the Ancient World* (Washington, D.C.: National Geographic, 1979).

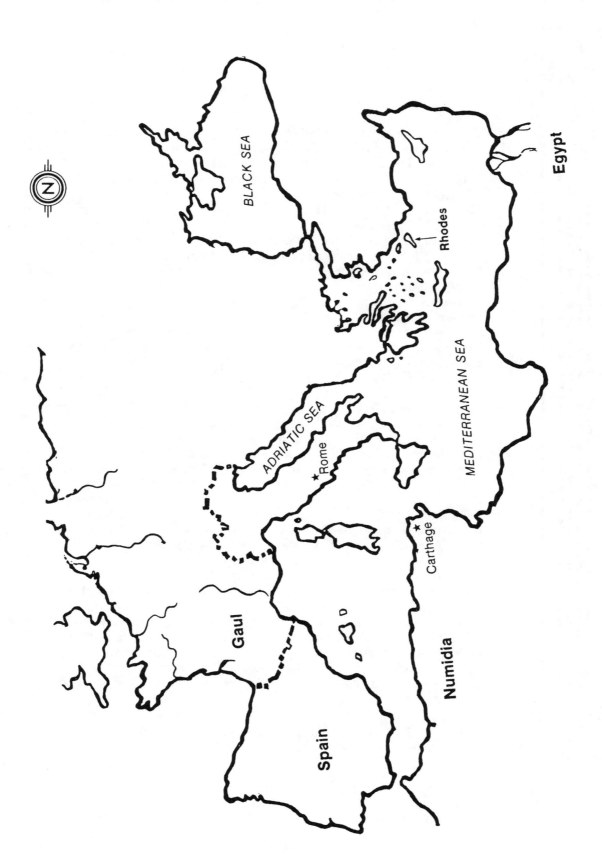

Mediterranean Area

# PREFACE TO
## *AB URBE CONDITA*

■ I am not presumptuous enough to boast that I can write a history that will be more accurate than my predecessor's works or more skilled in its presentation than theirs. It is enough just to undertake the task of retelling the deeds and events of the greatest people in the world. Should it happen that in the years to come my name is obscured and no one knows of my existence, it is of no account, since the nobility and greatness of my subject, namely the history of Rome, is more important than my own fame.

This is a monumental task to trace more than 700 years of history, starting at Rome's small beginnings and progressing to the present when our city now labors beneath its own vast size.[2] I do not doubt but that the origins of Rome are of less interest to my readers than contemporary events. They would have me hurry to the present when Rome's strength is waning. I shall consider my foray into early history to be a respite from the cares and troubles that our nation has endured for so many years.[3]

Those events that occurred before the founding of our city are more fitting for a poet's tale[4] than to be credited to the accurate records of history. I will neither affirm nor deny these events. It is permissible for antiquity to mix human deeds with divine ones and to create a more dignified beginning for a city. So great is Rome's glory in the matter of war that when Rome traces its ancestry to the very mighty Mars, all people should accept this, just as they accept Rome's dominion over them.

Whether the characters actually existed or not is beside the point. More importantly, the reader should consider the nature of the lives of these ancient personages, their strength and skills both at home and while fighting in foreign lands. It is through these attributes that the power of Rome began and expanded. Gradually our discipline waned and our morals declined, and the cycle continued until now when we are unable to see our own faults or endure the remedies that will cure our ails. This is why it is profitable to study the past, for in reading history one can see examples of what was beneficial to humankind and what should be imitated, and also witness the malevolence that should be avoided.

I hope I am not being deceived, but I believe there has never been a greater nation nor one more divinely blessed nor one more replete with goodness than ours. No other state was beset so late in its history with avarice and dissipation. For a long time the horror of poverty and frugality prevailed here, and only recently has wealth brought greed and the desire for pleasure, wantonness.

I pray that with favorable omens and vows the gods may inspire my work so that it will be well received.   —Livy

---

[2]Livy published the first book of his histories around 27-26 B.C. To see the extent of Rome's possessions at this time refer to a historical atlas (see Resources).

[3]Livy is referring to the numerous civil wars of the first century B.C., especially those between Julius Caesar and Pompey and between Antony and Octavian (Augustus).

[4]Livy probably refers to the poets Ennius and Naevius, who wrote down the legend of Romulus's ancestor Aeneas who escaped the ruins of Troy and fled to Italy.

## Romulus and Remus[5]

Proca, who was the fourteenth descendant of Trojan Aeneas, ruled Alba Longa and sired two sons, Numitor and Amulius. Though Numitor, the oldest, inherited his father's throne, Amulius usurped the power and banished his brother. Then he added crime upon crime by killing all his brother's male children to insure his position. Numitor also had one daughter, Rhea Silvia. She, however, seemed no threat to Amulius unless she should marry and produce heirs. Therefore, he forced her to accept perpetual virginity by becoming a *Vestal Virgin*—a great honor but in this case a frail disguise for Amulius's own scheme.

The Fates intervened in his plans, I suppose, because the great and powerful city of Rome was destined to arise. Rhea Silvia was raped and gave birth to twin boys, proclaiming their father to be none other than Mars, the god of war. It is uncertain whether she truly believed him to be the father or whether she thought such an illustrious sire would make her rape seem more respectable. However, neither gods nor humans could protect her and her offspring from the king's cruelty. Amulius immediately had Rhea Silvia bound in chains and thrown into prison. Then he ordered his henchmen to drown the babes in the Tiber River.

It so happened, perhaps again by divine intervention, that the Tiber had flooded its banks, leaving small channels and pools along the shore. When the men carrying the children were unable to reach the Tiber because of the flood waters, they placed the twins in a pool, assuming the river would eventually reach them, and they would drown. Instead, a gentle current floated the basket with the infants downstream and laid them on the riverbank. A she-wolf came to the river to drink and heard the wailing of the children. She was very gentle and suckled the boys with her own teats. The keeper of the royal flocks, Faustulus, found her nursing the twins and licking them with her tongue, much like a female dog and her pups.

Faustulus rescued them and brought them to his wife Larentia to raise as her own. There are some people who believe that Larentia's nickname was *Lupa* (meaning "Wolf") because she was a prostitute, and from this confusion of names the miraculous story of the she-wolf originated.

The boys, now called Romulus and Remus, eventually grew to manhood while tending the flocks of their adopted father and hunting wild beasts in the forest. They were both strong of mind and body and organized a group of young men to rid the countryside of brigands and robbers. Romulus and Remus attacked these outlaws and shared the stolen goods with their fellow shepherds.

At this time, a great festival took place on the Palatine Hill, and Romulus and Remus attended the festivities. Lying in ambush for them were the robbers, who were angry because of the booty stolen from them. They attacked the twins: Romulus escaped, but Remus was captured. They then took Remus to his grandfather, the exiled Numitor, for punishment, falsely accusing him of their own crimes.

Now, from the beginning, the shepherd Faustulus had hoped that Romulus and Remus were the actual heirs of Numitor. He knew that Amulius had ordered Rhea Silvia's twins to be drowned and that he had found the boys at about that same time. However, he had not wanted to tell them of his suspicions until it was necessary. After Remus's capture, Faustulus was afraid and revealed everything to Romulus.

Meanwhile, Numitor, who held Remus in his custody, began questioning the supposed thief. When he learned his age and that he was a twin, he became convinced the young man was his grandson. Meanwhile, Romulus led some shepherds in an attack on Amulius's palace, and in the fray, Romulus killed the usurper. Afterward, Numitor called together an advisory council and explained everything: how the twins were rescued, who

[5]Livy, *Ab Urbe Condita* I:3.

raised them, and about the death of the tyrant Amulius. Everyone saluted Numitor as the true king, and he regained his lawful position.

Romulus and Remus were not content to stay with their grandfather. Instead, they were determined to establish their own city in the same place where the she-wolf had rescued them. Because they were twins, it was impossible to say who was older, so they decided to allow the gods to choose. Whomever the gods favored would give his name to the new city and rule as king. Often the gods reveal their plans through birds, and by correct observation of the birds (*augury*), humans can discover what the higher powers desire. Romulus decided to sit on the Palatine Hill to observe the heavens, and Remus chose the Aventine.

Remus first received a sign from the gods, the appearance of 6 vultures, but then 12 vultures came into Romulus's view. Followers of both saluted each as king, one group assuming the kingship was rightfully due to Remus because he saw the birds first, others that Romulus should be king because of the larger number. An argument ensued, then fighting, and Remus was killed.

It is a more widely accepted story that Remus, in a fit of pique, jumped over the walls of the new city, mocking their short height. Romulus, angered, killed his own brother. Thus, Romulus alone ruled the new city, which was called Rome from its founder's name. ■

# TEACHER IDEAS

## Discussion Questions

1. What does Livy see as the value for studying the past?

2. What type of person does Livy consider the first century B.C. Roman to be?

3. What greatness does Livy admit that Rome possesses?

4. What did Amulius do to try to prevent Rhea Silvia from having children?

5. How did Romulus and Remus and their band of men help their community?

6. Who rescued Romulus and Remus from the kind she-wolf?

7. Why were the henchmen of Amulius unable to place the babes in the Tiber River?

8. Which brother do you think the gods actually preferred to be king? Why?

9. What does Livy mean in the preface to *Ab Urbe Condita* when he says, "we are unable to see our own faults or endure the remedies that will cure our ails"? Do you see any modern parallels to Livy's observation? Be specific.

10. Livy says that the Fates intervened in Amulius's plans "because the great and powerful city of Rome was destined to arise." The Romans truly believed that their city was unique and that the gods wanted them to civilize and rule the Mediterranean world. Do you believe in fate? Do you think your future is predetermined, or can you shape your own destiny?

## History Lesson: The Legendary Kings
### (as told by Livy)

Romulus was the first legendary king of Rome, and six others succeeded him until the establishment of the Republic. Because no records from that time existed, it was not difficult for later Romans to create an illustrious past for their city. Readers, however, should not discount all of Livy's information as inaccurate. Rome really was ruled by an elected king for many years. Chosen from the noble families and confirmed by all citizens, the king of Rome led the army in war, was the chief priest, and presided as the judge in legal disputes. He was a very important figure.

Romulus ruled for 37 years (753-716 B.C.). A king more devoted to war than peace, his death is shrouded in mystery. While reviewing the troops, he vanished during a sudden, violent storm. It was believed that the gods had carried him to heaven to join their ranks, and he was worshipped by the Romans as the god Quirinus.

His successor, Numa Pompilius (716-672 B.C.), a Sabine, felt Romulus had neglected the civil side of his duties. Numa appointed priests to oversee the various cults. He adjusted the old lunar calendar to fit the solar year and set aside religious days when no business could be enacted. Numa's zeal for religious matters did not end there; he established the Vestal Virgins, who guarded Rome's eternal flame and created the office of *pontifex maximus*—chief priest. He also built the temple of Janus. When its doors were open, they symbolized a nation at war (meaning Janus had left to help the Romans); when the doors were closed, the city was at peace. During Numa's reign the doors were closed.[6] As Livy himself says, "Each king (Romulus and Numa) in his own way, one with war, and the other with peace, increased the state."[7]

---

[6]The temple doors were only closed two other times in Rome's history: after the First Punic War and after the Battle of Actium during the time of Augustus.

[7]Livy, *Ab Urbe Condita* I:21.

Tullus Hostilius (672-640 B.C.), even more warlike than Romulus, ruled next. His biggest military challenge came from the Albans, who waged perpetual raids against Roman farmers. Although Tullus refused a diplomatic solution, he agreed to resolve the warfare through a fight between the Horatii (a set of Roman triplets) and a trio of Albans, the Curiatii. As the battle progressed, two of the Romans were killed and the three Albans were wounded. The sole remaining Horatius triplet immediately ran. The Curiatii triplets pursued, but each one's wound held him back, and the Roman was able to pick them off one at a time. Rome was thus victorious.

Tullus waged other wars successfully, and during his rule, the number of citizens doubled and Rome added the Caelian Hill to its territory. In 640 B.C., however, his tenure came to a sudden end when a thunderbolt killed him.

For the next 24 years, Rome was guided by Ancus Marcus (640-616 B.C.), the grandson of Numa. Involved in the reaffirmation of the religious aspects of the city, the Latins thought Ancus was weak, and they attacked the city. Ancus, both a civic and military leader, successfully defended against this military threat. The Janiculum Hill was annexed to Rome, and the first bridge across the Tiber was built during Ancus's reign.

After Ancus's death, one of his advisors, Lucius Tarquinius Priscus (616-578 B.C.), assumed the throne of Rome. Tarquinius, the first Etruscan monarch of Rome, brought many Etruscan customs to the city, most notably the notorious gladiator games. He and his wife, Tanaquil, raised the orphan Servius Tullius. Ancus's sons had Tarquinius murdered, but Tanaquil kept his death a secret until Servius could take over as king. Like his predecessors, Servius was also a great leader (578-534 B.C.). He waged war against the city of Veii to annex territory, started the census, divided the people into classes, and added the Quirinal and Viminal hills to Rome.

Then, in 534 B.C., the throne was seized by Tarquinius Superbus, who ruled Rome without a proper election. Servius was murdered, and Tarquinius eliminated any senators who opposed him. Though a capable general, his basic disregard for other people's rights and arrogance caused his downfall (see chapter 3). Tarquinius was the last king of Rome.

## SUGGESTED TOPICS FOR FURTHER RESEARCH

1. early Latin tribes of Italy

2. augury

3. Phoenician settlements in Sicily

4. Greek settlements of Italy

5. Mars, god of war

### Language Arts

## VOCABULARY BUILDING

Bases:

- *cide* from Latin verb *caedo*, meaning "to kill"
- *cise* from Latin verb *caedere*, meaning "to cut"

In English, the base *cide* carries two meanings:

- "killer" (e.g., *pesticide* means "a chemical used to kill pests"); and
- "the act of killing" (e.g., *suicide* means "the act of killing oneself")

1.  Match the deed (column A) with the victim (column B).

    | A | B |
    |---|---|
    | regicide | brother |
    | matricide | mother |
    | genocide | child |
    | fratricide | sister |
    | homicide | king |
    | sororicide | father |
    | patricide | group |
    | infanticide | person |

2.  Define the following words and use each in a sentence.

    excise

    incise

    incisor

3.  Fill in each blank with a word from exercise 2 above.

    a.  The skeleton's _____ looked worn down from constant chewing.

    b.  The surgeon _____ the lump and sent it to pathology for diagnostic tests.

    c.  The artist used his knife to _____ a pattern onto the heavy cardboard.

## ETIOLOGICAL MYTHS

Often, myths were created to explain the name of a place or a natural phenomenon (see chapter 13). These are called etiological myths. For instance, the city Athens was named for the Greek goddess of wisdom, Athena, who created the olive tree for the citizens of the then unnamed city. Because olives were widely used in the diet of the ancients, Athena was honored when the city was named Athens.

The story of Romulus as the founder of Rome is also an etiological story. Inhabitants of the town no longer regarded *Rome* as an Etruscan word and created a hero whose name resembled the city's own.

## ACTIVITY: Names of Modern Cities

1.  Research the naming of six of the following U.S. cities (e.g., *Philadelphia* is a Greek word meaning "brotherly love"): Pierre, Los Angeles, Denver, Bismarck, Baton Rouge, St. Louis, Memphis, Chicago.

2.  For the following classically named cities, determine the state(s) in which they are located and identify their classical reference: Romulus, Carthage, Hannibal, Juno, Cincinnati, Rome, Cicero, Seneca, Augusta, Minerva.

3.  Create and write your own myth that explains the name of the city in which you were born or now live.

## Cultural Lesson: The Guardians of the Roman House—
## Vesta and the Lares and Penates

Vesta was an ancient Italian goddess worshipped by the Latins long before Rome was an established city. She symbolized the fire found in the home, and her place of worship was the hearth. The importance of the worship of Vesta began in primitive times when the benevolent presence of a fire discouraged wild animals, warmed the family, and cooked the food. Fire was a cherished commodity, and without the aid of matches, a difficult one to produce. It became imperative to maintain a fire at all times, and each settlement kept its own communal fire from which all could borrow brands to use in their homes. When pioneers set out for new environs, they took with them a coal from their homeland's hearth. The eternal fire of Rome was said to have come from Troy with Aeneas.

To protect this fire, Numa, the king after Romulus, established the priestesses of Vesta. As Livy says, "He bestowed upon them a stipend from the government and with the purity of virginity made them respected and revered as sacred beings."[8] At first, there were only four Vestals, but this number was shortly increased to six. Young girls from respected families were chosen by lot to serve the goddess for 30 years, beginning before each girl's tenth birthday. The first 10 years of service were dedicated to learning the duties of the priesthood, the next 10 to carrying out those duties, and the final decade was spent teaching the new initiates. Their chief duty was to maintain the eternal fire, for the Romans believed that should it die out, their city would, too. They also presided over the sacrifices and prayers dedicated to the worship of Vesta. They came under the control of the chief priest of Rome, the pontifex maximus, who could punish them if they neglected the flame. Should any Vestal violate her vow of chastity, she was buried alive, and her lover immolated.

Along with the public worship of Vesta was the private devotion; Romans considered their hearths as Vesta's sacred domain. However, Vesta was not the only deity found in an ancient Roman home. Two other important deities were the Lares and Penates. The Lares were the good spirits of a family's deceased ancestors who protected its descendants by watching over the inhabitants and keeping danger out of the house. Every Roman home had a shrine (called a *lararium*) dedicated to these spirits usually in the *atrium* (see chapter 15). In very poor families, the hearth itself stood for the shrine. In the lararium were statues of the Lares, young men holding a drinking horn in one hand and a vessel in the other. Whenever household members went on a journey, they would say a special prayer to the Lares for their safety and on their return, give thanks once again. Every day the father of the house made a small offering of food or wine to these benign spirits.

Along with the Lares, other protectors (the Penates) resided in the Roman home. These spirits guarded the storeroom or food cupboard. The Penates insured that this cache always remained full so that the inhabitants of the house never went hungry. The Romans kept a dish of salt and a small plate of fruit on the hearth for the Penates, and a daily prayer of thanksgiving was offered to them.

According to legend, Aeneas brought the public Lares and Penates to Rome, where they were worshipped by everyone on certain religious holidays. The key to the prosperity of Rome rested in the strength of the Roman family, which was protected by these three good deities, Vesta, the Lares, and Penates.

### DISCUSSION QUESTIONS

1. Do any vestiges of the worship of these three deities remain today (e.g., the Olympic flame, vows of chastity)?

2. Imagine yourself as a pioneer who is starting a new community in a foreign land. What would you bring to safeguard your family? What would you bring to remind you of your homeland?

---

[8]Livy, *Ab Urbe Condita* I:20.

**Lararium**

## Et Alia: Mottoes of the 50 United States

Many state mottoes are Latin. Look up the mottoes of 10 of the following states in a *World Almanac* or other source and give the English translation for each. Why do you think each state chose its particular saying to represent it? If your state is not on the list, be sure to include it.

| | |
|---|---|
| Arizona | Mississippi |
| Arkansas | Missouri |
| Colorado | New Mexico |
| Connecticut | North Carolina |
| Idaho | Oklahoma |
| Kansas | South Carolina |
| Maine | Virginia |
| Massachusetts | West Virginia |
| Michigan | |

# RESOURCES

Asimov, Isaac. *The Roman Republic*. Boston: Houghton Mifflin, 1966.

Crump, Donald J., ed. *Mysteries of the Ancient World*. Washington, D.C.: National Geographic, 1979.

Grant, Michael. *Myths of the Greeks and Romans*. New York: New American Library, 1989.

McDonald, Alexander H. "Livy." *Encyclopaedia Britannica*, 1967 ed., vol. 14, 157-60.

*The Oxford Classical Dictionary*. Edited by N. G. Hammond and H. H. Scullard. Oxford, England: Oxford University Press, 1970.

Rose, H. J. *Handbook of Latin Literature*. New York: E. P. Dutton, 1960.
    This title describes the life of Livy.

Stewart, George. *American Place Names*. New York: Oxford University Press, 1970.

*Times Atlas of World History*, 3d ed. Maplewood, N.J.: Hammond, 1985.
    See page 89 for a map of the Augustan world.

Wolk, Allan. *The Naming of America*. Nashville, Tenn.: Thomas Nelson, 1977.

*World Almanac*. New York: Pharos Books, 1990.

# II

# The Sabine Women
## (750 B.C.)

### INTRODUCTION

Once Romulus established himself as king, he turned his attention toward creating a city superior to all others on the Italian peninsula. First, he fortified the Palatine Hill location by building walls that circumscribed an area much larger than was immediately needed to accommodate the population. Next, he dedicated the city to the gods through the performance of religious rituals and established a government of laws with an advisory senate of 100 members.

Rome was completely surrounded by other tribes all eager to occupy the seven hills. One of these neighboring tribes was the Sabines. Like the Latins, this Indo-European group had migrated to Italy during the second millennium B.C. and had settled in southern Italy, as well as the area around the Tiber River. The Latins and the Sabines spoke a similar language, and the Sabines occupied the Quirinal Hill adjacent to Romulus's Palatine community.

In the story that follows, Livy recounts the fanciful tale of the kidnapping of the Sabine women by the Roman senators who were in desperate need of brides. This abduction account contains some truth, for the Sabines actually did intermarry with the Romans around this time. After the debacle with Romulus, the Sabines continued to occupy the nearby Apennine Hills and to harass the Romans over the next two centuries. At the time of the last king of Rome (509 B.C.) one Sabine chieftain brought his clan of 4,000 under Roman jurisdiction, but even the inclusion of this large family did not dissuade other Sabine groups from raiding Roman territory. Finally in 449 B.C. the Romans won a decisive battle against their old foes. Hostilities between these two groups gradually decreased over the next century and a half until the Sabines became absorbed into Roman society.

1 PALATINE
2 AVENTINE
3 CAPITOLINE
4 QUIRINAL
5 VIMINCIL
6 ESQUILINE
7 CAELIAN
8 JANICULUM

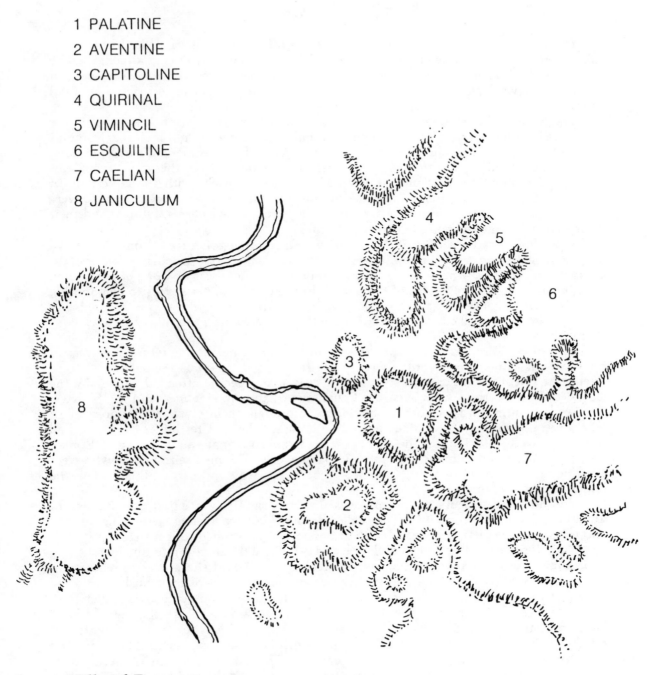

**Seven Hills of Rome**

### The Sabine Women[1]

■ Romulus, now king, began to manage the affairs of state. First, he fortified the Palatine Hill by building walls around it as a defense against any enemy attack; then he duly performed religious rites to the gods. Afterwards, he convened his advisory council to establish laws for the city, since laws are the main ingredient in securing a civilized nation.

The walls of Rome were made larger than the present population warranted in the hope that it would soon grow. But when the number of people did not increase, Romulus opened the city as an asylum for less desirable people. Free people and slaves, seeking greater opportunities and refuge from their pasts, flocked to the city. From this augmented population, Romulus selected 100 senators to help with the governing of Rome. Perhaps he chose this number because it was satisfactory or because there were only 100 men worthy of becoming senators. They were called *patres* (fathers) and their descendants became the patrician class of Rome.

The administrative affairs of the new city seemed to be going well. Rome was equal to any neighboring tribe in military strength but lacked one important element to guarantee its survival—namely women, without whom there was no hope of continuing the Roman race. On the advice of the patres, Romulus sent ambassadors to neighboring cities to seek alliances with them through intermarriage. Nowhere was his embassy received kindly, and all cities refused to allow their female citizens to marry the unsavory men of Rome.

Therefore, Romulus devised a clever plan to foil his neighbors' refusals. Games in honor of the Equestrian Neptune were made ready, and Romulus invited everyone to attend the celebration. Eager to see the new city, many people attended, especially the closest neighbors, the Caeninians, the Crustumians, the Antemnates, and the Sabines. The largest contingent was from the Sabines who brought their wives and children, all of whom were hospitably entertained in Roman homes. When the festivities began, and all spectators were intent upon the games, a prearranged signal was given, and Roman youths attacked and kidnapped the young Sabine girls. The men seized those who were exceptionally beautiful or who happened to be in the way and carried them off to the homes of the senators.

The horrified parents of the maidens fled and rightfully accused the Romans of violating the rules of hospitality. They called upon the gods to avenge these crimes of rape and injustice. The girls, too, resented their abductions and called for revenge.

Romulus personally went to each one and explained the situation to them, assuaging their anger. He assured them that with marriage they would share in the greatness of Rome, and with children, share in the respect and endearment of their husbands. They must soften their anger, he said, and give their love to those whom fortune had given their bodies. Often from injury arises regard, and Romulus assured them they would have better husbands because each one would strive to appease his wife's loss of parents and relatives. The Roman men seconded Romulus's pleadings and explained that desire and love forced them to take such drastic measures. This coaxing, which is found to be extremely effective on a woman's emotions, finally softened the maidens' objections.

However, the parents of the kidnapped girls refused to condone the situation and roused other states to wage war against the Romans. The Caeninians were the first to attack Roman territory, but they were easily routed by Romulus and his army. Then the Antemnates and the Crustumians each singly assaulted the Roman troops, but both were defeated.

---

[1]Livy, *Ab Urbe Condita* I:8.

Finally the Sabines came, by far the largest group and the most threatening, since they had a clever plan to gain entry into the Roman citadel. Spurius Tarpeius was in charge of the Roman garrison guarding the stronghold. Titus Tatius, the Sabine king, easily bribed Spurius's daughter with gold to open the gates for his troops. Once inside, they killed her so the citadel seemed to have been entered by force or perhaps to set an example that a traitor should never be trusted. There is another story commonly believed that the Sabines wore heavy gold bracelets on their left arms and large jeweled rings on their fingers. Tarpeius's daughter asked if she could have what they had on their left hands as payment for opening the doors. They complied by crushing her with their shields carried on their left sides. No matter which version one believes, the outcome was that the Sabines captured the Roman citadel and held it for several days. Finally, both armies lined up between the Palatine and Capitoline hills to begin their battle.

When the fighting began, the Sabine women whose injuries had started the war, ran directly into the flying missiles and stood facing the two hostile battle lines. They shouted that it was not right for fathers-in-law and sons-in-law to shed each other's blood. They would be killing the fathers and grandfathers of their children. They said, "Turn your anger against us. We are the cause of this war, we are the cause of the wounds to our husbands and parents. It is better for us to die than to live as widows and orphans."

The words of the women moved both armies, and a sudden hush fell over the crowd. Then the leaders walked forward and agreed to sign a treaty. Not only was peace restored, but the Romans eagerly invited the Sabines to join their city, forming one nation from two.

From this unhappy war and sudden happy peace, the Sabine women became more dear to their husbands and fathers, and especially to Romulus himself. Thus, when he divided the patricians into 30 *curiae*, he named them after the Sabine women. ■

# TEACHER IDEAS

## Discussion Questions

1. What types of people migrated to the new city founded by Romulus?

2. What three matters did Romulus attend to first while establishing his city? Do you agree with his priorities? Why or why not?

3. How many men became senators? Why this number?

4. Who was Titus Tatius, and how did he gain entrance to the Roman citadel?

5. How did the Sabine women react to their abduction?

6. What honor did Romulus bestow upon the Sabine women?

7. What did Livy say to indicate that he believed Spurius's daughter deserved her fate?

8. What ruse did the Romans devise to seduce their neighbors to visit Rome?

9. What does Livy mean when he says, "This coaxing, which is found to be extremely effective on a woman's emotions, finally softened the maidens' objections"? What does this statement reveal about Livy's opinion of women? Have these opinions changed over the past 2,000 years? If so, how?

10. Review the character of Romulus as described by Livy in chapters 1 and 2. Do you think he was justified in using deception against others to further the ends of his people? Do you find him a hero or an unprincipled man? Does his commission of fratricide diminish his worth? What qualifications do you admire in a political figure? Does Romulus possess these qualifications?

## History Lesson: The Nobles, Patricians, and Plebeians

Ancient Rome was divided into two distinct classes: the patricians and the plebeians. Both classes were Roman citizens, but each possessed different social and political privileges. Under the kings of Rome, the patricians were the wealthy land owners, and the plebeians were small farmers or clients of the aristocracy. After the expulsion of the kings, the patricians monopolized all government offices, the priestly colleges, and the senate house. They dominated the popular assembly because they controlled more votes than the plebeians, despite the latter's larger number. Essentially, the plebeians had no voice in the government of Rome.

Until 445 B.C., the plebeians could not intermarry with the patricians, and should a plebeian owe money to a patrician, he was subject to pay off his debt in the form of personal servitude. The imbalance of privileges between these two classes was so great that not long after the Republic was established, the plebeians rose up in protest. Many plebeians who had fought in Rome's army and were forced to neglect their own farms found themselves indebted to the aristocratic patricians. Unwilling to concede to involuntary servitude, the plebeians marched out of Rome and threatened to form their own city. Since they comprised the bulk of the Roman army, the patricians quickly conceded to their demands. The plebeians were given representatives to protect their interests. Called the *Tribunes of the Plebs*,[2] these officials could not initiate law but had the power of *veto* (meaning "I forbid") over all other magistrates' acts.

---

[2]There were only two tribunes when this office was first established, but eventually there were ten such positions.

This class struggle continued on a peaceful basis for 200 years. In 367 B.C., the first plebeian was elected *consul*, and finally, all offices were open to the plebeians. A new group of wealthy magistrates, both patricians and plebeians, became known as the *nobles*.

From the old traditions of the patrician aristocracy, the nobles inherited a rigid standard of conduct especially in the realm of professional activities. For example, it was considered improper for the upper class nobles to engage in any work (e.g., trade or banking) for pecuniary gain. These entrepreneurial pursuits were left to the middle-class knights. However, the nobles could own vineyards and land to produce crops such as grain and olives. As Rome expanded its territory, these aristocrats acquired large estates in both Italy and abroad to sustain their financial needs.

Another appropriate vocation for a noble was that of a politician. Since no salary was given to any magistrate and the cost of election campaigning was expensive, it was difficult for anyone without a private income to hold office. This often led to corrupt administrators who were forced to accept bribes or skim from the government coffers to refill their own purses.

The legal profession was also open to the nobles. Attorneys could not receive fees from clients, although valuable gifts were not refused.

Many nobles began their political careers with a stint in the army. As a military officer, nobles could share in the profits made from the spoils of war or the sale of slaves.

The aristocratic nobles (comprised of the patricians and plebeians from the days of the kings) were the most powerful group in Rome. They dominated all political offices, served as generals in Rome's great army, and owned large estates. They were the shapers of the Republic and the Empire who led Rome throughout its 1,000-year history.

## SUGGESTED TOPICS FOR FURTHER RESEARCH

1. *comitia tributa*

2. Hortensian Law (287 B.C.)

3. *comitia curiata*

4. the Sabines

5. clients and their relationship to patricians

### Language Arts

## VOCABULARY BUILDING

The following are English words derived from Greek and Roman mythological characters.

*Herculean:* (from Hercules) Tremendously difficult or demanding (i.e., a Herculean task). King Eurystheus forced Hercules to complete 12 seemingly impossible tasks. By his shrewdness and prowess Hercules performed them all. For example, in his second labor, Hercules needed to kill the nine-headed monster Hydra. Whenever he chopped off one head, two grew in its place. He succeeded by burning the neck with a brand as soon as he lopped off a head, thereby preventing the growth of any new heads.

*Sisyphean:* (from Sisyphus) Endless and to no avail (i.e., a Sisyphean task). Sisyphus, king of Corinth, angered Zeus, the king of the gods, by revealing the deity's secret. He was punished by being made to spend eternity in Hades with a relentless task: he must forever roll a rock uphill only to have it immediately roll downhill upon reaching the top and then roll it back uphill, repeating the process over and over again.

*Mercurial:* (from Mercury) Being quick and changeable in character (i.e., a mercurial temperament). Mercury was the messenger of the Roman gods and goddesses. On his feet were winged sandals and his cap also had wings to help speed him on his way. He carried a magic wand, the caduceus. He was shrewd, cunning, and a master thief. He was also the god of commerce and journeys.

*Procrustean:* (from Procrustes) Designed to produce uniformity at any cost (i.e., procrustean laws). The Greek hero Theseus met and slew the giant Procrustes who abducted travelers. It was Procrustes's habit to fit his victims to an iron bed. If they were too long, he lopped off their limbs; if too short, he stretched them.

*Protean:* (from Proteus) Changeable or versatile (i.e., a protean actor). Proteus, son of Poseidon, was the shepherd of the sea. Seals, whales, and other marine creatures made up his flock. He knew everything about the past, present, and future, but would not voluntarily reveal his knowledge. Whoever wished to gain his knowledge had to capture him while he was sleeping, bind him tightly, and hold fast while Proteus changed his shape into any creature he imagined. Eventually, he would return to his normal form and answer his captor's questions.

*Tantalize:* (from Tantalus) To tease or torment (i.e., to tantalize your victims). The mortal Tantalus was loved by the gods, especially by his father Zeus, whom he often invited to visit his palace. One day Tantalus murdered his only son and served him in a meal to his honored guest. Zeus refused to partake and punished Tantalus by confining him to Hades forever where he stands in a pool surrounded by fruit trees overhead. Each time he reaches for the food, the wind blows the branches out of reach, and should he attempt to partake of the water, it drains into the ground. He is eternally thirsty and hungry.

## WORD USE AND RECOGNITION

1. In groups of two to three, use each of the previous words in a sentence.

2. Locate an instance (in newspapers or magazines) of the use of these words or a picture of one of these mythological characters and bring them to class.

## CREATIVE WRITING

Do you think the Sabine women, who were innocent victims, really believed that they were the cause of the hostility between their tribe and the Romans or were they resigned to their fate and simply wanted the killing to stop? From the point of view of a captured Sabine woman, write a letter to her father explaining why her desire for peace had consumed her earlier wish for vengeance.

## MOVIE WATCHING

The movie *Seven Brides for Seven Brothers* is loosely based on the story of the Sabine women. View it and describe its storyline similarities to Livy's account.

## Cultural Lesson: Development of Romance Languages

Latin is not really a "dead" language because more than half a billion people in the world today speak languages derived from Latin. These languages, known as Romance languages from the phrase *romanice loqui* (meaning "to speak in a Roman manner"), constitute the second largest group (after the Germanic group) of languages today. They are: Italian, Spanish, Portuguese, French, and Romanian, as well as the regional dialects of Sardinian (island of Sardinia), Provencal (France), and Catalan (northeast Spain).

These Romance tongues developed from *vulgar*, or spoken, Latin. It is important to realize that oral Latin was stylistically different from classically written Latin as found in the works of Caesar or Livy. The ancient Roman considered it proper to write in an ornate, conservative style, reminiscent of old Latin. For instance, the numerous proper forms of nouns and verbs were discarded in everyday speech because they were too complicated to remember or too awkward for speech. But when actually writing for publication, the more sedate and structured manner was followed.

This distinction between oral and written language is no longer as prevalent in today's world. Modern technology, television, and the wide distribution of newspapers and magazines have narrowed the gap between spoken and written languages. Such was not the case in the days of Cicero who himself said that the style of oratory and the written word was called *sermo urbanus* (city speech) and everyday conversation was called *sermo rusticus* (rustic speech). Classical students can study vulgar Latin from the graffiti left on the walls of Pompeii and Herculaneum (see chapter 13) or the inscriptions etched on Roman tombstones. The first century A.D. author Petronius (see chapter 17), the first novelist, broke from the traditional mores of writing and included common speech in his stories. This less complicated Latin, simpler in grammar and more colorful in vocabulary, became the predecessor of the Romance languages. Large-scale writing of vulgar Latin appeared in the fourth century A.D., when Latin became the official language of the Roman Catholic Church.[3]

As Rome's power spread throughout the Mediterranean world so did Latin, and as long as Rome held control, Latin was the official language. With the invasion of the barbarians (fifth century A.D.) and the collapse of the Roman Empire in the West, no centralized speech remained. Instead, as these communities became more isolated, distinct language patterns emerged. The Emperor Charlemagne, king of the Franks (A.D. 768-814), tried to restore classical Latin to his domain, but there were not enough educated people to speak it. In A.D. 813, he issued a decree stating that the clergy should use *lingua romana rustica* (rustic Roman languages) that the congregation could understand the rituals of the church.

The first distinct written French appeared in A.D. 842, the first Spanish in A.D. 950, and the first Italian in A.D. 960, though these languages had undoubtedly been spoken for some time. The Romance languages resemble their mother tongue and each other. Their speech is musical because of the greater emphasis placed on vowels as opposed to hard-sounding consonants. Their verb forms are similar to Latin, and there is a great resemblance in vocabulary. For example, consider the following terms for the number 1,000:

| Latin | French | Italian | Portuguese | Spanish | Romanian |
|-------|--------|---------|------------|---------|----------|
| mille | mille | mille | mil | mil | mie |

Latin has definitely changed over the past 2,000 years; its descendants, the Romance languages, are alive, and today they are spoken all over the world. French is spoken in Belgium, France, the Canadian provinces of Quebec and Ontario, western Switzerland, and Haiti; Spanish is spoken in Spain, Mexico, Cuba, Puerto Rico, the Dominican Republic, Central America, South America (except Brazil), and parts of the United States; Portuguese is spoken in Portugal, Brazil, Mozambique, and Angola; Italian is spoken in Italy; and Romanian is spoken in Romania.

---

[3]St. Jerome (A.D. ca.382) revised the early Latin version of the Bible, called the *Vulgate*.

## ROMANCE LANGUAGE COGNATES

Fill in and complete the chart (see figure 2.1) with the use of foreign language dictionaries.

| English | Latin | Spanish | French | Italian |
|---|---|---|---|---|
| one | unus | | | uno |
| five | quinque | cinco | | |
| ten | decem | | | |
| good | bonus | bueno | | |
| father | pater | | | padre |
| difficult | difficilis | | difficile | |
| rose | rosa | rosa | | |
| love | amor | | | amore |
| better | melius | | meilluer | |
| fruit | fructus | | fruit | |

Fig. 2.1. Romance language cognates.

# RESOURCES

Elcock, W. D. *The Romance Languages*. London: Faber & Faber, 1960.

Grant, Michael. *History of Rome*. New York: Charles Scribner's Sons, 1978.

———. *Myths of the Greeks and Romans*. New York: New American Library, 1989.

Hirchelheim, F. M., and Cedric Yeo. *History of the Roman People*. Englewood Cliffs, N.J.: Prentice Hall, 1962.

Posner, Rebecca. "Languages of the World." *Encyclopaedia Britannica*, 1988 ed., vol. 22, 638 ff.

*Seven Brides for Seven Brothers*. Metro Goldwyn Mayer/United Artists, 1957. Film/video.

# III

# The Rape of Lucretia
## *(509 B.C.)*

## INTRODUCTION

Prior to the dominance of Rome, one group of people ruled northern Italy—the Etruscans. A powerful and wealthy alliance of 12 cities, Etruscan society was highly civilized. By the sixth century B.C., these people ruled the territory stretching from west of the Tiber to the Alps and as far south as Naples. This area was called Etruria. The Etruscans were merchants who traded with the cities of mainland Greece and northern Africa. Archaeological evidence demonstrates that they were great builders, skilled in mining, medicine, and astronomy.

At the time of Rome's inception (753 B.C.), the Etrurian cities controlled the Po Valley situated in what is now northern Italy. Legend states that Tarquinius Priscus migrated from the Etruscan town of Tarquinii to Rome and became the fifth king after Romulus. He transformed Rome from a small agricultural community into a prosperous city. Tarquinius defeated the Latins, erected a vast sewer system (still in existence today), laid out the Forum and Circus Maximus, and built a temple on the Capitoline Hill. He was murdered after a productive 38-year reign, according to Livy's account.

Servius Tullius was duly elected king by the senate, but he was murdered by Lucius Tarquinius Superbus (Tarquin the Proud), his son-in-law and son of Tarquinius Picus, who seized power. Historians accept this traditional story as essentially valid due to evidence that the last king of Rome was an Etruscan tyrant who usurped the throne by military force. While Tarquin the Proud ruled, according to Livy, he abolished all plebeian rights and murdered any patrician with whom he disagreed or whose wealth he coveted. Tarquin's eventual downfall resulted from his son Sextus's heinous rape of the innocent Lucretia. Banished from Rome, Tarquin made several unsuccessful attempts to regain the throne and died an old man bereft of all his family whom he lost to the perils of war.

Tarquin's expulsion from Rome did not, however, destroy Etruscan influence elsewhere. Etruria was still the most powerful presence in northern Italy, and in 476 B.C., the Etruscan city of Veii captured the Janiculum Hill on the west bank of the Tiber. It was not until

**Fasces**

21

265 B.C. that Etruria fell to Rome, but the latter's debt to this once great culture was far-reaching. The ceremonial trappings of office (i.e., the *fasces* and *lictors*), the gladiator troops, chariot races, the art of augury, and the engineering feats of the aqueducts all began with the Etruscans.

This next chapter tells about the last few years of Tarquinius's rule and his expulsion by the Roman nobles who established an aristocratic republican government that lasted until 28 B.C. when Augustus became the first emperor of Rome.

### The Rape of Lucretia[1]

■ Tarquin the Proud, the Etruscan tyrant, now ruled Rome. One day in his royal palace, a huge snake slithered out from behind a wooden pillar and frightened the noble household. The king himself was not overly concerned with the reptile's appearance, thinking it might be an omen sent by the gods. He decided to send a delegation to Greece to seek an explanation of this portent from the most famous oracle at Delphi. Since Tarquin did not trust just anyone to carry back the oracle's interpretation, he chose two of his sons, Titus and Arruns, to travel over the unknown lands and uncharted seas to Greece. The boys were accompanied by Lucius Junius Brutus, their cousin and son of Tarquinia, the king's sister.

Brutus purposely feigned an idiotic posture and allowed his comrades to nickname him Brutus, which means "stupid one." Actually, he kept concealed a strong hatred for his uncle whom he knew had killed his brother and confiscated his property for personal gain. Beneath this disguise of slow-wittedness lay the liberator of the Roman people. The princes took him to Delphi more as an object of ridicule rather than as a true friend.

After the oracle had deciphered the mystery of the snake's appearance, Titus and Arruns decided to ask which one of them would eventually rule Rome. From the deep cave echoed this response to their inquiry: "He will hold the greatest power in Rome whichever one of you is the first to kiss his mother." The brothers vowed to keep the oracle's utterings a secret from their other brother Sextus who remained in Rome and promised to toss a coin to see which one of them would first kiss their mother when he returned home.

Brutus, however, interpreted the oracle's words in another way. Pretending to trip, he fell to the ground and kissed the earth, realizing that Mother Earth was the mother of all living beings. Then the three returned home where the Romans were preparing to make war upon a neighboring tribe, the Rutulians. Tarquin wished to conquer the wealthy city of Ardea to enrich his own private coffers. Extensive building of public works had impoverished the king's resources and antagonized his overtaxed subjects. Tarquin hoped to lessen the Romans' hostility toward himself and regain his popularity by looting the treasure of the Rutulians.

The war was not immediately successful in open battle so the Roman troops began a long siege upon Ardea. As often happens in an assault of this type, there were frequent idle moments for the officers, and the three sons of Tarquin spent their leisure time drinking and eating. One evening, they were all imbibing in Sextus Tarquinius's quarters and boasting about their wives' pulchritude and virtue. Bolstered by the wine, they argued heatedly for a long time. Collatinus, one of the revelers, vowed that talk was unnecessary since his wife Lucretia far excelled all other women. Then he proposed an interesting contest. Collatinus proclaimed: "Let us all mount our horses immediately and surprise our wives this evening. We will see what they are doing in our absence and settle this argument once and for all."

They all agreed to Collatinus's plan, drank more wine to fortify their spirits, and flew to Rome on swift steeds. The Tarquin princes discovered their wives enjoying a luxurious banquet, wasting their time in idle chit-chat and base frivolity. Then they proceeded to Collatinus's home where they found Lucretia surrounded only by her maid servants weaving quietly at her loom.

Everyone agreed Lucretia had won the contest for the most virtuous woman. She received them all hospitably into her home and graciously served food to her guests. Lucretia's chastity and beauty aroused Sextus Tarquinius's lust. He vowed to possess her even by force. The men returned to camp. A few nights later, Sextus secretly left camp and hurried to Collatinus's house. Because he was a friend of her husband, Lucretia

---

[1]Livy, *Ab Urbe Condita* I:56.

offered him dinner and afterward showed her guest a sleeping chamber. She retired for the night while Sextus eagerly waited until the household was quiet and all seemed safe.

Carrying his sword, he entered Lucretia's room where he found her asleep. With his left hand he grabbed her breast and said, "Hush, Lucretia, I am Sextus Tarquinius. My sword is in my right hand, and if you cry out, you will die." Then he confessed his love for her and begged her to succumb to his desires, mixing threats with prayers of entreaty. Lucretia saw no means of escape, but she refused to consent to his demands. Desperate, he threatened her with death, but also to no avail; Lucretia remained steadfast. Finally, Sextus said he would disgrace her in her husband's memory. After killing her, he said he would murder a male slave and place his naked body in her bed so people would say she had died in adultery. At this Lucretia relented, and after Sextus had raped her, he left, feeling arrogant in the knowledge that he had assaulted this woman's honor.

Lucretia promptly sent a message to her father in Rome and her husband in Ardea. She urged them to come quickly along with a faithful companion since a great evil had occurred to her. Spurius Lucretius came with Publius Valerius and Lucius Junius Brutus accompanied Collatinus on this tragic journey. They found a despondent Lucretia sitting on her bed. At the arrival of her family, Lucretia burst into tears, and when Collatinus asked what was wrong, she confessed Tarquinius's rape. She said that her virtue, a woman's greatest possession, had been stolen from her. To Collatinus she exclaimed that traces of a strange man were in his bed; she affirmed that only her body had been touched and that her heart was still innocent. She asked that they all pledge revenge upon the adulterer, Sextus Tarquinius, who returned hospitality with brute force.

They all promised to punish the perpetrator of this heinous crime and then tried to comfort Lucretia with words saying she was forced and not at fault. It is only the mind that can do wrong, not the body, and she was blameless of any intention or design.

She responded to their tender ministrations by saying, "You must see that Sextus Tarquinius is given his due. I, though innocent of wrongdoing, cannot be free from punishment." Then she took a knife concealed beneath her dress, pressed it to her breast, and fell upon the blade taking her own life.

While Lucretia's father and husband wept, Brutus removed the knife from her wound and holding it aloft, still dripping with her warm blood, shouted, "I swear by this most chaste blood and the gods above that I will pursue Lucius Tarquinius Superbus and all his offspring with sword, fire, and all the power I possess. Nor will I allow them nor any others to rule over Rome." Then Brutus handed the knife to Collatinus and all were amazed by the transformation of Brutus. They swore to follow his command and to help to remove the kings from Rome.

The family carried Lucretia's body from the house and laid it in the Forum. People gathered around, and when they learned of Sextus Tarquinius's perfidy, they complained of personal injustices they had suffered at the hands of this despotic family. The telling of these crimes inflamed the crowd; the people chose Brutus as their leader for their revolt. This bold band of youths seized their weapons and marched to Rome (509 B.C.) to free Rome forever from the rule of the kings. ∎

# TEACHER IDEAS

## Discussion Questions

1. Why did Tarquin the Proud lay siege to Ardea?

2. What contest did Collatinus propose to his comrades?

3. Why did the Tarquin brothers want Brutus to accompany them to Greece?

4. What threat finally convinced Lucretia to succumb to Sextus's demands?

5. What is Brutus's relationship to Tarquinius Superbus?

6. Who is the mother of all humankind?

7. What was Lucretia doing when her husband and friends surprised her?

8. Why did the Tarquin brothers venture to Greece?

9. Describe Sextus's personality using specific examples. What do you think motivates him to rape Lucretia?

10. Was Lucretia's reaction extreme? Why did she believe herself innocent, yet somehow deserving of punishment? Do you think the credo "death before dishonor" is appropriate for modern humans? Did Livy believe it was appropriate? Why or why not?

## History Lesson: Magistracies of the Republic

Rome had been ruled by a monarchy for almost 250 years when Brutus led the people against Tarquinius Superbus. With the elimination of the kings, a republican government was established that guided Rome through its many conquests. At first, there was little distinction between the monarchy and the Republic. The patricians continued to dominate Roman society and oppressed the plebeians under both political structures.

The supreme authority of the kings was transferred to the consuls,[2] two men who were elected yearly and shared all duties. They were the commanders of the army, the judges, high priests, and administrators of the city. In military matters, they shared the power of command on a day-to-day basis if they were both in the field in the same location.

In the affairs of the city, the consuls divided the business on a monthly basis. Rome was never without two consuls, for if one died, another was elected immediately. This joint tenure and short one-year term ensured that one consul would not gain too much power. As time went on, the consuls' authority became subordinate to the senate, but the office existed until the early sixth century A.D.

The election of the consuls rested with the *comitia centuriata*, an assembly of all Roman citizens based on military participation. This was not a true democratic body in the sense of "one man one vote" because the patricians had more voting power than members who owned less property. The comitia centuriata was called into session by the senate, which could greatly influence its vote. The comitia centuriata elected all higher magistrates (consuls, *censors*, and *praetors*), was the court for capital crimes, made declarations of war, and passed laws. The last two duties,

---

[2] The first two consuls were Brutus and Collatinus.

however, required approval of the senate, which lessened the comitia's authority. As Rome became more involved in wars to acquire territory, the participation of the plebeians in military matters became crucial, and the patricians lost some of their control over this assembly.

The other popular assembly was the *comitia tributa*, an assembly of all Roman citizens based on tribal association. It was dominated by the plebeians whose number far exceeded that of the patricians. The duties of this assembly were to elect the lower magistrates, the tribunes and *aediles* (municipal officials), and the religious officers, the *pontifex maximus* and *augurs* (priests who practiced augury). It also served as the court for all lawsuits brought by the tribunes and aediles and passed resolutions of these magistrates. In 286 B.C., laws passed by this body became binding on everyone without the senate's approval.

As life in Rome changed so did the personality of the comitia tributa. Once revered as the representative of the people, it became corrupt and an easy pawn in a politician's manipulative hand. Although it met until the third century A.D., it became politically passive and really only rubber-stamped the emperor's decrees, initiating no business of its own.

The senate, which tradition said was established by Romulus, was originally an assembly of the clans' chiefs who served as advisors to the kings. The number of senators corresponded to the number of clans, and Tarquinius Superbus fixed that number at 300. When a king died, the senate took control until a new one was appointed.

During the Republic, the senate continued as an advisory body, convened by any magistrate who wanted its expertise on a domestic or foreign matter. Although theoretically only an advisory body, its permanence as an institution ultimately led to its assumption of power. It directed all foreign affairs and provincial governments, fixed taxes, and distributed funds for public works. The *standard* (flag) of the Roman army *senatus populusque romanus* (the senate and people of Rome) acclaimed its revered place in Roman history.

**Standard**

## SUGGESTED TOPICS FOR FURTHER RESEARCH

1.  comitia centuriata and comitia tributa

2.  censors

3.  class of knights

4.  pontifex maximus

5.  use of dictatorship during times of crisis

### Language Arts

## VOCABULARY BUILDING

Bases:

*ac(u)*, *acr* from Latin adjective *acer*, meaning "sharp, keen"

1.  Define the following words and use each in a sentence:

    acupuncture  acute

    acrid    acumen

    acrimony

2.  Which of the previous words are nouns? Which are adjectives?

3.  Fill in the blanks with the words from exercise 1 above.

    a.  I suffered an _____ attack of appendicitis and had to be rushed to the hospital.

    b.  His answer was so filled with _____ that I was somewhat taken aback.

    c.  His _____ remarks hurt my feelings.

    d.  _____ is a Chinese method for relieving pain.

    e.  His business _____ allowed him to achieve financial success.

## CREATIVE WRITING

Write a letter from Lucretia to her husband Collatinus explaining her despair or write a letter from Collatinus to Lucretia that urges her to persevere in her tragedy.

### Cultural Lesson: Oracles

The ancients believed that the will of the gods was revealed to mortals through oracles and other vehicles. Dead spirits were thought to understand the mind of the immortals, and people visited places considered to be the entrances to Hades in the hopes that the dead would appear and answer their questions. The sacred spring in Bath, England was one such place.

Dreams were also considered revelations sent by the divinities. In ancient Greece, sick people slept in the temple of Asclepius, the healer god. Priests would then interpret their dreams, which would help the invalids find a cure.

More common were oracles revealed by signs. The most famous oracle of this type was located at Dodona, in the Epirus region of Greece, where a temple dedicated to Zeus stood near a large oak tree. When the leaves of this tree moved, the priests of the sanctuary interpreted the rustling signs, which were supposed to give answers. Pilgrims came to hear Zeus's messages. They would reveal their problems to priests who listened to the rustling signs of the leaves, which answered the inquirer's questions.

The most prominent oracles were revealed by verbal utterings and the most famous was the oracle of Apollo at Delphi in Greece. This is where the Tarquin brothers journeyed at the bequest of their father. Apollo was the god of light and truth who sees and knows all things. Apollo's priestess, the Pythia, sat in the inner room of the Delphic temple on a gilded tripod. Cold vapor would rise from a rift in the earth and drive her into a state of frenzy. Her unintelligible words were then recorded by an assistant who wrote them in verse and presented them to the inquirer. These verses were written in an unclear way so that they could be interpreted many ways.

During the Persian invasion of Greece, the Athenians asked the oracle at Delphi to help their city. The oracle spoke: "Trust your citadel of wood," and the Athenians fortified the Acropolis with wooden scaffolding. The commander, Themistocles, however, realized the true meaning of the prophetic utterance. The "wood" was the Athenian fleet, and so the Athenians took to their ships and engaged and defeated the Persians at the Battle of Salamis.

In the story of the sons of Tarquin, Brutus realized that Mother Earth was the mother of all humankind. By responding with ambiguous verses, the oracle maintained its reputation for being accurate.

Anyone could consult the oracle. In early times, the Pythia was available only one day a year, but as her reputation grew, she was there more often.

The Romans were generally skeptical about oracles and their ability to interpret divine will. In Italy near Cumae, there was a Greek settlement where a priestess of Apollo, known as the Cumaean Sibyl resided. During the days of Tarquin the Proud, she came to the king and offered to sell him nine books that contained rituals and rites to appease the gods. When Tarquin refused to buy them, she burned three. She offered him the remaining six, but he refused again, and she burned three more. Finally, the king's curiosity was aroused, and he looked at the books. Realizing their worth, he bought the remaining three for the price of the original nine. Tarquin housed the Sibylline books in the temple of Jupiter on the Capitoline Hill. In 83 B.C., they were lost in a fire. The Roman senate then sent envoys to various places to make a new collection. These were kept in a new temple until 12 B.C. when Augustus transferred them to the temple of Apollo on the Palatine where they remained until A.D. 410 when marauding barbarians destroyed them. Only the Roman senate could consult these books. They were used not to predict the future, but rather resorted to in times of great disaster to learn what must be done to expiate the gods' anger.

## THE ORACLE'S ANSWER

Write an oracle's reply to the Tarquin boys' initial question concerning the importance of the snake. What might the oracle have said? What would the priest record? Remember, the replies were generally in poetic form, so write your reply in verse.

## Et Alia: Geography

1. Using a map of the Mediterranean, trace the Tarquin brothers' route from Rome to Delphi. Remember, Livy says they went by land *and* sea.

2. How far a trip would it be by sea? How far by land? (Use an atlas.)

3. How can you travel to Delphi today? How long would it take you from your town to Delphi? How many different means of transportation would you use? Compare your answers with those of your classmates. Who got there faster? Who took a shorter route in terms of mileage?

# RESOURCES

Asimov, Isaac. *The Roman Republic*. Boston: Houghton Mifflin, 1966.

Cornell, Tim, and John Matthews. *Atlas of the Roman World*. New York: Facts on File, 1982.

Grant, Michael. *History of Rome*. New York: Charles Scribner's Sons, 1978.

Talbert, Richard, ed., *Atlas of Classical History*. New York: Macmillan, 1985.

Trever, Albert. *History of Ancient Civilization*, vol. 2. New York: Harcourt, Brace, and World, 1939.

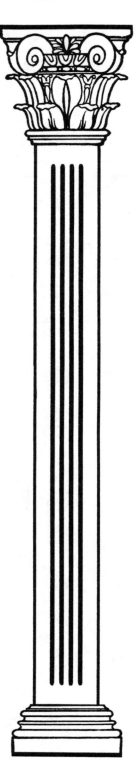

# IV

# Three Heroic Tales
## *(500 B.C.)*

### INTRODUCTION

The expulsion of the Etruscan kings did not insure peace to the city of Rome. The unification of Italy took another 250 years and was achieved only through bitter conflict and continual war. In 486 B.C. at Lake Regillus, the Romans defeated the Latin League, a group of allied Italian towns. The two contenders ratified a treaty that united them against their common enemy, the Etruscans. The latter's power and influence in Italy was on the decline, and it was now the perfect time for Rome to assume control over the entire Italian peninsula.

The following stories describe the daring deeds of three heroic figures (Horatius, Mucius Scaevola, and Cloelia) who helped Rome destroy the Etruscan influence in Italy. They all shared a common characteristic: their willingness to sacrifice their own lives for the salvation of their homeland. All accomplished superhuman feats and survived impossible odds.

Livy himself doubts the historical accuracy of their stories. Over the centuries, Roman tradition had exaggerated the deeds of its past heroes and heroines. Roman scholars generally agree that Livy's account of these legendary figures was not intended to represent historical fact but to arouse feelings of patriotism and cultural pride.

### Horatius at the Bridge[1]

■ The Roman rebellion against the Etruscan kings succeeded, and a republican government was established in place of the monarchy. Tarquin the Proud and his family escaped and took refuge with Lars Porsenna, the king of Clusium, a powerful city in Etruria. Together, these two monarchs conspired to reestablish Etruscan rule in Rome. Both believed in the supremacy of kings, and felt that if Tarquin's removal remained unchallenged, the lofty institution of kingship would be permanently threatened.

With a large army, Porsenna marched directly toward the Tiber. The Roman senate was terrified, not only of Lars Porsenna's reputation and strength, but also of its own citizens' reaction to this attack. Fearing that the Roman people might prefer peace to liberty and permit the kings' entrance to the city, the senate offered the citizens many enticements. The government appropriated from private enterprise the buying and selling of salt in order to guarantee low prices to everyone. The plebeians were also exempted from taxes and import duties unlike the wealthy citizens who carried the burden for all. The people were pleased, and despite a terrible siege by the Etruscans, they remained loyal to their new government.

As soon as the enemy approached, the Roman farmers fled to the city for protection. Defensive walls surrounded three sides of the city, and the Tiber River provided a barrier on the other. However, a single wooden bridge spanned this waterway and would have given access to Porsenna's army if it had not been for the courage and resolution of one brave man—Horatius Cocles. On that day, the fate of Rome rested with him alone.

By chance, Horatius was standing watch on the bridge when he spied the Etruscans capture the Janiculum Hill. Then the enemy stormed the bridge, routing the Roman soldiers stationed there. Horatius witnessed his own men abandoning their weapons and ranks while rushing toward the safety of the city. He grabbed each one and shouted in his face that he was deserting in vain. Once the bridge was taken, the enemy would inevitably overtake the Palatine and Capitoline hills.

Instead, Horatius argued, it would be better if they would destroy the bridge with fire or tear it down with whatever tools were necessary. He would stand on the bridge and alone, if possible, defy the Etruscan assault. Straightway, he leaped into the fray and stupefied the enemy by his audacity. Two other soldiers, Spurius Lartius and Titus Herminius, ashamed of the Roman retreat, joined Horatius in this seemingly futile battle. Together they held off the first fierce onslaught, but then, when only a small part of the bridge was still intact, Horatius forced Spurius and Titus to seek safety.

Alone now, Horatius fixed his savage-looking eyes on the Etruscan nobles and chided them by proclaiming them slaves of proud kings who, unable to enjoy their own liberty, came to destroy others' freedom. It seemed as if his words mesmerized the nobles because not one of them moved. Then they all looked at each other and with a shout, hurled their weapons at Horatius. He deflected the spears with his shield and remained firm in his resolve to stand alone. The Etruscans tried to push him down when the noise of the bridge collapsing reached their ears. Fear held all immobile. Horatius prayed out loud, "Oh, Father Tiber, please welcome these weapons and this soldier into your reverent waters." Then he jumped headlong into the river and swam unscathed toward the safety of his men.

The state of Rome was so grateful to Horatius that it erected a statue of him in the *comitium* and endowed him with as much land as he could plow in one day. ■

---

[1]Livy, *Ab Urbe Condita* II:9-13.

Mucius Scaevola[2]

■ Since his attempt to enter Rome was frustrated by Horatius's valiant stand at the Tiber bridge, Porsenna decided to besiege Rome. Part of his army was stationed on the Janiculum Hill and another on the flat plain near the banks of the river. No supplies could enter the city, and Porsenna patiently awaited Rome's starvation and inevitable surrender.

However, another brave young man appeared, Gaius Mucius, who detested the idea of Etruscan kings ruling free Romans. First, he considered infiltration of the enemy's lines without anyone's knowledge, but he realized this plan carried some risk. He might be caught by the Roman guards and thought to be a traitor escaping the destitute situation in the city. Therefore, Gaius went to the patres and pleaded, "Oh fathers, I wish to cross the Tiber and if possible, to enter the enemy's camp not as a robber or avenger, but if the gods allow, for a much greater purpose."

The august senators approved his plan, and Mucius, concealing a sword beneath his tunic, slipped unnoticed into the Etruscan camp. The troops were gathered around the king's platform because it was payday. Mucius easily hid among the dense crowd and watched the proceedings. On the dais sat the king Porsenna and his scribe, both dressed in similar attire. The soldiers approached the secretary who kept the records, and Mucius was uncertain which man actually was the king. He dared not ask, since his ignorance would reveal his identity. Heedless of the danger, he swiftly attacked, and as fate willed, murdered the wrong man. Though he tried to escape and rushed through the crowd with his bloodied sword, the king's guards overpowered him.

When Mucius was dragged before Porsenna, out of fear he issued a brave proclamation, "I am a Roman citizen; they call me Gaius Mucius. As your enemy, I wished to kill an enemy. I am less concerned with my own death than I am resolved to cause your death, King. It is the fate of any Roman to do brave deeds and to endure them. I am not the only man to feel this way. After me stands a long line of youths eager to seek the same glory. Make yourself ready, for every hour of your life will be spent defending yourself against these men. You should not fear battle, but instead one man's attack against yourself. No place is safe for you, not your palace, not your bedroom."

Porsenna was angered at Gaius's boast, as well as terrified at the prospect of such unrelenting peril. He ordered his soldiers to threaten Mucius with torture unless he disclose immediately the particulars of this assassination plot. Undaunted, Gaius Mucius shouted, "See, Etruscans, how cheap is flesh to those who seek great glory," and then he thrust his right hand into the sacrificial fire burning on the altar. It appeared as if his mind were immune to the excruciating pain. The king, astonished at this miracle, jumped out of his seat and ordered the youth removed from the flames. Then he proclaimed, "Go, young man, indeed, go. You have dared to harm yourself more than me. If such bravery had been displayed by one of my people, I would have bestowed great honors on him. For you, I will allow safe passage back to your homeland."

Then Mucius, as if he were repaying Porsenna's kindness, responded, "Since you have honored my bravery, I will honor your kindness and give you the information you wished to obtain with threats. There are 300 gallant young men of Rome who have all sworn to attack and kill you as I attempted to do. I drew the first lot; the rest, each one in his own time, will come forward until fortune grants one of them success."

Porsenna was truly frightened by the prospect of losing his own life. He sent peace envoys to Rome with Mucius who was given the *cognomen* (last name) Scaevola (Left-handed) because of the loss of his right hand. The ambassadors discussed conditions to end the siege and establish a permanent peace between the two nations. In vain, the Etruscans requested the return of Tarquinius Superbus to power, a demand that was overwhelmingly denied. However, the Romans did return captured land to the Etruscans and gave them hostages to secure the removal of the king's troops from the Janiculum Hill and Roman territory.

In gratitude to Gaius Mucius Scaevola, the patres bestowed upon him land across the Tiber that later was called the Mucian Meadows. ■

---

[2]Livy, *Ab Urbe Condita* II:9-13.

## Cloelia[3]

■ There were also women who assisted in Rome's struggle for freedom. One young woman, Cloelia, who was among the hostages in Porsenna's camp, eluded her guards and led a group of girls to safety by swimming across the Tiber to Rome.

When Porsenna heard of the prisoners' escape, he was extremely angry and demanded Cloelia's immediate return. But then his anger turned to admiration, and he declared her deed superior to Horatius's and Mucius Scaevola's. He would not consider the treaty broken but instead would promise the girl's safety if she were returned to him. He would insure her virginity and restore her to her parents once his troops were safely out of Roman territory.

Cloelia stayed at Porsenna's house unharmed, and the king further honored her bravery. She was allowed to choose whomever she wished of the hostages to be returned to Rome. As was fitting a young maiden, she asked that the little boys be sent home since they would suffer separation from their families the most.

Once peace was firmly established, the Romans rewarded Cloelia's courage with a new type of honor. On the *Sacred Way*, a statue was erected depicting the young girl astride her horse. ■

---

[3]Livy, *Ab Urbe Condita* II:9-13.

# TEACHER IDEAS

## Discussion Questions

1.  To whom did Horatius pray before diving into the river?

2.  What two monarchs wished to reestablish the kingship in Rome?

3.  What concession did the government grant to its citizens to ensure their loyalty during the Etruscan war?

4.  What rewards did the state grant to Horatius, Mucius, and Cloelia?

5.  What lie did Mucius fabricate to scare Porsenna?

6.  Why didn't Mucius know which man was the king?

7.  What does *Scaevola* mean?

8.  What hostages did Cloelia choose to return to Rome? Why?

9.  Do you think Mucius was rash or brave? Was his sacrifice necessary? Could he have accomplished his task without losing his hand? Explain your answers.

10. Livy stated in his preface to *Ab Urbe Condita* (see chapter 1) that he wanted the reader to "consider the nature of the lives of these ancient personages, their strength and skills both at home and while fighting in foreign lands." He goes on to say, "It is through these attributes that the power of Rome began and expanded." Compare the characters of these three heroic figures. Describe their individual "strength and skills." How would these qualities contribute to Rome's greatness?

## History Lesson: Etruscan Power in Italy

The Etruscans were wealthy traders whose power reached its height in the sixth century B.C. What is known about their civilization derives largely from the archaeological evidence found in their tombs. Richly decorated with murals and filled with artifacts, the Etruscan mausoleums reveal the day-to-day life of these Italian people. Unfortunately, few Etruscan records remain to further elucidate this culture, a problem compounded by the fact that only a few hundred words of the Etruscan language have been deciphered.

As the Etruscans tried to enlarge their sphere of influence to include the southern part of the Italian peninsula, they came in contact with the Greeks who inhabited the area and who were also great maritime merchants. Conflict naturally arose over control of the seas. As the Etruscans pushed south, they overran the Latin towns. Rome's location was important because it was the gateway to the South. Tarquinius Priscus came from the city of Tarquinii, about 40 miles northwest of Rome, and peacefully established himself on the throne of Rome. With the addition of an Etruscan ruling class, the two cultures, Latin and Etruscan, began to meld.

About the time when Tarquinius Superbus, Priscus's son, was thrown out of Rome (see chapter 3), the Greeks began to wage war against the encroaching Etruscans in earnest. In 474 B.C., they defeated the Etruscans and their Carthaginian allies in a naval battle. Other Latin cities took advantage of the Etruscan vulnerability and began to rebel against Etruscan dominance.

The Etruscans did not relinquish their power easily. Lars Porsenna, the Etruscan king and antagonist of Mucius Scaevola, attempted to reestablish Etruscan rule in Rome and, in fact, managed to recapture the city for a time (notwithstanding the legend that Horatius successfully held off the entire Etruscan army from entering Rome). However, beleaguered continuously by the Greeks, the Etruscans eventually conceded their southern holdings and withdrew north to Cisalpine Gaul.

In 405 B.C., the Romans commenced a siege of the Etruscan town of Veii. Finally achieving victory after a ten-year siege, the Romans sold all the inhabitants into slavery. By 265 B.C., the Romans had conquered all of Etruria, and an alliance was made between these two powers. During the Second Punic War (see chapter 5), Etrurian towns supported Rome in its battle against the Carthaginians. Finally, in 87 B.C., all Etruscans were granted full Roman citizenship by passage of the *Lex Julia*. Though Etruscan political independence was gone, Etruscan culture endured with the assimilation of these two peoples.

## SUGGESTED TOPICS FOR FURTHER RESEARCH

1. Etruscan tombs

2. Etruscan art

3. Etruscan engineering

4. role of women in Etruscan society

5. Etruscan language

### Language Arts

## VOCABULARY BUILDING

Prefix: *Circum* from Latin preposition *circum*, meaning "around"

1. Define the following words (and phrase) and use each in a sentence:

   circumlocution          circumvent

   circumnavigate       circumstantial evidence

   circumspect

2. Which of the previous words (and phrase) are nouns? Which are adjectives? Which are verbs?

3. Are the underlined words (and phrase) used correctly in the following sentences?

   a. The jury believed the  circumstantial evidence  and convicted the thief.

   b. I  circumnavigated  the globe in my new airplane.

   c. His  circumlocution  was direct and to the point.

   d. John's  circumspect  behavior created distrust in all who knew him.

   e. The army  circumvented  the enemy's troops and avoided battle.

## LEGENDS

1. Choose two of the following early American (part mythological and part real) heroes and heroines for study. Read and compare their characteristics to those of the three Romans described in this chapter. See Resources.

   Pecos Bill:                  Texas cowboy and inventor of the "cattle drive."

   Daniel Boone:                Frontiersman who settled the wilderness of Kentucky.

   Paul Bunyan:                 Giant lumberjack from the north woods who had many adventures with Babe, his blue ox.

   Davy Crockett:               Frontiersman, politician, and defender of the Alamo.

   John Henry:                  Ex-slave who worked on the railroads after the Civil War.

   Annie Oakley:                Sharpshooter and entertainer of the old West.

   Molly Pitcher (McCauley):    Revolutionary war heroine.

   Slue-foot Sue:               Contemporary of Pecos Bill.

   Harriett Tubman:             Leader of underground railroad.

2. A heroic figure can be real or imaginary or both. Who is your hero or heroine? What characteristics does he or she possess that you admire?

3. Compare the heroic figures of the following eras: ancient Rome, early America, and modern times. Write a short paragraph that explains how public opinion of heroic figures has changed.

## CREATIVE WRITING

Write a newspaper article or a one-minute television news spot reporting the deeds of Horatius, Mucius Scaevola, or Cloelia.

## Cultural Lesson: The Modern Calendar, a Roman Creation

We are indebted to the ancient Romans for shaping our modern calendar. The number of months, the number of days in each month, and the name of each month find their origin in the calendar of ancient Rome. The word *calendar* is derived from the Latin word *kalendae*, which was the first day of every month, *Kalendae Februariae* being February 1.

In the early days of ancient Rome, the calendar was based on the cycles of the moon. There were ten lunar months, four with 31 days and six with 29 days, numbered one through ten. Four remain in use: September (seventh), October (eighth), November (ninth), and December (tenth). According to tradition, Tarquinius Priscus instituted this system.

However, it quickly became apparent that these calculations were inaccurate. Numa, Romulus's successor, added two months at the end of the year. The calendar then contained 354 days and began with March (in 153 B.C., January became the first month). Whenever days were needed to reconcile the lunar calendar with the sun's cycle, the government increased the length of the last month of the year, February. Hence, our own extra day during leap year occurs that month.

In 45 B.C., Julius Caesar introduced the solar calendar. He calculated the year to be 365¼ days long and established the number of days in the months as we now know them ("thirty days hath September...").

The names of the months have interesting Roman origins. January is named after the god Janus, a native Italian deity who had two heads, one to look forward and one to look back. On the first of January, one traditionally reminisces about the past year and makes resolutions for the future.

February derives its name from an ancient Roman festival. In Rome's early days, the city was threatened by wolves that preyed on flocks of sheep. During this month, a festival was held, the *Lupercalia*, dedicated to ridding the community of these predators. Strips of goat skin (called *februa*) were given to two young boys who, after smearing their heads with goat milk and blood, ran through the crowded streets and slapped the spectators with the februa. Whoever was touched was blessed with increased fertility and protection of their flocks. As the city grew, wolves were no longer a threat, and the emphasis of the festival changed. Barren women ran through the streets of Rome to be struck by the sacred goat skin strips in order to enhance their fecundity.

March derives its name from the god Mars, the god of war and the immortal sire of Romulus and Remus. Mars, considered to be the father of all Roman people, was honored by having this month named after him.

The etymology of April is not absolutely clear. Ovid, a Roman poet, states in his book the *Fasti* that April comes from the Roman verb *aperire*, meaning "to open." April is the month when spring arrives and flowers bloom ("open"). Other scholars associate April with the Latin word *aper* (boar), possibly connecting a spring hunting ritual to the name.

May's name probably came from Maia, a minor divinity worshipped in ancient Rome as the goddess of the fields. Called the *Bona Dea* (Good Goddess), she helped the crops come to fruition. A celebration in her honor was held on May 1, and May was, of course, an excellent month for planting seeds.

June's name is derived from Juno, the queen of the gods. She was especially liked by the Romans because in the fourth century B.C. the sacred geese guarding her temple warned the Romans of a sneak attack by the barbarian Gauls. The city was saved, and she was honored by having the sixth month named after her.

July honors Julius Caesar, the conqueror of Gaul and creator of the calendar. After his death, the senate renamed the seventh month July in his honor (it was called *Quintilis* in the old calendar).

In 8 B.C., the first emperor, Octavius Augustus, gave his honorary title to August, the eighth month. *Augustus* means "lofty one."

September, October, November, and December were among the original 10 lunar months, taking their names from the words for the numbers seven (*septem*), eight (*octo*), nine (*novem*), and ten (*decem*).

### ACTIVITY: Renaming the Calendar

If you could choose new names for the 12 months that would reflect American history and culture, what would they be? Explain your choices.

# RESOURCES

Blair, Walter. *Tall Tale America*. Chicago: University of Chicago Press, 1987.

Christofani, Mauro. *The Etruscans*. New York: Galahad Books, 1978.

Crump, Donald J., ed., *Mysteries of the Ancient World*. Washington, D.C.: National Geographic, 1979.

Grant, Michael. *The Etruscans*. New York: Charles Scribner's Sons, 1980.

Hamblin, Dora Jane. *The Etruscans*. New York: Time Life Books, 1975.

Macaulay, Thomas. *The Lays of Ancient Rome and Miscellaneous Essays and Poems*. Lanham, Md.: Biblio. Dist., 1968.
This title includes a poetic rendering of "Horatius at the Bridge."

Macnamara, Ellen. *Life of the Etruscans*. New York: Dorset Press, 1973.

# V

# Scipio and the Virgin
## *(210 B.C.)*

## INTRODUCTION

After the collapse of Etruscan power and the defeat of other Latin tribes, only one group of foreigners remained in Italy—the Greeks in the south. In 275 B.C., Rome vanquished this rival, and the entire peninsula finally belonged to the once small city on the Tiber. The unification and control of Italy had taken more than two centuries, and Rome's complete success led to an inevitable confrontation with the city of Carthage.

This wealthy Phoenician colony, located on the northern coast of Africa, had dominated the trade routes of the western Mediterranean for 300 years. Its sphere of influence stretched from present-day Gibralter and the eastern coast of Spain (*Hispania*) to Libya, the islands of Sardinia, Corsica, and southern Sicily. Carthage sent ships as far west as Britain and excluded all rivals from trading in the western Mediterranean including Rome. The Romans, previously uninterested in managing trade routes, had signed several treaties with Carthage resigning all rights to maritime trade. Now, with the conquest of southern Italy, Rome resented this closed policy.

In 265 B.C., war broke out between Rome and Carthage over the control of Sicily. For the next 24 years, these powers fought, neither achieving complete victory. By 241 B.C., Carthage, her resources depleted, sued for peace. Rome, itself, had lost more than 200,000 men and 500 ships, but the terms of peace replenished its treasury. Carthage was forced to pay the very large sum of 3,200 talents of silver over the next 10 years, as well as yield the control of Sicily and the other islands west of Italy to its victor.

Beleaguered by the large debt to Rome, Carthage established colonies in southern Spain to conduct silver mining and used the resources from this area to pay off the monetary obligation early. Peace lasted between the two until 218 B.C. when the Carthaginian general Hannibal besieged the Spanish city of Saguntum, a Roman ally. Two Roman generals, Gnaeus Scipio and his brother Publius Cornelius Scipio, succeeded in ousting the Carthaginians from Saguntum, but in 211 B.C., both men were slain in battle, and Rome lost all territory south of the Iberus River.

Hannibal made his historic march over the Alps with elephants in the hopes of surprising Rome. The Romans chose Publius Cornelius Scipio (today referred to as the "Junior") as their general to match military wits with Hannibal. Scipio, only 24 years old, promptly marched to Spain, seized the Carthaginian city of New Carthage (*Carthago Nova*), and by his tactful treatment of the Spanish prisoners won them over to Rome's cause. In 202 B.C., at the battle of Zama, the younger Scipio confronted his enemy and emerged victorious.

**39**

In the treaty approved after the war, Carthage (in Africa) ceded all its territory to Rome, was required to pay 200 talents of silver per year for 50 years, surrendered all war elephants and ships, except 10, and was forbidden to wage war on anyone without Rome's consent. This once mighty nation was effectively crushed, and Rome now controlled the western Mediterranean.

For the next 50 years, Carthage lived up to the terms of the treaty of the Second Punic War. However, in 146 B.C., when the Numidians began to harass the city, Carthage waged war against Numidia without Rome's consent. Carthage had appealed to Rome for assistance, but its pleas were ignored. Thus, Rome seized this opportunity to destroy its old foe. Led by Scipio Aemilianus, the Roman troops stormed the city of Carthage, sold all the inhabitants into slavery, and burned the city to the ground. To insure the annihilation of Carthage, the Romans plowed salt into the fields so no crops could grow.

The following story from Livy describes the exploits of the young general Publius Scipio during the Second Punic War. A brilliant military strategist, Scipio became a hero in Rome with his success against Carthage. However, this episode is about his humanitarian treatment of the Spanish natives and not about his battle expertise. After Rome's victory at New Carthage, Scipio divided up the spoils and found himself the recipient of a beautiful maiden. Should Scipio keep her for his own amusement or return her to her family? Livy explains the situation.

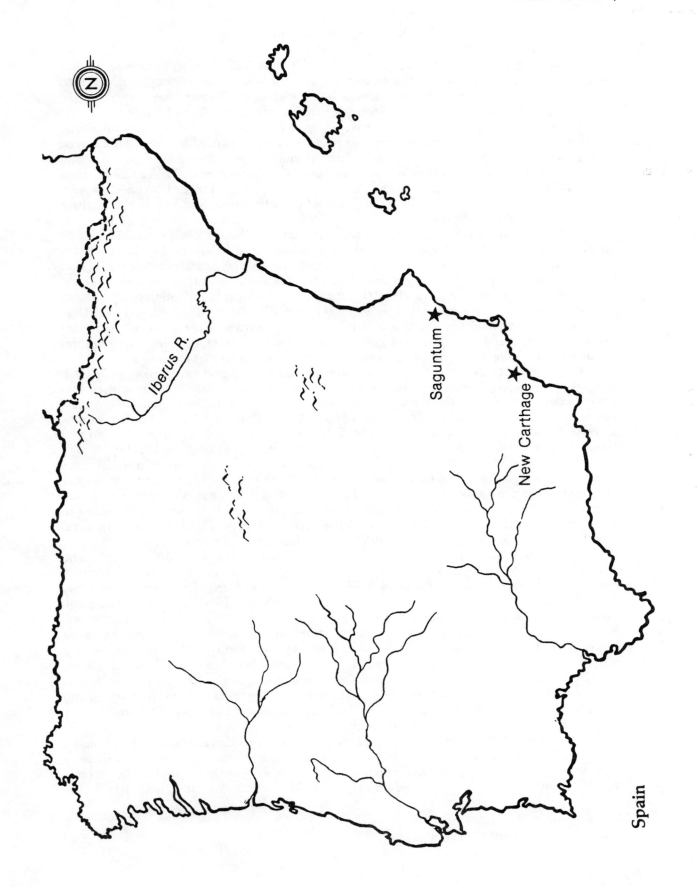

## Scipio and the Virgin[1]

■ The Roman troops attacked the city of New Carthage, slaughtering every adult male who resisted their assault. The citadel was the last bastion to fall, but finally it, too, surrendered, and the Spanish city formed a truce with its Roman captors. Then the victors devoted themselves to the collecting of the numerous spoils and booty.

About 10,000 captured free male citizens were ordered freed by the general Scipio and their possessions that survived the devastation of war restored to them. He decreed that the 2,000 artisans become servants of the Roman state and that they could obtain their freedom in the future if they would manufacture arms for Rome. The remaining men and healthy slaves he consigned to the fleet of eight ships seized from Carthage. Besides these groups, several other Spanish tribes were taken as hostages, and Scipio treated them as if they were allies of Rome.

Many weapons were appropriated from the city: 120 large catapults, 281 smaller ones, 23 large ballistras (stone throwers), 52 small ones, and large and small scorpions (missile throwers). In addition, 74 military standards and large quantities of gold and silver were also seized. These items were brought to Scipio, as well as 276 gold saucers, each weighing almost a pound, 18,300 pounds of unwrought and minted silver, and myriad numbers of silver utensils. The Romans found 400,000 modiums (slightly less than 2 bushels each) of wheat and 270,000 of barley. In the harbor, they seized 63 merchant ships and confiscated their cargos of grain, arms, bronze, iron, cloth, hemp, and timber. All articles were weighed and catalogued and given to the *quaestor* for safe keeping.

After recording the lists of spoils, Scipio ordered the soldiers to summon the Spanish hostages. He stated that they need not be concerned for their safety because they had come under the power of the Roman people who preferred to bind people with kindness rather than fear and to make allies by faith and alliance rather than by the harsh means of slavery. He counted the Spaniards and noted the names of the various tribes and then sent messengers to their homes so that relatives could retrieve their family members.

In this group of captives was a young maiden whom the soldiers brought to Scipio as a prize. She was so beautiful that wherever she went, all eyes turned toward her. Scipio, after questioning her about her home and family, learned that she was betrothed to a man named Allucius, the leader of the Celtiberians. Without hesitation, Scipio sent word to her parents and fiancé that she was safe. When Allucius arrived and disclosed his great love for the girl, Scipio spoke privately to him with these kind words:

"As a young man," he said, "I speak to you, a young man, so that there will be no embarrassment between us. When your betrothed was captured and brought to me by my troops, I learned from her of the great love you both share. I, myself, if the duties of my country did not demand so much of my attention, wish that I could enjoy a loving and lawful relationship with a woman. But my time is not my own; it belongs to Rome." Scipio continued, "I wish to give you this small gift and lessen your concerns. Your betrothed stayed in my quarters under my personal protection with the same respect she would have received in her own home. I return her to you, untouched, still a virgin, worthy of your love. I ask only that you become a friend of the Roman people. If you believe me to be a good man, know this, that there are many men in Rome like myself and there is no people today in the entire world whom you would less wish to be your enemy or prefer more to be a friend to your compatriots."

Allucius was filled with joy and at the same time with embarrassment. While holding Scipio's hand, he prayed to all the gods to favor this young general in some way since he himself could never repay Scipio enough for his kindness. Shortly afterward, the parents of the maiden arrived with a large amount of gold to ransom their daughter from the

---

[1]Livy, *Ab Urbe Condita* XXVI: 46.

Romans. When they realized that Scipio had already released her, they insisted that he accept the gold as a personal gift. He conceded and ordered the money to be placed at his feet. Then he summoned Allucius and pointing to the treasure on the ground said, "Besides the dowry you are about to receive from your future in-laws, this will be my wedding present to you."

Allucius, happy with these gifts and honors, returned home with his bride and praised Scipio's merits. He told his tribe that a young man similar to a god had arrived who conquered cities with arms and people with kindness. A short time later Allucius brought 1,400 Celtiberian horsemen to Scipio to aid in his war against Carthage. ■

# TEACHER IDEAS

## Discussion Questions

1.  How old was Scipio when this story took place?

2.  What Spanish town was besieged by the Romans?

3.  To what tribe did Allucius belong?

4.  In 146 B.C., what happened to the city of Carthage?

5.  What was more important to Scipio than his own desires?

6.  Scipio's treatment of Allucius resulted in the Spaniard reciprocating in what manner?

7.  How many weapons were seized by the Romans?

8.  What labor did Scipio assign to the healthy captured slaves?

9.  Do you believe that Scipio returned the gold for purely honorable reasons or did he have an ulterior motive in mind?

10. What does Scipio mean when he says to Allucius, "there is no people today in the entire world whom you would less wish to be your enemy or prefer more to be a friend to your compatriots"?

## History Lesson: Hannibal (247-181 B.C.)

After the First Punic War, Hamilcar Barca, a great Carthaginian general, moved to Spain where he helped expand his country's interests. He founded the city of Barcino (modern day Barcelona), which he named for himself, and settled his family there. According to legend, he forced his young son Hannibal to swear undying hatred toward the people of Rome. After Barca's death, the Carthaginians entered into a treaty with the Romans guaranteeing that they would remain south of the Iberus (Ebro) River and refrain from attack on the city of Saguntum.

In 221 B.C., command of the Carthaginian forces fell to 26-year-old Hannibal. A natural leader, Hannibal led his troops north to subdue hostile Spanish tribes. Despite the treaty, Hannibal seized Saguntum, prompting the Romans to declare war. They quickly sent an army under Publius Cornelius Scipio Senior to Spain, but when Scipio arrived, Hannibal had vanished. In a daring move, Hannibal had marched his soldiers over the Alps. It was inconceivable to the Romans that anyone could attack from this direction.

Scipio sailed back to Italy and engaged Hannibal in battle. The Roman general was badly wounded but survived, rescued by his son and namesake. Hannibal was victorious again. The Romans sent another army, which also failed to defeat the Carthaginian forces, causing Rome to concede Cisalpine Gaul to Carthage.

Hannibal then marched south, detoured around Rome, and tried to persuade the Italian towns to join his forces. In 217 B.C., Rome lost yet another battle to Hannibal. Frustrated over these continued losses, Q. Fabius Maximus, a Roman general, adopted a different policy and refused to engage Hannibal in direct battle. Instead, he separated and defeated small segments of Hannibal's army, gradually reducing the size of his enemy's forces. Fabius was given the name *Cunctator*—the "delayer"—for his successful tactics. Shocked at this seemingly cowardly approach, Rome, in a rash move, sent 80,000 infantry under the consuls Varro and Paulus to Cannae, about 200 miles southeast of Rome. Rome's superior numbers suggested a victory, but Hannibal's brilliant strategies won the battle. Paulus died and Varro committed suicide over his disgrace.

Rome had now lost over 100,000 men, and its allies started to desert. Instead of giving up, however, the Romans raised another army and sent it to Spain under Publius Scipio (the Senior) and his brother. No longer would Rome fight Hannibal directly. Instead, Rome attacked other Carthaginian forces. In the engagement between the two armies, both Scipios were slain.

For the next 10 years, Hannibal remained in southern Italy but never again engaged Rome in a decisive battle. By returning to Fabian's policy of divide and delay, Rome managed to wear down the Carthaginian general and his forces. Hannibal lost most of his veteran soldiers. Hasdrubal, his brother, tried to bring reinforcements, but a message he sent was intercepted by the Romans. Instead of meeting his brother, Hasdrubal was surprised by the Romans who routed the Carthaginian forces and sent Hasdrubal's head to Hannibal as a grisly announcement of their victory.

Hannibal turned south and for several years eluded Rome. In 202 B.C., Scipio Junior decided to attack Carthage directly, and just when the city was about to capitulate and sign a treaty, Hannibal arrived to rescue his homeland. These two great generals met at the Battle of Zama in 202 B.C. Rome was victorious, and Hannibal's 19-year reign as Rome's greatest foe came to an end.

Hannibal withdrew from military service and became a statesman. However, Carthaginian leaders were jealous of his popularity. When Rome suggested that Hannibal was in league with its enemy, Antiochus, the king of Syria, Carthage seemed ready to betray its revered general. Hannibal escaped to Syria and helped Antiochus wage an unsuccessful war against Rome. He then fled to Bithynia to the court of Prusias. The Romans pursued him there and demanded his surrender. Prusias realized it would be foolish to deny Rome its request. Hannibal, now 65 years old and in exile from his country, poisoned himself rather than become a prisoner of Rome.

## SUGGESTED TOPICS FOR FURTHER RESEARCH

1. First Punic War

2. Second Punic War

3. Third Punic War

4. Roman warships

5. Publius Scipio's life after the Battle of Zama

## Language Arts

## VOCABULARY BUILDING

Base: *uni* from Latin adjective *unus*, meaning "one"

1. Define the following words and use each in a sentence:

   unit      unique

   unison     universe

   united

2.  Which of the previous words are nouns? Which are adjectives?

3.  Fill in the blanks with the words from exercise 1 above.

    a.  The _____ is comprised of many solar systems.

    b.  "Let us all sing in _____," said the music teacher.

    c.  We are all _____ individuals.

    d.  _____ we stand. Divided we fall.

    e.  A centimeter is a _____ of measurement in the metric system.

4.  Study the following Roman numbers and their derivatives and then define each word:

    | Number | Derivative |
    | --- | --- |
    | duo (two) | duality, duet, duplicity |
    | tres (three) | triceps, trident, trio |
    | quattuor (four) | quadrangle, quadriplegic, quadrant |
    | quinque (five) | quintet, quintuplet, quintessence |
    | sex (six) | sextant, sextuplet, sextet |
    | septem (seven) | septuagenarian, septuplet, September |
    | octo (eight) | octagon, October, octave |
    | novem (nine) | novena, November |
    | decem (ten) | decimeter, December, decimate |

**ESSAY WRITING: Dido's Curse**

Often the ancients would invent a story to explain an actual historical event. For instance, the myth of Romulus (see chapter 1) explains the origin of the name *Rome* (derived from Romulus's name), associates Rome with the gods (by saying Mars is Romulus's father), and discloses the reason for Rome's location (where the wolf discovered the twin babies).

The strong antagonism between Rome and Carthage that resulted in three devastating wars also had a fictional interpretation. According to legend as written down by the Roman poet Virgil, Aeneas was the actual founder of Rome and the ancestor of Romulus. After escaping from the ashes of Troy, he wandered the Mediterranean region searching for a new homeland. He and his companions were rescued from a terrible storm by Dido, the queen of Carthage. Aeneas and Dido fell in love, and though he loved her and stayed with her in Africa for one year, he left to journey to Italy. Dido was heart-broken and committed suicide at his departure. While dying, she invoked the gods with this prayer, a curse against Aeneas and his Roman descendants:

> These last words, I pray as I pour forth my life. May you, Oh Carthaginians, plague his [Aeneas'] race and all future generations with enmity and hatred. Grant this gift to my ashes. Let there be no love, nor alliances between our peoples. May some avenger arise from my people who will pursue these Trojans with arms and destruction, now and forever. When this comes to pass, grant, oh gods that my shores will oppose his, that waves will oppose waves, and arms will oppose arms, and may mine and his people fight forever.[2]

Carefully read Dido's soliloquy. From what you know of the Punic wars, write a short essay (one page) about her curse. Did her wish come true? Look closely at what she says.

---

[2]Vergil, *Aeneid* IV: 620-9.

## Cultural Lesson: Roman Numerals

It was important for Roman officials to keep accurate records. In Livy's account, Scipio Junior has the quaestor catalog all articles taken during the Spanish conquest. An abacus was used for mathematical figuring up to 1,000,000. Most modern societies have adopted Arabic numerals, but occasionally Roman numerals are still used (e.g., on clocks, to date films, etc.).

The origin of Roman numerals stemmed from using one's hands to count, starting with the smallest finger: I, II, III, IIII. The gap between the forefinger and thumb resembled the letter "V," the number 5. An X-shape (designating the number 10) was formed by placing an upright "V" on top of an upside down "V."

Study the following Roman numbers. Remember, there is no zero.

| | | |
|---|---|---|
| 1 = I | 6 = VI | 50 = L |
| 2 = II | 7 = VII | 100 = C |
| 3 = III | 8 = VIII | 500 = D |
| 4 = IIII or IV | 9 = VIIII or IX | 1000 = M |
| 5 = V | 10 = X | |

A letter placed *before* a letter of greater value subtracts the value of the former from the latter. Subtraction can be done only with one unit. Study the following examples:

```
  4 = IV
  9 = IX
 40 = XL
400 = CD
900 = CM
```

A letter placed *after* a letter of greater value adds to the value.

```
  6 = VI
 12 = XII
 18 = XVIII
600 = DC
```

Roman numerals are written from left to right. Thus, 3,754 is written as MMMDCCLIV. Study the following break-down of this number:

```
 M = 1,000
 M = 1,000
 M = 1,000
 D =   500
 C =   100
 C =   100
 L =    50
IV =     4
       ─────
       3,754
```

## ACTIVITY: Roman Numerals

Write the following numbers in Roman numerals:

| | | |
|---|---|---|
| 1,492 | 1,066 | 337 |
| 844 | 210 | 2,001 |
| 73 | 1,945 | your birth year |

### Et Alia: Maps

Go to the library and find a map of Roman territories before and after the Punic wars (see Resources). Using the map in figure 5.1, complete the following:

1. Locate the following cities and label each one in *red* ink:

   | | |
   |---|---|
   | Rome | Saguntum |
   | Carthage | Athens |
   | New Carthage | Alexandria |

Fig. 5.1. Mediterranean Area.

2. Locate the following rivers and bodies of water and label each one in *blue* ink:

   | | |
   |---|---|
   | Ebro River | Adriatic Sea |
   | Tiber River | Mediterranean Sea |
   | Nile River | Black Sea |
   | Atlantic Ocean | Aegean Sea |

3. Locate the following islands and countries and label each one in *black* ink:

| | |
|---|---|
| Corsica | Numidia |
| Sardinia | Gaul |
| Sicily | Crete |
| Italy | Greece |
| Spain | Egypt |

4. Color lightly the following in crayon:
   * Rome's possessions in 264 B.C. (in *red*)
   * Rome's possessions in 238 B.C. (in *blue*)
   * Rome's possessions in 218 B.C. (in *yellow*)
   * Rome's possessions in 201 B.C. (in *green*)

# RESOURCES

Asimov, Isaac. *The Roman Republic*. Boston: Houghton Mifflin, 1966.
    This title covers the Punic wars.

Grant, Michael. *History of Rome*. New York: Charles Scribner's Sons, 1978.
    This title details the Punic wars.

Hamilton, Edith. *Mythology*. New York: New American Library, 1940.

*Iliad of Homer*, trans. Ennis Rees. New York: Macmillan Publishing, 1977.

Lamb, Harold. *Hannibal*. Garden City, N.Y.: Doubleday, 1958.

*Past Worlds*. Maplewood, N.J.: Hammond, 1988.
    Refer to maps on pp. 168-79.

Scullard, Howard Hayes. "Scipio," *New Encyclopaedia Britannica*, 1988 ed., vol. 10, 555-56.

Starr, Chester G. "Carthage," *Encyclopedia Americana*, 1990 ed., vol. 5, 723-25.
    This is a good reference for maps.

*Times Atlas of World History*. Maplewood, N.J.: Hammond, 1978.
    Refer to maps on pp. 86-91.

Vergil, *Aeneid*, trans. Robert Fitzgerald. New York: Random House, 1981.

# VI

# Spartacus
## (73 B.C.)

### INTRODUCTION

The barbaric custom of pitting one man against another in a fight to the death was a favorite pastime of ancient Romans. It is believed that gladiatorial combat originated with the Etruscan custom of killing slaves or captives as sacrifices during the funerals of wealthy men. In 264 B.C., Marcus and Decimus Brutus presented the first "show" (*munus*) in Rome at the funeral of their father, but it was not until 30 B.C. that a permanent stone amphitheater was built to house these brutal contests.

**Gladiators**

The word *gladiator* means "swordsman." The participants were mostly captured slaves or condemned prisoners. During the time of the Empire when these shows reached their height in popularity and depravity, however, even senators and women were known to fight in the arena.

The gladiators often belonged to a trainer who kept them incarcerated in a martial arts school and hired them out for exhibitions. Gladiators were grouped and named according to the weapon with which they were most proficient. A wide variety of weapons was used. For example, Thracians carried a round shield and a curved dagger; Samnites used a large rectangular shield and an axe; an Essedarius fought from a chariot; the Laquearii used only a noose; the Dimachaerus carried two swords. Sometimes teams of two combatants fought each other with the same weapon, and sometimes pairs with different weapons met in combat.

The shows were often sponsored by politicians who hoped to gain popular support by entertaining the masses with a free exhibit. Advertising handbills announced the contest in advance; and the night before the game, the gladiators were fed their last meal, which the public could watch. The morning of the contest began with a parade of gladiators marching around the arena in festive dress. After saluting the sponsor or emperor with these immortal words, "Ave imperator morituri te salutamus,"[1] their weapons were carefully examined to insure integrity and sharpness. A mock battle with wooden swords followed to ready the crowd, and then, with a trumpet signal, the real contest began.

---

[1]"Hail leader, we about to die, salute you."

The enormity and barbarity of these games are shocking to contemplate. Death was the main objective. Until the third century A.D., contests were held *sine missione*, in which no one survived. The sparing of a gladiator's life often rested with the humanity of the fickle crowds. In A.D. 116, Emperor Trajan celebrated his conquest of Dacia (modern Romania) with a show that lasted four months and employed 5,000 pairs of gladiators. It was not until Christianity conquered the hearts and souls of the emperors that this heinous "sport" was finally abolished. The doors to the gladiator arenas were closed by Constantine in the East in A.D. 326 and, finally, by Honorius in the West in A.D. 404.

The following story tells of the valiant escape of a small band of gladiators from a school in southern Italy. Led by the Thracian slave, Spartacus, these men, with their numbers increased by the joining up of local farmers and shepherds, managed to evade the entire Roman army from 73-71 B.C. They gained two years of freedom for themselves and embarrassed Rome with their constant victories.

Although this tale is a part of Roman history, it is written by the Greek author Plutarch (A.D. 50-120), who lived and taught in Rome for several years. His principal work, *Parallel Lives*, is a series of biographies of famous men. Each biography most often compares a Greek and Roman statesman (e.g., Alexander the Great to Julius Caesar or Nicias to Crassus). Plutarch also wrote essays on ethical themes and nine other books on numerous subjects. Forty-six of his biographical accounts have survived, one of which ("Life of Crassus") contains the following story of Spartacus.

## Spartacus[2]

■Lentulus Batiatus, a cruel man, owned a troop of gladiators that he trained (at Capua) for combat. Most of the gladiators were slaves from Gaul or Thrace. Batiatus kept them confined and chained in small quarters at all times, and conditions were appalling. Two hundred of them attempted an escape, though only 78 succeeded. They stole knives and other utensils from the kitchen to use as weapons, and once they reached the main road, the band ambushed a wagon loaded with arms for the gladiator school. Now, better supplied, they hid in the hills and elected three leaders, making Spartacus their supreme commander. He was from a nomadic Thracian tribe and possessed great physical strength as well as an intelligent mind. Spartacus seemed more like a cultured Greek than a Thracian. It was said that when he was first captured and taken to the market in Rome for sale, a snake coiled around his head while he slept. His wife, also a captured slave, was a prophetess who interpreted this omen to mean that one day Spartacus would gain great power but suffer a terrible death. She had escaped from Batiatus's establishment with her husband and was a member of his band of renegades.

After the gladiators fled, a small party of soldiers from Capua tried to recapture them but were easily beaten. Spartacus and his troops then were able to replace their weapons with authentic army equipment pilfered from the defeated troops. Again, they escaped to the safety of the hills. Next, came the Roman praetor Clodius with 3,000 soldiers who surrounded the base of Mt. Vesuvius. There was only one entrance to the top of these steep cliffs, which Clodius heavily guarded thinking this would trap the gladiators. However, wild vines grew everywhere, which the slaves cut down and wove into strong ladders. They lowered the ladders down at night, and all escaped to the bottom except one man who remained to throw weapons down to his comrades before he joined them on the flat plain below. The Romans were unaware that any of these events took place. Spartacus surrounded the Roman camp, launched a surprise attack, and won the encounter easily. Due to his successes, many shepherds and farmers joined his group, and he used some as scouts or infantry soldiers and auxiliary forces. Rapidly increasing in size and strength, his original small group of less than 100 soon blossomed into an imposing army of many thousands.

Most anxious to put down this insurrection, the Romans immediately dispatched more troops under the leadership of the praetor Publius Varinus. His deputy commander initially attacked the fugitives with 2,000 troops, but he was defeated. Then another commander, Cossinius, was sent with a large force, but Spartacus spied on his movements and almost succeeded in capturing him while he was in his bath. Cossinius escaped, and Spartacus followed him to the main camp where a battle ensued, and the Roman was killed. Then Spartacus defeated Varinus, captured his lictors, and even the very horse the praetor was riding.

Despite these continued successes, Spartacus realized it was impossible to defeat all of Rome. He began to lead his army toward the Alps, hoping to cross the mountains and allow his men and their families to return to their original homes in Gaul and Thrace. However, his men could not see the wisdom in his plan. Overconfident, they preferred to remain in Italy ravishing and pillaging the countryside.

The Roman senators were very disturbed by all these events, embarrassed by Spartacus's continued victories against their seasoned troops, and concerned about the destruction of the people and property of Italy. Both consuls, Gellius and Lentulus, set out to put an end to this predicament. Gellius immediately attacked a small group of German slaves who had joined the rebellion and succeeded in routing them. Lentulus's luck, however, was not as good. Although his force far outnumbered Spartacus's troops,

[2]This story is derived from Bernadotte Perrier's English translation of "Life of Crassus" from Plutarch's work *Parallel Lives*, which was written in ancient Greek. See Resources.

the gladiators managed to capture all the Roman equipment. They then marched toward the Alps in hopes of escape and were confronted by Cassius, the governor of Cisalpine Gaul. Despite his 10,000-man army, Cassius was defeated and barely escaped with his life.

This last debacle so enraged the Roman senate that it divested the consuls Lentulus and Gellius of all military rank and appointed Marcus Crassus as supreme commander. In the meantime, Spartacus was heading for Picenum, and Crassus stationed his troops on the border of this district to wait and engage in battle. He ordered Mummius to take two legions and scout out Spartacus's movements while staying clear of the marauders. Mummius, however, thinking that he had a good chance to defeat Spartacus, attacked and was soundly defeated. Many of his soldiers were killed and some escaped only by discarding their weapons and running away.

Crassus, greatly angered at Mummius's rash and costly mistake, personally confronted each and every soldier and made them swear that they would never again retreat and abandon their weapons. Crassus then selected 500 men from those he considered the most cowardly and divided them into 50 squads of 10 men each. He chose one man at random from each squad and ordered him executed. *Decimation* (executing one of every 10 men) was a way of punishing soldiers, but it had not been in use for many years until Crassus punished his troops' cowardice in this manner. The entire army was required to witness the savage executions.

Once assured of his troops' loyalty, Crassus marched against the enemy. Spartacus slipped away and hastened to the sea where he paid pirates from Cilicia to sail his band to Sicily. He hoped to seize that island and start a slave revolt there. The untrustworthy Cilicians stole the money and sailed away. Unable to escape, Spartacus took his troops to the peninsula of Rhegium. Crassus followed and after studying the terrain, decided to build a huge ditch across the isthmus. It was 40 miles long and 15 feet wide, with a strong wall on top. Surprisingly, it took his troops only a short time to complete the fortification. At first, Spartacus thought this was sheer folly but soon realized that he was walled in, unable to move out or get supplies to his troops. He waited for a snowy night and filled up part of the ditch with earth and timber and managed to lead one-third of his army across the ditch and over the wall.

Crassus, concerned that the gladiators might try to march against Rome itself, was relieved when he learned that there was now great discord in the ranks of the outlaw gladiators. Due to disagreements, many of Spartacus's men had abandoned their commander and were camped near Lake Lucania. Crassus attacked this contingent and was almost successful, but Spartacus appeared and rescued his men.

Previously, Crassus had written the senate requesting that Generals Lucullus from Thrace and Pompey from Spain be sent to help him. Now, however, he realized that his own credit for success against the gladiators would be jeopardized if he shared victory with others. Therefore, he hastened to complete the war before these two generals arrived.

First, he decided to attack a group of gladiators, led by Canicus and Castrus, which had separated from the main group. Crassus ordered a 6,000-man force to surround the camp and take possession of a hill without being seen by the enemy. They camouflaged their helmets but were detected by two women who alerted the men. Fighting began, and the Roman troops surely would have been lost, but Crassus brought reinforcements to their rescue. Both sides fought bravely in this fierce battle, but 12,300 renegades died.

Then Crassus turned his energy to the pursuit of Spartacus who was camped in the mountains of Petelia. Two contingents of Roman soldiers were defeated in the first engagement with Spartacus's forces. Ironically, this success became the seed of Spartacus's destruction. His fellow slaves were so confident of victory that they refused to obey their commander's order to retreat. They forced their officers to lead them back to Lucania where Crassus and his main body of soldiers waited. While the Romans were digging defensive ditches, the slaves attacked, initiating a confrontation. Spartacus stood by his men and took command, ordering all his men into battle formation.

It is said that when his horse was brought to him, Spartacus killed the animal with his sword, saying that if he won, he would commandeer a good Roman horse, and if he lost, he would not need one. He then rushed straight toward Crassus himself, and the two centurions who protected the general fell to his attack. Finally, when his troops were routed and forced to flee, Spartacus stayed to face the enemy and died fighting.

The gladiators' rebellion was over. It took numerous lives on both sides, including Spartacus, who died in battle; 6,000 of his followers, who suffered crucifixion on the Appian Way, and another 5,000, who managed to escape to northern Italy, were soon annihilated. ■

# TEACHER IDEAS

## Discussion Questions

1. Define *decimation*. Why was it used by the Roman general?

2. Why did Spartacus push his men toward the Alps?

3. Who was the general who eventually defeated Spartacus, and how did he accomplish his victory?

4. Where was Spartacus's homeland?

5. Identify the Roman legions that fell to Spartacus's band.

6. What fortifications did the Romans build to trap Spartacus?

7. How did Spartacus die?

8. What omen predicted Spartacus's greatness?

9. Why do you think Spartacus was so successful against the Roman army? What advantages did he have? What were his disadvantages?

10. Do you think that the two years of freedom won by Spartacus's daring escape justified the loss of so many men, women, and children? What would you have done under similar circumstances?

## History Lesson: Great Generals of the First Century B.C.

### GAIUS MARIUS (157-86 B.C.)

Marius came from an obscure family and found success in the army by distinguishing himself in battle. His fame and popularity increased during his leadership of Roman forces in several conflicts.

When Jugurtha usurped the throne of Numidia from his cousin and killed all Italian traders residing in Africa, the Roman senate declared the Jugurthine War (111 B.C.). Marius achieved much military success during this war, but the actual conclusion to the war was falsely credited to him. In 105 B.C., Sulla, Marius's quaestor, convinced Jugurtha's father-in-law to betray the outlaw. Credit for this idea went to Marius, and the slighting of Sulla's participation began the animosity between these two men.

During Marius's tenure in Africa, a large-scale migration of Germanic barbaric tribes occurred when 500,000 men, women, and children were searching for new land. Crossing the Alps, they marched into Spain and made a demand for land that the Romans refused. After two Roman armies (approximately 80,000 soldiers) were defeated by the barbarians in 105 B.C., Marius was appointed to confront the situation. Due to his careful reorganization of the army, Marius created an efficient military machine. He set rigid training requirements for his troops, increased the size of the legion, and improved his military equipment. As a result, the barbarian hordes were no match for his force. In two battles, Marius's armies nearly wiped out the Germanic tribes.

To increase the number of troops, he eliminated the property requirement for soldiers so that the poorer classes could join, transforming the army into an entirely volunteer organization. Military service provided a soldier a comfortable retirement. The compensation system, however, encouraged soldiers to transfer their loyalty to the general who gave him these favors instead of the state. This created a situation where one man could control an entire legion and thus opened the way for the civil wars.

Shortly after the defeat of the Germanic tribes, Rome found itself threatened by a revolt of its Italian allies (*socii*) who demanded full citizenship rights and representation in the senate. Led by Sulla and Marius, Roman forces recaptured the rebel cities, but in 88 B.C., the cities of Italy were accorded all citizen rights as long as they declared loyalty to Rome.

Problems then occurred on another front. The King of the Pontus, Mithradates III, taking advantage of the chaos caused by the situation, seized Roman territory, thinking that Rome would not have the resources to engage in two wars at once. However, when he massacred (88 B.C.) all Romans and Italians living in Asia (approximately 80,000), the Romans reacted with a vengeance. The senate gave Sulla command of the army, but Marius, now 67 years old, wanted one last command. Sulla, however, forced Marius to flee Rome and then set out for the East to do battle. Marius returned to Rome and for five days and nights slaughtered all his political opponents. He managed to get himself elected consul for the seventh time, but his success was short-lived because only 18 days after his election, he died.

## LUCIUS CORNELIUS SULLA (138-78 B.C.)

Unlike Marius, Sulla came from a noble Roman family. During the Jugurthine War, he displayed his diplomatic skills by resolving the conflict and during the rebellion of the cities, he exhibited his military prowess. Sulla's popularity and competence angered Marius who aspired to be the sole commander of Rome.

When the senate named Sulla general to head the troops against Mithradates, the animosity between these two men erupted. Sulla's loyal army helped him force Marius's retreat. He then headed east and handily defeated Mithradates both on land and sea. The Greek cities that had sided with the king found themselves the victims of Rome's wrath. Sulla marched through Greece, looting the sacred treasuries of Delphi and Olympia and forcing the disloyal cities to pay a heavy tribute.

Meanwhile, Marius had reestablished himself in Rome and nullified all of Sulla's laws. The senate tried to end this civil dispute through diplomatic channels but failed. When Marius died, his loyal followers were too disunited to withstand Sulla's assault. In 79 B.C., Sulla marched to Rome and like his predecessor, eliminated his opponents in a terrible blood bath. More than 4,700 men were killed, including 90 senators and 2,600 merchant class knights. Sulla became dictator (82-79 B.C.) and tried to reestablish the old Roman constitution, which affirmed the senate's power. Once his measures were in force, he resigned and retired to his farm.

## GNAEUS POMPEIUS MAGNUS (106-48 B.C.)

Pompey was only 23 years old when he helped Sulla in the fight against Marius. His prestige was enhanced by his successful handling of two other major conflicts, the rebellions of Lepidus in Rome and Sertorius in Spain. He also joined Crassus in the Spartacus affair, and his success did not stop there. In 67 B.C., Pompey was given 500 ships and more than 120,000 troops to eliminate the pirates who harassed Roman ships in the Mediterranean. Within three months, he had cleaned out their sanctuaries and secured the sea for Rome. He also took part in subduing Mithradates and capturing Jerusalem (66 B.C.).

His continued success worried the senate who thought they might have another Sulla or Marius on hand. When Pompey returned home, the senate failed to offer him its support and transferred its loyalty to a "new" man—Julius Caesar. Seemingly unalarmed by the senate's defection, Pompey allied himself with Caesar and Crassus in forming the First Triumvirate, an extralegal alliance in which all three men promised to advance each other's careers. It was, however, only a matter of time until each general wanted to run the state alone. Pompey and Caesar (Crassus had already died) fought for dominance at the Battle of Pharsalus and Pompey was defeated.

## SUGGESTED TOPICS FOR FURTHER RESEARCH

1. Plutarch's works

2. life of Crassus

3. Jugurthine War

4. rebellion of Sertorius

5. rebellion of M. Lepidus

### Language Arts

## VOCABULARY BUILDING

Prefixes:

- *bio/bi* from Greek noun *bios* meaning "life"
- *mon* from Greek adjective *monos* meaning "single, alone"

1. Match the word (column A) with the definition (column B).

| A | B |
|---|---|
| biopsy | account of a person's life |
| monocle | capable of decomposition by natural processes |
| biodegradable | single corrective lens |
| monogamy | having certain functions carried out by electronic equipment |
| biography | diagnostic study of tissue from a living being |
| monolith | having one spouse |
| biology | a large pillar of stone |
| bionic | science of life |

2. Find five more words that are derived from *bios*.

3. Find five more words that are derived from *monos*.

## CRITICAL THINKING

Not all Romans embraced the gladiatorial entertainments with equal enthusiasm. In the first century A.D., a Stoic writer by the name of Lucius Annaeus Seneca (Nero's tutor, see chapter 10) wrote 124 essays in the form of letters to his friend on specific moral issues. One such essay addressed the depravity of the gladiator shows:

*Epistulae VII*[3]

You ask, Lucilius, what I think you should avoid—a crowd. It is impossible to frequent large groups of people without losing some of one's character. I confess my weakness to you in this regard. Whenever I go out amongst people, I bring back with me some quality of character I sought to avoid. Vice becomes attractive and clings to my person. The worst possible condition is to sit in some gladiator show where pleasure easily seduces one to enjoy evil. Every time I go, I return more greedy, more self-serving, and more desolate than when I went—even more cruel and malevolent than I thought possible.

Just the other day I went to a noon show expecting to see some sport or wit, at least to relax a little. But this did not happen. In my previous association with the games, I judged them to be merciful. Now all pretense of humanity has been eliminated. Pure murder remains! These men have nothing to protect them; their entire bodies are exposed to every type of attack. The fans prefer this all-out slaughter to the more gentle contests of the past. They wear no helmets, no shields to ward off the iron swords. What is the sense in their not wearing this armor? What use is skill in such a fight? Both defenses merely postpone the inevitable—DEATH!

In the morning, combatants are thrown to lions and bears. At noon, the victors are at the mercy of the fickle crowd, which throws them against more opponents until they are all dead. The people justify such cruelty by saying, "He was a robber" or "He murdered a man and so deserves this fate." The crowd excites the foes with these cheers: "Burn! Kill! Strike!" Then the crowd questions why the gladiators rush against the sword so timidly or why they kill with too little audacity. They "boo" if one does not die willingly. Should there be a halt in the action, the crowd shouts, "Let's slit some throats so something will happen."

I am convinced, Lucilius, that only bad can come to those who participate in such evil.

## DISCUSSION QUESTIONS

1. What is Seneca's main criticism of the gladiator shows?

2. Compare Seneca's reaction to being a gladiator game spectator in ancient Rome to your reaction to being a spectator at a modern sports event.

3. Do spectators react differently at different activities? How might you feel at a boxing match? a car race? a soccer game? a ballet performance? a baseball game? a bullfight?

4. Write an essay that refutes or supports Seneca's thesis. Use your own experiences to confirm your theory.

## MOVIE WATCHING

See the movie *Spartacus* (see Resources) and compare it to the factual information given in Plutarch's "Life of Crassus."

---

[3]See Seneca, Resources.

## Cultural Lesson: *Ludi Scaeni* (Roman Theater)

The government hosted free entertainments (*ludi*) throughout the Roman world during public holidays and religious festivals. The most popular shows were the *munera gladiatoria* (gladiator games) and the *Bestiarii*, in which wild animals fought to the death.

In the area of the theater, it was comedy that captured the hearts of Romans. Rome's greatest playwrights, Plautus (250-184 B.C.) and Terence (birth date unknown-159 B.C.), produced a great number of comedies. Plautus's *Menaechmi*, the inspiration for Shakespeare's *Comedy of Errors*, suggests what must have appealed to the ancient Roman theatergoer: sight gags, mistaken identities, and farcical plots.

Other less-sophisticated entertainments also became popular. The mime (*mimus*) was well liked but should not be confused with modern silent acting. Instead, the performer(s) presented a variety of skits, songs, and dances resembling a vaudeville revue. Dramatic presentations might have been part of the mime, as well as acrobatic romps or puppet shows. Burlesque plays satirized scenes from everyday life. A unique characteristic of the mime was that women participated, unlike more serious drama in which men played all roles. Although these women were not held in high esteem, nevertheless, some of them became famous. Mark Antony (see chapter 9) chose the mimer Cytheris as his mistress, and Empress Theodora, an actress, became the wife of Justinian (527 A.D.)—after he repealed a law that forbid any Roman senator from marrying someone of the theatrical profession.

Pantomimes were also given during these festivals. These were ballet performances, most of which were based on mythology or tragedy (e.g., "The Trojan Woman" and "Leda and the Swan"). The performer said nothing, relying solely on gesture and movement to portray the story. Use of closed masks allowed the actors to play several parts. Flutes, pipes, and percussion instruments supplied the music.

The first plays were presented outdoors with no stage or seats. In 145 B.C., a wooden theater was built, but it was only a temporary structure that was removed once the holiday ended. In 55 B.C., Pompey erected the first permanent stone theater (26,000 seats) on the Campus Martius. In 13 B.C., the Theater of Balbus (7,700 seats), and later, the Theater of Marcellus (14,000 seats) were completed. Although large by modern standards, when compared to the size of the Circus Maximus, which was used for chariot racing (250,000 seats), they were perhaps not so spectacular to the Romans.

The Romans adapted the Greek theater design by cutting down on the orchestra circle and enlarging the entire structure. The backdrop to the stage was often three stories high. Trap doors allowed actors to sneak on stage, cranes could hoist them aloft, and revolving screens offered scenery changes. Even special sound effects were used, like the simulation of thunder and lightning.

Since there was no artificial light, all plays, mimes, and pantomimes were given during the daylight hours. Canvas canopies were stretched over the top to shield the spectators from the sun. Food vendors hawked their wares. The state presented the ludi for free for all citizens to enjoy. The Romans believed the lower classes could be appeased with these entertainments. "Give them bread and circuses!" was the establishment's answer to proletarian needs.

## DRAMATIC PRESENTATION

As a group, read a play from Plautus or Shakespeare and present one act to the class. Suggestions: Shakespeare's *Comedy of Errors* or *Twelfth Night*; Plautus's *Menaechmi, Amphitruo, Miles Gloriosus,* or *Mostellaria.*

# RESOURCES

Arnott, Peter D. *The Ancient Greek and Roman Theatre*. New York: Random House, 1971.

Carcopino, Jerome. *Daily Life in Ancient Rome*. New Haven, Conn.: Yale University Press, 1940.

Fast, Howard. *Spartacus*. New York: Dell Publishing, 1980.

Johnston, Mary. *Roman Life*. Chicago: Scott, Foresman, 1957.

McCullough, Colleen. *The First Man in Rome*. New York: William Morrow, 1990.

Perowne, Stewart. *Death of the Roman Republic*. Garden City, N.Y.: Doubleday, 1968.

Plutarch. *Parallel Lives*. Loeb Classical Library, 1984.
    This anthology of biographies covers the lives of Pompey, Marius, Sulla, and Crassus.

Seneca, Lucius Annaeus, *Letters from a Stoic*, ed. Robin Campbell (Middlesex, England: Penguin Classics, 1969).

Shakespeare, William. *Comedy of Errors*. New York: Bantam Books, 1963.

_____. *Twelfth Night*. New York: Bantam Books, 1988.

*Spartacus*. Universal Pictures, 1960. Video (185 minutes).

Wallace, Lew. *Ben Hur*. Westwood, N.J.: Barbour, 1988.

# VII

# Druids of Gaul
## *(55 B.C.)*

### INTRODUCTION

Gaius Julius Caesar was born in 102 B.C. to a patrician family. As an adult, however, he allied himself politically with the popular party to advance his career. At age 19, he wed Cornelia, the daughter of a supporter of Marius, the leader of the popular party. In 82 B.C., the dictator Sulla, an optimate, gained control of the government and ordered Caesar to divorce his wife. When Caesar refused, Sulla confiscated all his property and relieved him of his political post. Caesar secreted himself away for several years until it was safe for him to re-emerge. He then joined the army and served with great distinction.

When Sulla died in 78 B.C., Caesar returned to Rome and earned recognition as a great orator and prosecutor. On route to the island of Rhodes where he was to study rhetoric, he was captured by pirates and held for ransom. Once freed, Caesar commandeered a cotillion of ships, pursued his kidnappers relentlessly until they were captured, and then crucified the culprits.

During the next decade, Caesar held numerous political offices, including praetor, aedile, and quaestor. In 61 B.C., he served as governor of Spain and excelled both as a military commander and civil administrator. It is at this time that the extralegal coalition, the First Triumvirate, was formed. Three men, Pompey, a general, Julius Caesar, a politician and military commander, and Marcus Crassus, a wealthy civilian, joined forces to promote each other's political interests. To seal the bargain, Julius Caesar's daughter, Julia, married Pompey.

After serving out his consulship, Caesar became governor of Gaul for five years, and the senate assigned him four legions for use in subduing the barbarians. It took nine years for the complete subjugation of this territory, and during this time, Caesar also invaded Germany and Britain.

When Julia died in 54 B.C., and Crassus the following year, the triumvirate dissolved. Pompey, jealous of Caesar's success and popularity, persuaded the senate to declare Caesar a public enemy if he did not disband his army. It was considered an act of treason for any Roman general to bring his troops into Italy, but Caesar refused to relinquish control of his legions. Standing at the Rubicon River, the northern boundary, Caesar hesitated about the momentous decision he was about to make. With the utterance *"Alea iacta est"* (The die is cast), he marched his army across the Rubicon and initiated a civil war with his old friend and political ally, Pompey. Within three months, Caesar controlled Italy, and Pompey had fled to Greece where the two generals met in battle. Although outnumbered two to one, Caesar routed his rival.

Pompey then fled to Egypt (48 B.C.) where he was assassinated before Caesar's arrival. Caesar dallied awhile in Egypt, siring a son, Caesarion, with Queen Cleopatra and then returned to Rome. He was declared dictator for a year, but when he made known his desire to hold that position permanently, he earned the enmity of many Romans led by Brutus and Cassius. A group of senators assassinated Caesar on the Ides of March in 44 B.C. His death, however, solved nothing for the government of Rome. The Republic was already lost, ravaged by years of civil war and an ineffectual senate. Julius Caesar had paved the way for the beginning of the Roman Empire, and it was his adopted son Octavian (Augustus) who became the first Roman emperor.

Caesar was not only a brilliant military commander and politician but a skilled orator and writer. Unfortunately, all his speeches are lost, as are his poems and grammar books. Only his memoirs, consisting of seven books on the Gallic War and three on the Civil War remain. When in Gaul, Caesar carefully kept field notes about his army's activities and confrontations. Later, he polished his observations into a formal manuscript for publication.

Included are two passages from his book *Gallic War*. The first chapter is a description of the Gauls and Germans, their customs, religious practices, marriage rites, and even the unusual animals Caesar's troops encounter. It is the only eyewitness account available of these two groups of people and affords an interesting look at a barbaric culture in the first century B.C.

## The Gauls[1]

◼ In Gaul, there are only two classes of people of any importance, the Druids and the knights. The common man is treated almost like a slave, kept in the bonds of servitude by the enormity of the taxes imposed upon him, as well as the injustice of the powerful lords. Burdened with debt, the ordinary man indentures himself to the noble class, which executes the same legal rights as a master holds over a slave.

The Druids, one class of nobles, control all religious matters. They also decide all public and private disputes. Yearly, the Druids assemble in a sacred place in the middle of Gaul to act as judges. If any crime or murder has been committed, if there is a controversy over an inheritance or a boundary line, the Druids resolve the disagreement. They establish the fine to be imposed or the punishment to be enacted. Should any person not abide by the court's decision, he is excluded from participating in sacrifices—which every Gaul considers the most severe penalty. Any individual who opposes the Druids' decree is marked as a wicked and godless man, and all people avoid him. They flee his approach and refuse to speak with the accursed lest some misfortune befall them just by this contact. No rights will ever be restored to the accursed, who is ostracized from his tribe forever.

There is one Druid who acts as chief over the other priests. When that person dies, if anyone excels from the rest, a new chief is appointed. If there are several Druids of equal merit, the succession of the leadership is chosen by a vote, or sometimes by a force of arms if a peaceable solution is impossible.

The Druids retain special privileges among the Gauls. They are exempt from taxation and excused from military service. Induced by these rewards, many young boys desire to become Druids or are persuaded to do so by parents and friends. During their training they are forced to memorize a great number of verses. In fact, they believe it is harmful to write down these verses although they do use Greek characters for public and private business. They shun writing for two reasons. Foremost, they wish to keep their knowledge secret from the common people. Also, they believe that if the priests rely too heavily on writing, this might diminish their powers of memory. (I, too, believe this—that writing reduces the skills of learning and memorization.) Since it takes a long time to train to become a Druid, they are bound to this profession for 20 years.

In religious matters, the Druids emphasize that the spirit does not disappear after death but transfers to another body. They believe that this fact will promote courageous deeds since the fear of death is removed. The Druids also act as teachers to the young, discussing many things about the great size of the universe, the nature of life itself, and the strength of the immortal gods.

The second noble class is that of the knights who are the military leaders of the Gauls and whenever war is declared, the knights are in charge. (I would like to add that before I came to Gaul, war was almost a yearly occurrence.) The Gauls, and especially the knights, enjoy inflicting injuries on other tribes. The knights are very wealthy and influential lords and have many retainers and clients attached to them.

All people of Gaul are involved in the religious rite of human sacrificing. They believe that it is impossible to appease the gods unless a human life is given in exchange for a life. Therefore, anyone who is gravely ill or who participates in battle, either burns men as sacrificial victims or promises to do so when his ordeal is over.

The Druids administer these sacrifices, which are public spectacles. Huge figurines are woven from straw and stuffed with live humans. The straw is set ablaze and the person trapped inside dies. They generally sacrifice robbers or other lawbreakers, believing that criminals are more appealing to the gods. But should their supply of villains run out, they readily select innocent people as victims.

---

[1]Caesar, Julius, *Gallic War* VI: 13.

The Gauls deem Mercury[2] to be the most powerful deity. He is the originator of all arts, the patron of roads and journeys, and assists in the profit making of business and trade. They believe that they are descended from the god of the underworld, Pluto, and for this reason, they define all time not by the number of days but by the number of nights.

After Mercury and Pluto, they rank Apollo, Mars, Jupiter, and Minerva as important gods and hold the same opinion of them as our own people, namely, that Apollo cures diseases and that Minerva introduced handiworks and crafts. Jupiter rules the sky, and Mars is the god of war. After engaging in battle, they generally consecrate whatever goods they have looted to Mars. They gather up animals and other pillaged belongings and place them on a shrine. I have seen many of these shrines in Gaul untouched and undefiled. No one dares to rob them or conceal the spoils of war among his own possessions since the punishment for such sacrilege is torture.

The Gauls are different from almost everyone else in their attitude toward children. Until a child reaches military age, he cannot approach his parents in public or even speak to them. A man holds the power of life and death over his wife and children. Should he die under suspicious circumstances, his relatives will interrogate his spouse, and if she is found guilty of murder, she is burned or tortured to death.

A noble's funeral is a lavish affair. All of the deceased's favorite possessions, even animals, are cremated along with the body. Not too long ago, even servants and clients were added to the funeral pyre, but this custom has now ceased. ■

---

[2]Caesar gave Latin names to Gallic deities.

The Germans[3]

■ The Germans are quite different from the Druids. They have no class of Druid priests, nor do they practice human sacrifices. They only worship the gods they can visibly see, namely, the Sun, the Moon, and Fire. They spend their entire lives in the pursuit of hunting or making war. Unmarried men are greatly respected, and abstinence from sex is thought to increase one's strength and energy. It is considered disgraceful for a man to have sexual relations with a woman before he is twenty. On the other hand, they are not embarrassed by nakedness, and both sexes bathe undressed together in rivers. Normally they only wear small fur pieces to cover their private parts.

The Germans have no interest in farming, and most of their food is milk, cheese, and wild animal meat. No one owns a piece of property, but the leaders of a tribe distribute a parcel of land for a family's use for one year only. They do this for a variety of reasons: the most important being that they fear domesticity saps one's desire for war. They also are concerned that a powerful individual might acquire large tracts of land and force others to leave their homes. If they stayed more than a year, people would build strong houses and this would weaken their natural resistance to heat and cold. Also, wealthy individuals might arise and with wealth comes disputes over possessions. Under this system of yearly land ownership, each person is equal to another. ■

---

[3]Caesar, Julius, *Gallic War* VI: 13.

Animals from the Hercynian Forest[4]

■ In the past, the Gauls were more courageous than the Germans, and due to over-population, they often crossed the Rhine River to wage war and settle new colonies, populating the fertile area around the Hercynian Forest. This forest is so immense that it takes a traveler nine days just to cover its width. Many unique types of animals live there. There is an ox that resembles a stag in the shape of its body, but on its forehead branches a single antler. From the top of this antler several prongs extend out laterally, and both sexes of this species display this ornament.

Another unusual animal is an elk that is shaped like a goat, although a little larger. Their horns are stunted, and their legs have no knee joints. Consequently, they must stand to sleep, and if they fall down by accident, they are unable to right themselves. These elks use trees for couches, leaning on them when they rest. Hunters follow the tracks of these elks and observe their resting places. They then uproot the trees or partially cut the trunks so that when the animals lean on them, they fall down. Unable to stand up, the elks are easily trapped.

The third unusual animal is called an *auroch*, which is almost, but not quite, as large as an elephant. They are shaped like bulls and possess tremendous strength and speed. Whenever a man kills an auroch, he brings back its horns as proof of his bravery. These horns are huge, and the Gauls encase their tips with silver and use them as drinking cups at lavish banquets. ■

---

[4]Caesar, Julius, *Gallic War* VI: 13.

# TEACHER IDEAS

## Discussion Questions

1. Why did the Druids refrain from using written records?

2. What did the Gauls consider to be the most severe punishment?

3. Why did the Gauls perform human sacrifices?

4. What two privileges do the Druids enjoy?

5. Name three of the Druids' duties.

6. What types of food did the Germans eat?

7. What two pursuits did the Germans enjoy most?

8. For what were the auroch's horns used?

9. What do you think of Caesar's skill of observation? Has he given his reader a detailed account of the people of Gaul and Germany? Do you think he is accurate? Can you find anything in his account that might not be true? What types of information has he presented to his audience?

10. From your knowledge of the level of sophistication of the Romans of the first century B.C., what might their reaction have been toward the people of Gaul?

## History Lesson: Optimates and Populares

Political parties as we know them did not exist in ancient Rome. The government was run by individuals who had money and power. These wealthy individuals known as Nobles belonged to both the patrician and plebeian classes. They excluded all others from public office and dominated the senate while the assemblies were compelled to assent to their wishes (see chapter 3, History Lesson). However, as the size of Rome's territorial holdings expanded, the senate found itself unable to cope with the new demands. The time had finally arrived for someone to challenge the senate's exclusive power, which existed only through custom, not by any written law.

The Optimates were the dominant group in the senate who wished to maintain the status quo. The Populares were also members of the noble class who used the backing of the urban proletariat to push through their legislation. By controlling the office of tribune and the assemblies, they could veto the senate's actions as well as initiate their own reforms.

Tiberius Gracchus (133 B.C.), a popular noble, urged change. He supported the small farmers whom he felt were the backbone of the state and the nucleus of the Roman army. The senatorial Optimates disagreed because the destruction of the large farms would cost them the loss of their own real estate. Tiberius saw the senate's disunity as an opportunity to push his reforms. Backed by the urban poor who had flocked to Rome looking for work, he managed to see his ideas passed into law. The senate reacted by murdering him violently. Armed with clubs, the senators themselves beat Tiberius Gracchus to death and ordered the execution of 300 of his supporters.

His murder did not stop the impetus for change. In 123 B.C., Gaius Gracchus, Tiberius's younger brother,[5] was elected tribune. With the support of the masses, he was able to enact many laws aimed at breaking the senate's monopoly over the government. In turn, the senate spread vicious lies about Gaius who, as a consequence, lost the office of tribune. Like his brother, Gaius was assassinated at the direction of the senate. To compound its atrocious behavior, the senate, without the benefit of trial, ordered the execution of 3,000 Gracchi reformers.

Tiberius and Gaius successfully created a new political group in Rome—the Populares, which checked the senate's powers. However, after Tiberius's and Gaius's deaths, many individuals controlled this group not for altruistic reasons but to advance their own ambitions. Marius was a Populare, as was Julius Caesar, both of whom used the urban masses to help check their Optimate opponents, Sulla and Pompey. The political chaos of the first century B.C., and the senate's inability to maintain its position of authority, allowed these men to claim ultimate power. The natural result was the demise of the Republic and the birth of the Empire (27 B.C.).

## SUGGESTED TOPICS FOR FURTHER RESEARCH

1. agrarian reforms of the Gracchi

2. Battle of Pharsalus—Caesar versus Pompey

3. office of tribune

4. Roman territorial expansion during the first century B.C.

5. Cornelia, mother of the Gracchi brothers

## Language Arts

### VOCABULARY BUILDING

Prefixes:

- *inter* from Latin preposition *inter* meaning "between"
- *intra* from Latin preposition *intra* meaning "within"
- *bene* from Latin adverb *bene* meaning "well"
- *male* from Latin adverb *male* meaning "badly"

1. If *factor* means "doer" and *murus* means "wall," what do the following words and phrases mean?

   benefactor       intermural sports

   malefactor       intramural sports

2. What is the difference between an *interstate* and an *intrastate* highway?

3. Would you rather have a benign tumor or a malignant one?

---

[5]The Gracchi brothers were the grandsons of Publius Cornelius Scipio Africanus (see chapter 5).

4. Define the following words and use each in a sentence:

| | |
|---|---|
| malady | intermediary |
| benefit | intermittent |
| malaria | intravenous |

## CRITICAL THINKING

One hundred and fifty years after Julius Caesar described the tribes of Gaul and Germany, Cornelius Tacitus (see chapters 10 and 11) wrote a lengthy essay about the Germans called *Germania* and published circa A.D. 99. Since Caesar's day, the Romans had come in contact with the Germans both through war and commerce. Much of the information Tacitus presents has been substantiated by archaeological evidence, but not every detail is accurate. Following are five excerpts from *Germania*:

4.  I agree with most men who believe the Germans have not married with other nations and therefore are an unmixed and distinct race. That is why most of them look the same with savage blue eyes, red hair, and large bodies. They cannot endure much toil and labor or withstand the discomforts of thirst and heat, but they are accustomed to the cold and hunger.[6]

16.  It is well known that the Germans have no cities. They do not even locate their houses near each other but prefer to keep them separate. Each man surrounds his own dwelling with space unlike our homes, either as a precaution against fire or because they are just inexperienced in the craft of building. They do not use stone but unadorned timber. They also dig underground caves and lay dirt on top as a shelter from the cold winter or as a storage area for their produce.[7]

17.  Everyone, male and female, wears the same piece of clothing, a cloak held with a pin or a thorn. They must sit near the hearth all day when it is winter to keep warm. Wealthy people wear a tight cloak which clings to their limbs. Wild animal pelts are also used. Women might have a linen garment colored purple, and since it does not extend over their arms in the manner of sleeves, their arms are naked and even part of their breast is exposed.[8]

18-19.  The sanctity of marriage is upheld by all Germans. For among all barbarians they alone have only one wife, and she does not bring a dowry to her husband, but he to her. The bride does not want frivolous or luxurious presents but prefers oxen, a horse with reins, a shield, a spear, or a sword. She believes that by accepting these gifts, she pledges herself to the marriage. She comes to the union as a partner to her husband in all danger and adversity. She will endure with him the fruits of peace or the pain of war. German women live lives of unassailable virtue. They are not seduced by licentious public shows nor corrupted by the excitement of banquets. Adultery for both men and women is rare in so large a country. Should a woman be caught in an affair, she is immediately punished by her husband who cuts off her hair and drives her naked through the village while he beats her.[9] No German scoffs at debauchery

---

[6]Tacitus, Cornelius, *Germania* 4.

[7]Ibid. 16.

[8]Ibid. 17.

[9]Tacitus, Cornelius, *Germania* 18.

nor considers it acceptable to corrupt or be corrupted. To limit the number of children or to kill one already born is considered a crime. Good morals are stronger there than good laws elsewhere.

23.   The Germans drink a beverage similar to wine made from barley and wheat. Their food is simple, uncultivated fruits, game, and thickened milk. Without sauces or excessive preparation they satisfy their hunger. There is not the same temperance, however, toward drinking. It is conceivable that should their enemy appease their voracious appetite for drunkenness by supplying as much alcohol as they desired, they could conquer them by corruption rather than by arms.[10]

## COMPARISON AND CONTRAST

1.   Compare the attitudes of Caesar and Tacitus toward the Germans. Are they alike or different?

2.   Compare the German houses with that of the Roman house of the first century A.D. (see chapter 15).

3.   Research Roman clothing and compare it to that worn by the Germans.

4.   Tacitus is an excellent historian, but his personal opinions are revealed in his essay. In chapter 18 of *Germania*, whom do you think Tacitus is comparing to the virtuous German? What does he see as virtuous? What does he see as immoral?

5.   Compare German eating habits to those of the Romans (see chapter 12).

### Cultural Lesson: Dating the Roman Way

The Romans did not simply number the days of each month as we do now. Instead, three days of each month had special names from which all dates were reckoned backwards. These special dates were:

- the *Kalends*: the 1st of each month;
- the *Nones*:   the 7th of March, May, July, and October, and the 5th of all other months; and
- the *Ides*:   the 15th of March, May, July, and October, and the 13th of all other months.

Let's see how this worked. Be careful! When counting backward, the date itself must be included. Calculate *III Idus Februarias*, or three days before the Ides of February. The Ides fall on February 13. Count backward *including* the Ides. Day one=the Ides (the 13th). Day two=the 12th. Day three=the 11th. So III Idus Februarias=February 11.

Let's do another. Calculate *V Kalendas Maias* or five days before the Kalends of May. Day one=the Kalends (the 1st). Day two=April 30. Day three=April 29. Day four=April 28. Day five=April 27. So V Kalendas Maias=April 27.

An exception: The day before each marking date was simply stated Pridie Idus/Kalends/Nones. *Pridie* means "the day before."

---

[10]Ibid. 23.

**ROMAN DATES**

Translate the following Roman dates:

1. Pridie Idus Martias

2. V Idus Februarias

3. VIII Kalendas Maias

4. VI Nonas Maias

5. IX Kalendas Junias

6. Idibus Juniis

7. XVIII Kalendas Sextiles

8. Nonis Octobribus

9. VI Idus Novembres

10. Kalendis Decembribus

What does "Beware the Ides of March"[11] mean?

## Et Alia: Gracchi and Scipio Family Tree

Make a family tree for Tiberius and Gaius Gracchus (see figure 7.1), the founders of the popular party and the descendants of Publius Cornelius Scipio (see chapter 5). All the family members have similar names, so be careful! Hint: Barbatus, the founder of this clan, should be at the top of your tree and the Gracchi brothers at the bottom of the tree. The following names should be included on your tree:

Tiberius Sempronius Gracchus and Gaius Semptonius Gracchus—brothers

Tiberius Sempronius Gracchus—father

Cornelia Scipio—mother

P. Cornelius Scipio Africanus Maior—maternal grandfather

Aemelia Paulus—maternal grandmother

P. Cornelius Scipio Africanus and Gn. Cornelius Scipio Africanus—brothers of Cornelia

P. Cornelius Scipio—maternal great-grandfather

Gn. Cornelius Scipio Calvus—brother of P. Cornelius Scipio

L. Cornelius Scipio—maternal great-great-grandfather

L. Cornelius Scipio Barbatus—maternal great-great-great-grandfather

---

[11]Shakespeare, William, *Julius Caesar*, Act 1, Scene 2.

GRACCHI AND SCIPIO FAMILY TREE

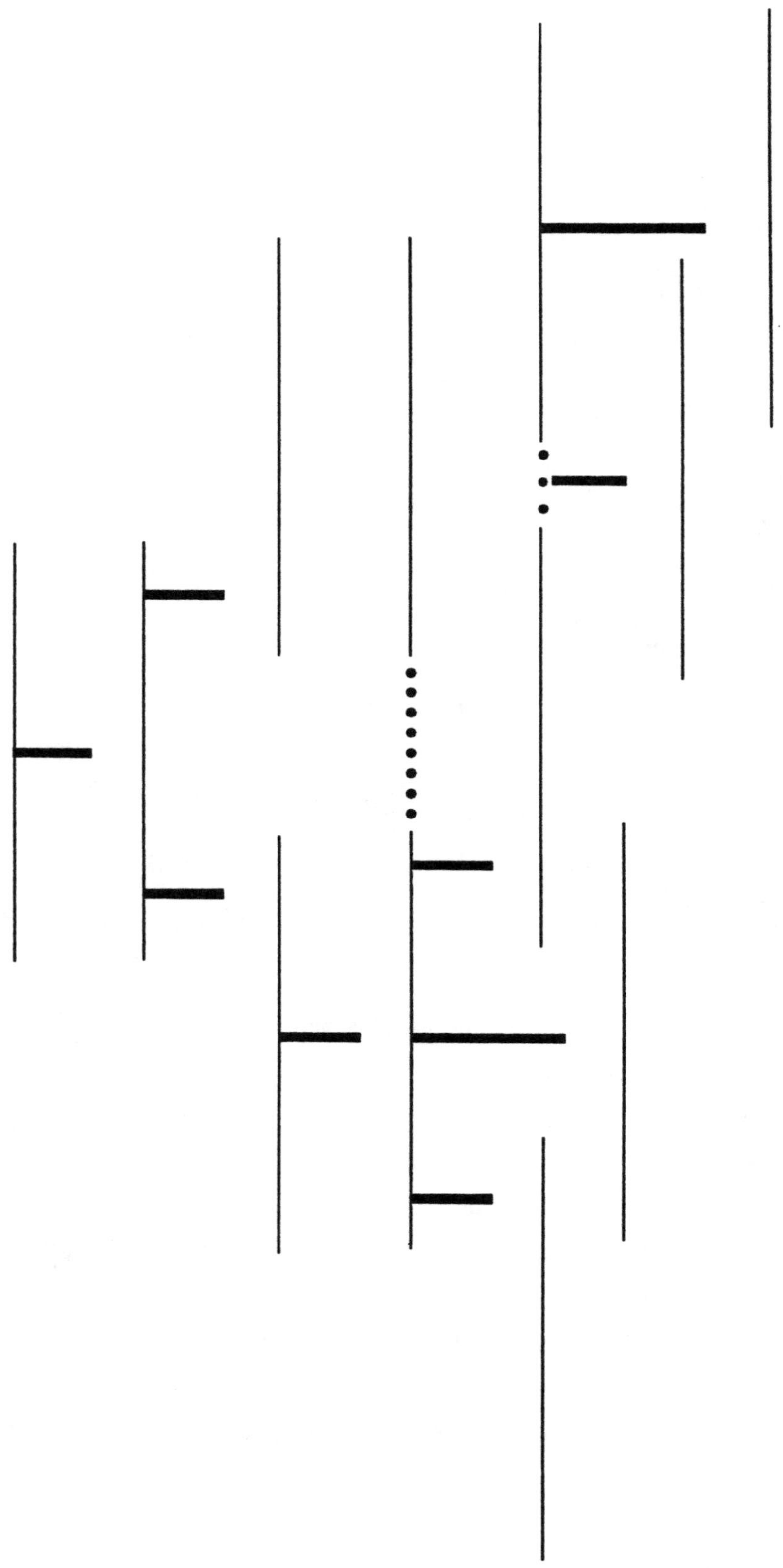

Fig. 7.1. Family Tree.

# RESOURCES

*The Battle for Gaul*, trans. Anne Wiseman and Peter Wiseman. Boston: David R. Godine, 1980.

*Julius Caesar*. Culver City, Calif.: MGM/UA, 1953. Video. (122 minutes).

*Julius Caesar*. Los Angeles: Republic Pictures, 1970. Video. (116 minutes).

"Optimates and Populares," *Encyclopaedia Britannica*, 1988 ed., vol. 8, 972.

Plutarch. *Parallel Lives*. Loeb Classical Library, 1986.
    Describes the lives of Tiberius and Gaius Gracchus, and Brutus.

# VIII

# Siege of Alesia
## (51 B.C.)

### INTRODUCTION

With well-disciplined troops, the Romans conquered the Mediterranean world and stretched their empire from Britain in the West, to Syria in the East and Egypt in the South. Amazingly, until the first century B.C., the Roman army consisted of only part-time soldiers who were recruited each year to serve wherever Rome might need fighting men. In 106 B.C., the general Marius reorganized the army into a professional force with each soldier enlisting for a period of 20 years.

The most common rank was that of a foot soldier. An infantryman received only nominal pay, less than a dollar per week, and from this small stipend he was obligated to supply his own clothing and equipment. However, he was rewarded with a share of the spoils of war and customarily retired with a small grant of land or monetary remuneration. He carried standardized arms, including a rectangular shield, two spears, one sword, and a dagger. While marching, his pack contained around 50 pounds of equipment including his grain ration (for making porridge), cooking gear, chains, tools for erecting siege works, a spade, rope, shovels, and axes.

Though the Roman legion consisted mainly of infantrymen, it contained other types of military personnel, including the cavalry. These horsemen were heavily protected by a helmet and chain mail and carried a small round shield, plus a thrusting spear and long sword. Cavalry horses were equipped with a bridle and saddle with no stirrups, so the cavalry used leg commands to turn their steeds. Other more specialized troops, such as archers, slingers, boatmen, and engineering experts, rounded out the Roman military forces. At the time of Augustus, the Roman army numbered approximately 350,000 men, including 25 legions (with more than 5,000 infantrymen in each), plus cavalry and auxiliary specialized troops, which numbered around 200,000 men. Miscellaneous forces completed this highly disciplined military force.

The next section, taken from Julius Caesar's *Gallic War*, describes the siege of Alesia, a town in eastern Gaul. The Gauls, led by a young noble Vercingetorix, made one last attempt to rid themselves of Roman domination. This unsuccessful revolt lasted three years (54-51 B.C.) and concluded with Vercingetorix's surrender of Alesia to the Romans. Julius Caesar removed Vercingetorix to Rome to languish in prison for six years while Caesar busied himself fighting the civil war against Pompey.

Finally, in 46 B.C., Caesar staged his great spectacular procession, which celebrated his victories over Gaul, Africa, the Pontus, and Egypt. He led the procession carried in a chariot drawn by four white horses. His troops marched behind, and following them, came the captives including

74

the once proud Vercingetorix (who was summarily executed after this triumph). Wagons loaded with gold, silver, jewels, and silk displayed the spoils of war plundered by Caesar's troops. To entertain the masses, Caesar arranged gladiator and beast shows, mock naval battles, and chariot races and filled 22,000 tables with comestibles to feed the crowds.

It was the greatest triumph ever to take place in Rome. Caesar was literally in control of the world. Only two years later, however, he died ignominiously at the hands of assassins on the floor of the senate house, a victim of his own ambition.

### The Siege of Alesia[1]

■ As the war waged by the Gauls against the Roman troops became difficult, their leader, Vercingetorix, retreated and led his troops into the town of Alesia. Situated on top of a high hill, Alesia appeared impregnable. On two sides of the site, rivers flowed to the bottom of the hill, and a large open plain three miles long stretched out from the base of the escarpment. Smaller hills surrounded the area protecting the town from all invaders. Due to its location, the town could be taken only by a long siege.

I pursued Vercingetorix to this location and proceeded to build siege works around the town for a space of 11 miles. I set up 23 towers at marked intervals along this line and posted troops to guard these posts day and night. Before our fortifications were completed, however, Vercingetorix ordered his cavalry to sneak out at night and scatter to various parts of Gaul to enlist more reinforcements. He calculated that the grain supply in the town would last only 30 days more, perhaps, if he parsimoniously doled out the food to the inhabitants.

Meanwhile, our Roman soldiers completed the mammoth task of fortifying such an expansive area. I ordered a 20-foot trench dug all around the town with straight sides and moved the towers back 400 feet from this trench. It was too difficult to protect so large a line, and I feared that the enemy might launch surprise attacks at night. Directly behind the towers, two more 15-foot ditches were excavated. I diverted water from one of the rivers to fill up the first ditch to act as an obstacle to the enemy. Next we built a 12-foot wall and placed a grillwork of pointed stakes on top to retard the enemy's attack should they try to bridge our lines.

Several times the Gauls attacked our forces and destroyed some of the battlements. Therefore, I decided to strengthen the armaments. In front of the ditches, more five-foot trenches were dug and filled with tree branches sharpened to points so that whoever entered would be impaled upon them. Smaller three-foot pits in a diagonal pattern came next, with thick tree trunks buried at the bottom. The trunks jutted out of the ground only about a depth of four fingers, and then sticks and twigs were thrown on top to conceal the trap. Eight rows of pits of this type were excavated at three-foot intervals. In front of these, large logs with iron hooks were placed over the ground. Once this line was completed on two sides, I ordered everyone to forage for a 30-day supply of grain and animal fodder so we would be able to remain at our stations without interruption.

**Centurion**

---

[1]Caesar, Julius, *Gallic War* VII: 68.

Thirty days passed, and no reinforcements had arrived to rescue the Gauls in Alesia. Their food supply was exhausted, and the various leaders met to discuss their options. Some proposed surrender as their only solution, while others recommended making an all-out attack while they still had strength. They selected the latter course.

Finally, the Gallic chieftains arrived with 80,000 new cavalry and 250,000 infantry and set up their troops on a hill only about one mile from our fortifications. The next day, the battle lines were drawn. The Gauls placed their cavalry on the open plain and stationed the footsoldiers on higher ground behind them. Once the Alesian troops saw their fellow countrymen, they took courage and immediately marched from the town. They filled the first trenches with dirt and wicker and prepared their battle lines.

In turn, I ordered my cavalry to attack theirs on the plain and readied my other troops for action. Scattered among the Gauls' forces were archers and lightly armed soldiers. These were very successful against our cavalry, which yielded to the onslaught. Confident they would win, the Gauls raised a roar of screaming and howling to boost their spirits. The battle raged from noon until sunset, but neither side was clearly victorious. Then our German allies attacked and killed the archers, and the rest of our troops pressed the enemy and drove them back toward the town.

The next day, both sides rested, but on the following night, the Gauls on the outlying hills sneaked toward our trenches. They brought large numbers of ladders, hooks, and other equipment, which they threw at my men guarding this location. At the same time, by preappointed signal, Vercingetorix led his men out of the town, but our soldiers rallied to this unexpected dual foray and managed to beat back the enemy. Both sides experienced many injuries because it was difficult to see in the dark. As long as the Gauls stayed at a distance, they were successful, but when they approached our lines, they became impaled on the hooks and caught by the spikes in the ditches. Our Roman soldiers stationed on the towers effectively hurled missiles against the Gauls who eventually retreated.

Then the Gaul leaders conferred about their next battle plan. They selected 60,000 troops distinguished for their bravery and sent them at night to station themselves on a hill north of town. Since this hill was so large, we had not been able to build any fortifications there, but two legions commanded by Gaius Rebilus and Gaius Reginus guarded the base of the hill. The Gauls hid behind the hill and exactly at noon attacked our troops. Simultaneously, the Gauls' cavalry rode against our entrenchments, and Vercingetorix marched his troops out of the town. Consequently, three main attacks were going on at the same time, and it was difficult for our battle formation to hold. Our weakest point was at the hill, and the Gauls seemed to be advancing successfully there.

I stationed myself on top of a hill where I could watch the entire battle and was able to dispatch reinforcements wherever and whenever I sensed they were needed. The Gauls realized that their salvation rested in their ability to break through the Roman fortifications, and we Romans felt we would win if we could hold our line. Reginus and Rebilus's troops were exhausted and seemed to be losing ground. I dispatched five cohorts [80 men each] led by Labienus to help them. Then I visited my soldiers and urged them to remain strong because this day's battle would surely determine the outcome of the war.

Meanwhile, back on the plain, the enemy had managed to dislodge many of our soldiers fighting from the towers and had filled the ditches with earth and wicker. I sent young Brutus to reinforce these troops, then Gaius Fabius with more men, and finally, I brought in fresh numbers myself when the fighting became very intense. The enemy began to lose heart, so I pressed forward with four cohorts and cavalry to help Labienus on the hill. We maneuvered around the hill and attacked the enemy from the rear. We threw down our pikes and began a close engagement with swords. The enemy could not withstand this double onslaught and tried to retreat, but our cavalry cut them off. A great slaughter occurred, and most of the enemy lost their lives that day.

The next day Vercingetorix called his fellow Gauls together. He said that he had undertaken this war against Rome not for his own benefit but for the freedom of all Gaul. Since they must now yield to the conqueror, he offered himself for whatever purpose they wished, either to hand him over to the Romans alive or to placate their enemy by his death. They then sent envoys to me to negotiate the surrender.

In this way, the revolt of the Gauls led by Vercingetorix was put to an end. Afterward, I went to Bibracte to spend the winter, and, when word of our victory reached Rome, all Romans celebrated with a 20-day holiday. ■

# TEACHER IDEAS

## Discussion Questions

1.  Where was Caesar's weakest point during the battle? How did he strengthen it?

2.  Describe two of the fortifications built around Alesia.

3.  How long would the grain supply last at Alesia?

4.  Who commanded the two legions at the base of the hill?

5.  How many Gauls were engaged in the battle according to Caesar?

6.  What did Julius Caesar say to encourage his troops?

7.  How did the people of Rome celebrate Caesar's victory?

8.  Which troops did Caesar bring to the aid of Labienus?

9.  Does Caesar's estimate of the Gallic troops seem excessive? Why might he have chosen to exaggerate their numbers?

10. Julius Caesar published his account of the Gallic War so that the people in Rome would not forget him while he was absent. It was a shrewd move calculated to prevent his rivals from usurping his power. From the account of the siege of Alesia, what might a Roman have learned about Julius Caesar? Would his impressions have been favorable or unfavorable? Use specific references from the text.

## History Lesson: The Conquest of Britain

While Julius Caesar was fighting in Gaul, he planned an invasion of Brittania (England) whose people had often helped the Gallic tribes in their fight against Rome. Caesar felt it important to stop this alliance, and so on August 25, 55 B.C., he left the mainland with a small force and sailed to Dover. In his own words, this is what Caesar saw:

> With the first cotillion of ships I reached Britain around the fourth hour, and on the hills above, I saw the enemy heavily armed awaiting our arrival. The place was situated such that the sea was surrounded by very narrow cliffs and from this high location it was easy for the enemy to hurl their weapons with accuracy.
>
> I concluded that this was an unsuitable place for disembarkation. I waited for the rest of the boats to arrive until the ninth hour. When all were assembled, I signaled for our departure and we sailed about seven miles up the coast to an open plain where I could beach the ships.
>
> The barbarians realized our plans and immediately attacked with their cavalry and war chariots. My men were unable to leave the boats, which were forced to stay in deep water. It was difficult for the troops to jump off and at the same time fight because their hands were burdened with heavy weapons.[2]

---

[2]Caesar, Julius, *Gallic War* IV: 23.

Not meeting with complete success in his first expedition, Caesar retreated to Gaul only to return the following year—that time with a force of 800 boats carrying five legions and four cavalry units. After several decisive battles, he exacted a promise of tribute from the local tribes, but upon his withdrawal from Britain, the Britons stopped tribute payments.

Rome and Britain subsequently enjoyed a highly profitable commercial exchange for many decades. The island was rich in precious metals, cattle, grain, and slaves—all of which Rome wanted. This peaceful exchange eventually ended. The Romans were eager to find an excuse to invade the British Isles.

In A.D. 40, a British prince, Adminius, was exiled by his family. He sought refuge with Emperor Caligula, and, when his father demanded his return, the Romans refused. Hostilities erupted. The British raided Roman outposts, and Rome seized upon these attacks as an excuse to launch a large invasion.

In A.D. 43, Emperor Claudius (the mad Caligula had been murdered) launched a full-scale expedition. Approximately 50,000 troops, plus animals and supplies, crossed the channel under the command of Aulus Plautinus. His first objective was an assault against Adminius's brothers. Once this was accomplished, he sent troops against other tribes. The biggest obstacle to Britain's freedom from Roman domination was its own disunity. Many invaders had settled this small island, and local tribes were hostile to each other. They would not unite to resist a common foe.

Though many clans signed treaties with Rome, not all was peaceful. For years to come, the Britons continued to raid Roman settlements. The people of the lowlands were more easily pacified than the highlanders. Finally, Emperor Hadrian (A.D. 122) built a permanent wall to guard the northern boundary of the empire. Further advancement was stopped; Scotland contained no riches to fill the treasury, and the expense in maintaining legions so far from Rome was enormous. Rome's greatest influence on Britain was in the southern and middle regions where Roman civilization flourished.

## SUGGESTED TOPICS FOR FURTHER RESEARCH

1. Caesar's British expedition (see *Gallic War* IV: 20-37)

2. Boudicca, British queen who led revolt against Rome in A.D. 61

3. Hadrian's Wall

4. Vespasian's role in Claudius's British campaign

5. Roman baths in Bath, England

## Language Arts

### VOCABULARY BUILDING

Suffix:

- *ine* from Latin suffix *inus*, meaning "of or pertaining to." In English, the suffix *ine* means "like or pertaining to" (e.g., *feminine* means "like a woman").

In the following exercise, the suffix *ine* has been added to form an adjective that describes a type of animal (e.g., *ovine* means "like a sheep"). What animal is associated with the following adjective?

- aquiline
- asinine
- bovine
- canine
- columbine
- elephantine
- equine
- feline
- lionine
- lupine
- piscine
- porcine
- serpentine
- ursine
- vulpine

## CREATIVE WRITING

1. Caesar kept a field diary of his activities and then used these notes to write a more polished account later. Write Caesar's field diary of the siege of Alesia.

2. Write a field diary of the siege of Alesia from the point of view of Vercingetorix.

## DRAMATIC READING

As the Romans marched across Europe and Asia, they subjugated the local inhabitants and made them a part of their domain. As in the siege of Alesia, the conquered tribes did not always accept Roman authority without resistance. The following two speeches are taken from the *Agricola* written A.D. 97-98 by Tacitus. This short biography describes the exploits of Julius Agricola, the Roman governor of Britain (A.D. 78-85), who was Tacitus's father-in-law. During his tenure of office, Julius Agricola managed to subdue many tribes of Britain, as well as introduce the culture and civilization of Rome to this island. Read the following two speeches. With a partner, present a dramatic rendering of both excerpts. You may use a script. The first speech is that of Calgacus, a Brit, who is exhorting his comrades to fight the Roman invaders. The second excerpt is Agricola's rallying cry to his troops before the same battle.

**Calgacus:** As I look upon you my fellow countrymen, I have great confidence that today will be the beginning of freedom for all of Britain. You have all come here to ensure your liberty. The Roman fleet is now threatening us. In the past we have fought these invaders and sometimes we have won, sometimes we have lost. We, the noblest of all Britains, have lived in the most obscure region of this country. The remoteness and seclusion of our state have kept us free. There are no tribes beyond us, nothing but rocks and waves and hostile Romans whose arrogance is inescapable. They are robbers of the world. They have no more lands to destroy so now they look to the sea. If an enemy is rich, they are greedy; if poor, then they are eager for glory. Neither the land of the East nor of the West has satisfied them. They alone covet wealth and poverty with equal eagerness. To rob—to slaughter—to rape—this is what they call Empire. They have made the world a desert, and now they call it peace.

Forget all hope of kindness and show your spirit. Let us who have not been conquered carry our arms into battle, to fight for freedom and to show these Romans what kind of men Caledonia has given birth to.[3]

\* \* \*

---

[3]Tacitus, *Agricola* 30-32.

**Agricola:** It is now the seventh year, my comrades, in which by your courage, and loyalty, and by my efforts, you have conquered Britain. Together we have fought the enemy and the elements of this hostile place. I have never regretted having you as my soldiers nor have you seen fault with your leader. We now hold the outer limits of Britain not merely by rumor but with actual camps and with real soldiers. Often while you marched through the swamps and over mountains and rivers, I heard the bravest of you say, 'When will we meet the enemy? When can we draw up our battle line?' Your prayer has been answered. They are here now!

Good things happen to the victors; the vanquished will suffer. We are not familiar with this terrain, nor do we have many supplies, but we have our hands and our weapons. These are all we need! I know that retreat is not acceptable for an army or its leader. An honest death is preferable to an ignominious life.

These are the same men who attacked you last year and fled immediately when they heard your battle cry. The most brave of the Britons has died a long time ago. What is left is a timid and cowardly bunch. Let us finish 50 years of war in one day. Prove to the State of Rome that it could never fault its soldiers as the delayers of war.[4]

## Culture Lesson: Archaeology

The modern scholar who studies the world of ancient Rome relies on written sources such as Julius Caesar's *Gallic War* to help reveal the past. However, this is not the only type of record used by the classicist, who must also analyze the material remains of the Romans. The scientific study of these remains is called *archaeology*.

Tangible remnants of the past may be a result of random events—such as an ancient trash dump—or a deliberate occurrence—such as the minting of coins, the erecting of a bridge, or the building of a tomb. It is the job of the archaeologist to unearth these remains and analyze them. When there are written records that relate to artifacts, the archaeologist will coordinate both types of information.

How does the archaeologist know where to dig? Often a passage in an ancient text locates a town or site. In Caesar's siege of Alesia, he mentions building a camp near the hill. It might prove fruitful to dig near this location to find ancient weapons or signs of military activity. Sometimes modern builders unearth an earlier construction. Pompeii was discovered when an Italian farmer was digging a well and came upon the roof of a Roman temple. Also, when one good site is unearthed, this often leads to the discovery of a nearby one.

Once a location for a dig has been pinpointed, the archaeologist uses aerial photographs and extensive land surveys to aid in his or her search. Pictures taken from airplanes often reveal unusual growth patterns in the vegetation. If crops grow noticeably better in one spot, this may indicate a refuse pile or ditch underneath. If the crops seem stunted, a stone wall may be the problem. Surveys of the land are taken to produce a map of the area. Other scientific instruments are also helpful. Some detect buried iron objects or measure sound waves bouncing off underground chambers.

All this preliminary work helps the archaeologist determine whether the site warrants excavation. Then, with careful methods, he begins to unearth the site and to record the location of each and every object he discovers. Pottery is important to almost every classical site because it is an accurate tool for dating the finds. Also, coins reveal trade transactions between communities, as well as help in dating. Buildings themselves are evidence of the people's activities and interests. Looking at the ruins of Pompeii (see chapter 13), one finds taverns, baths, and arenas that bespeak of a society that enjoyed leisure activity. The large number of unearthed temples testify to the importance of religion to these ancient people.

---

[4]Ibid. 33-34.

After the site is excavated, the archaeologist carefully analyzes the finds and publishes the conclusions. It is also important for him or her to conserve the site and prevent deterioration of the artifacts. Some objects need to be restored such as the reshaping of a broken pot or the erection of a fallen column. It may be determined to remove some objects to put them into a safer environment such as a museum. If the actual site is to be open to public viewing, then preventive measures must be taken to preserve its integrity. Once all this is completed, the archaeologist's job is finished.

## BEING AN ARCHAEOLOGIST

1.  Analyze site contents: Bring in a week's worth of trash from two students' families, and examine, sort, and list the contents. Look for materials that might reveal dates. What can you learn about the diet of the family? What other conclusions can you draw from your analysis of each family's discards?

2.  Restore an artifact: Break a piece of crockery into many pieces. Have the class try to put it back together.

# RESOURCES

Cunliffe, Barry. *Rome and the Barbarians*. New York: Henry Z. Walck, 1975.

King, William J. *How We Know about Antiquity*. Oxford, Ohio: American Classical League, 1981.

Mackendrick, P. *The Mute Stones Speak*. New York: St. Martin's Press, 1960.

Mattingly, H., trans., *Tacitus on Britain and Germany*. Middlesex, England: Penguin Classics, 1960.

*Past Worlds*. Maplewood, N.J.: Hammond, 1988.
See p. 171 for depiction of Roman military camp.

Peddie, John. *Invasion, the Roman Conquest of Britain*. New York: St. Martin's Press, 1987.

Richmond, Ian. *Roman Britain*. New York: Penguin Books, 1978.

Sherratt, Andrew, ed., *Cambridge Encyclopedia of Archaeology*. New York: Crown Publishers, 1980.

Simkins, Michael. *Warriors of Rome*. London: Blandford Press, 1988.

*The Times Atlas of World History*. Maplewood, N.J.: Hammond, 1978.
See Rome's conquests to 44 B.C. on p. 86.

Watson, G. B. *The Roman Soldier*. Ithaca, N.Y.: Cornell University Press, 1969.

Wiseman, Ann, and Peter Wiseman, trans., *The Battle for Gaul*. Boston: David R. Godine, 1980.

*The World Atlas of Archaeology*. Boston: G. K. Hall, 1985.

# IX    Antony and Cleopatra
## (30 B.C.)

### INTRODUCTION

When Julius Caesar was brutally assassinated in 44 B.C., his co-consul was Marcus Antonius (Mark Antony). Antony had supported Caesar's desire to become absolute dictator and now seized upon his champion's death to further his own quest for power. Caesar had designated his grand-nephew, Gaius Octavius (Octavian), as his heir, but because Octavian was not in Rome at the time of Caesar's death, Antony absconded with Caesar's papers and embezzled the money bequeathed to Octavian. After forcing the conspirators to leave Italy, Antony wielded great power over the senate.

Everything seemed to be working according to Antony's design until Octavian, a young man of 18, arrived to claim his inheritance. Octavian persuaded the senate to exile Antony from Italy, and a battle ensued between the senate's troops (including Octavian) and Antony's forces. Although victorious, Octavian realized that it was to his immediate advantage to seek reconciliation with his rival, whose popularity and power far exceeded his own.

In 43 B.C., Octavian, Antony, and Lepidus joined together to form the Second Triumvirate, which lasted for five years. This trio wielded supreme power over all legislation in Rome and approved of the appointments of all magistrates. To insure their positions, the Triumvirate ordered the executions of more than 300 senators and 2,000 knights who might oppose their schemes.

Leaving Lepidus in charge of Rome, Antony and Octavian embarked in pursuit of Caesar's murderers, Brutus and Cassius. At the Battle of Philippi in 42 B.C., Antony's brilliant military maneuvers defeated both the army of Cassius and of Brutus who had previously routed Octavian's troops. As the clear victor of the battle, Antony decided to tour the eastern provinces before returning to Italy. In 41 B.C., he demanded that Cleopatra, Queen of Egypt, explain her financial support of the conspirator Cassius. This seemingly innocuous meeting was to be his downfall. Obsessed with Cleopatra's beauty and charm, he abandoned his fourth wife, Octavia, Octavian's sister. Then he continued to alienate the Roman senate by shirking his official duties until he eventually was declared a traitor to the state. His former colleague led forces against him, and Antony was defeated by Octavian at the Battle of Actium in 31 B.C.

The struggle for power that began in 44 B.C. after Julius Caesar's death finally came to an end. Antony and Cleopatra both committed suicide, and Egypt became another Roman province ending the Macedonian rule of that land since the time of Alexander the Great. Octavian returned to Rome in 28 B.C. and ruled successfully until his death in A.D. 14.

Antony and Cleopatra[1]

■ Cleopatra, Antony's greatest love, now entered his life. His passion for her was almost to the point of madness and corrupted all his redeeming qualities. While he prepared his campaign against the Parthians,[2] he ordered Cleopatra to come to Cilicia to answer charges that she had raised funds for Cassius in his war against the *triumvirs* [coalition of Octavian, Antony, and Lepidus formed in 42 B.C.]. The queen Cleopatra knew that she held great power over men, especially Roman men, since her beauty had enchanted Julius Caesar and Gnaeus Pompey (Pompey's son). She was a mere girl when she knew these two men; now she was a woman of 28 and was confident that she could bewitch Antony with gifts and her charms.

She ventured to meet the Roman general dressed in jewels and ornate garments, sailing up the river Cydnus in a barge laden with gold bullion. Purple sails billowed in the wind, and her oarsmen dipped oars made of pure silver into the water while flute and pipe music filled the air. Cleopatra reclined beneath a canopy of golden cloth dressed like the goddess Venus. Two boys disguised as Cupid stood on either side fanning the queen. Her sailing crew consisted entirely of beautiful women, some working the rudder, some the sails.

## Banquet

---

[1]This story is derived from Bernadotte Perrier's English translation of Plutarch's "Life of Antony" from his work *Parallel Lives*, which was written in ancient Greek. See Resources.

[2]Despite Antony's attempts, the Parthians were never subdued until 150 years later during the time of Trajan (see chapter 14).

Antony was greatly impressed by her ostentatious display. Cleopatra invited him to come to her barge, and there offered him a magnificent feast. Her beauty was not the kind that captures the viewer immediately, but her charm was irresistible. It was a delight to listen to her voice with which she passed from one language to another with ease. In fact, in interviews with Ethiopians, Troglodytes, Hebrews, Arabians, Syrians, Medes, Parthians, and others, she never required an interpreter.

Cleopatra succeeded completely in bewitching Antony so that he abandoned his plans to invade Parthia and withdrew to Alexandria with the queen. He behaved like a young man enjoying his first romance, frittering away his time in sensual pleasures. Lavish banquets were given every day. A friend of my grandfather's, Philotas, a physician, told a story that while he was studying medicine in Alexandria, he visited the royal kitchen and watched the preparation for one of the meals. When Philotas saw the large amounts of food being cooked and eight boars being roasted, he wondered at the large size of the guest list. Cleopatra's cook scoffed at his naivete and said that only 12 people were expected. Antony demanded perfection from the kitchen and so several dinners were prepared and readied at different times. The cooks never knew when Antony might call for the food and did not want the fare to be dry or cold.

Plato described four types of flattery, but Cleopatra knew one thousand. No matter what Antony's mood, whether serious or frivolous, she sensed how to charm him. She never let him out of her sight day or night. She drank with him, played dice with him, hunted with him, and even watched him exercise his weapons. At night when Antony disguised himself as a slave and frequented the streets to spy on and laugh at the common people, Cleopatra dressed as a maid servant and went with him.

It would be too laborious to describe all of Antony's pranks, but I will recount one as an illustration of his childish behavior. One day he went fishing but was catching nothing. Embarrassed before his paramour, he ordered some fishermen to dive into the water and hook their fish to his line. Then he pulled up his line and displayed his catch, but the Queen sensed the truth. The next day, they again went out with friends to fish, and Cleopatra ordered one of her servants to hook a salted fish from the Black Sea on to Antony's line. When he exhibited his fish, everyone burst out laughing. Cleopatra said, "General, leave the fishing to us poor Egyptians. Your sport is to hunt cities, kingdoms, and even continents."

In the midst of all these frivolities, Antony received two disturbing reports: one that his wife Fulvia and brother Lucius had taken up arms against Octavian but were defeated and forced to leave Italy, and two, that the Parthians (the original object of Antony's military campaign but abandoned because of his dalliance with Cleopatra) were becoming a threat in Asia. Upon receipt of these reports, he roused himself from lethargy and ordered a campaign against the Parthians. After setting out, an urgent letter from Fulvia forced him to abandon his plans and hurry to Italy. Fortunately, by the time Antony arrived, Fulvia had died, and Octavian did not blame Antony. The two generals, Antony and Octavian, were easily reconciled and reaffirmed the Second Triumvirate. This arrangement was sealed with the marriage of Antony to Octavian's widowed sister, Octavia. She was a beautiful woman of good character, and everyone hoped this union would restore harmony to Rome.

The next year a daughter was born to Octavia and Antony, and they spent the winter in Athens where news reached them of the defeat of the Parthians by Antony's commander, Ventidius. As a result of this victory, Antony's power increased, incensing Octavian who spread vicious rumors about his co-leader. In retaliation, Antony sailed with 300 ships to Italy to silence this dissension, but his wife, now pregnant with their third child, intervened. She persuaded her brother Octavian to make peace with Antony, who then set sail for Asia.

Although his passion for Cleopatra had lain dormant, it gathered strength as he approached Syria. He sent an escort to fetch her, and when she arrived, Antony showered her with numerous presents. He worsened his scandalous behavior by acknowledging that the twins Cleopatra bore him, a boy named Alexander and a girl named Cleopatra, were his legitimate heirs.

Antony's obsession with his Egyptian queen clouded his judgment. He started his campaign against the Parthians too early, being eager to spend the winter with Cleopatra. He forced his men to march 1,000 miles and to fight before they had a chance to rest, not even waiting for the siege equipment being carried in 300 wagons to arrive. His campaign against the Parthians was a disaster. The Romans lost 20,000 infantrymen and 4,000 cavalrymen, more than half to disease. Although they had defeated the enemy in 18 battles, none was decisive enough to conclude the war. Since it was now winter, Antony ceased all combat preparations and journeyed to a resort on the Mediterranean to rest with Cleopatra. She did not arrive immediately, and Antony drowned his sorrows with continuous drinking. She finally appeared bringing gifts of money and clothing for her lover's soldiers.

Meanwhile, Octavia, anxious to join her husband, sailed to Athens. There she received a note from Antony who advised her to stay in Greece since he was about to begin a new expedition. Although Octavia knew of Antony's perfidy, she wrote back saying that she had brought clothing, money, pack animals, and 2,000 hand-picked soldiers for his personal use. Cleopatra, concerned that Octavia's bribes might seduce Antony, devised a plan, pretending that she would die if Antony left her. Refusing all food, her body became emaciated, and whenever Antony left her room, she seemed on the verge of collapse. She maintained this behavior the entire time he was preparing to march to Syria. Antony, fearful that she might commit suicide, postponed his expedition.

Octavian was furious at Antony's insult toward his sister. Some believe that he had urged Octavia to go to Greece so that he would have an excuse to declare war against Antony. Octavian ordered Octavia to leave Antony's household, but she refused. She looked after all of Antony's children, including those of Fulvia. Unwittingly, Octavia's faithful behavior to her husband harmed Antony's reputation because most people abhorred his mistreatment of his honorable wife.

Antony added insult to injury, giving Octavian just cause for taking up arms. While neglecting his own children in Rome, he honored his Egyptian offspring with unprecedented generosity. In a large ceremony in Alexandria, while he and Cleopatra sat on golden thrones and their children on silver ones, he granted huge areas of land to them. He proclaimed Cleopatra Queen of Egypt, Cyprus, Libya, and Coele Syria and named Caesarion, her son by Julius Caesar, her consort. To the boy Alexander, he gave Armenia, Media, and Parthia (when he eventually conquered it) and to his other son Ptolemy, he gave Phoenicia, Syria, and Celicia.

Octavius Caesar reported these events to the senate and the people of Rome (32 B.C.), hoping to arouse their anger against Antony. Antony still had many friends in Rome, but eventually, his neglect of duty forced military action. These two generals met in battle. Antony's fleet consisted of 500 warships, some carrying eight or ten banks of oars. His army numbered 10,000 infantry and 12,000 cavalry. His land forces outnumbered those of Octavian, but he was convinced that the outcome of this civil war lay in a naval confrontation. Caesar's fleet consisted of ships designed for quick maneuvering. When the two fleets finally met at Actium near mainland Greece, they did not ram each other. Antony's ships were sluggish due to their immense size but heavily armored with metal plates and spikes of bronze so Octavian avoided them. The naval battle was conducted more like a land engagement. Three or four of Octavian's ships surrounded one of Antony's, and the sailors fought in close combat with missiles and spears. In the midst of this confusion, when neither side had gained a clear advantage, Antony saw Cleopatra flee with a squadron of 60 ships. Antony's reaction proved the old adage that a lover's soul dwells in the body of another. As soon as he saw her sail toward Greece, he abandoned his men and ran in pursuit of the Egyptian queen.

When he finally caught up with her, he boarded Cleopatra's galley and spent the next three days in a silent sulk. At Actium, his fleet continued to fight, but after a severe gale crippled many of the ships, his men surrendered. About 5,000 men had perished, and 300 ships were captured. Cleopatra returned to Egypt, and Antony joined her in Alexandria. He then left the city and went to live on the island of Pharos. He became a recluse shut away from everyone because he claimed he mistrusted all mankind. After a while, he left his hideaway and returned to the palace. There he began to live his old life of banqueting and drinking.

Cleopatra, realizing that this war was not yet over, gathered all sorts of poisons and tested their efficiency on prisoners. She discovered that quick-acting drugs caused the victim to die in agony, but mild poisons took too long. Then she experimented with the venom of lethal animals and learned that the bite of an asp produced drowsiness and numbness but no excruciating pain.

Antony and Cleopatra sent a delegation to Octavian, praying for leniency. The queen asked that her children might still inherit the throne of Egypt, and Antony that he might retire to a private life in Athens. Octavian rejected Antony's petition, but informed Cleopatra he would grant her wish if she would execute Antony. Upon her refusal, Caesar marched to Egypt. In the first battle, Antony was the victor. The next day, he sent his fleet against Octavian's forces, but instead of fighting, it saluted Caesar as a friend. Then Antony realized his cavalry was deserting him also. In despair, he stabbed himself in his stomach with his sword, but the wound was not immediately fatal. When the bleeding stopped, he asked his friends to finish the attempt. Instead, they abandoned him writhing in pain.

Finally, Cleopatra's secretary arrived and took Antony to the queen. She was secreted in a tomb and refused to open the doors. Instead, a pulley had to be lowered from a window, and Antony was raised up to the second story this way. Those who were there say it was terrible to see Antony covered with blood stretching his hands to his lover while the platform swung precariously in the air. As soon as she secured him inside, she covered his body with her torn garments. She beat her breasts and smeared her face with the blood from his wounds. She called him her lord, husband, and emperor. He asked her to cease grieving because he had once held the greatest power in the world, and it was not shameful to die a Roman, conquered by a Roman. He died shortly afterward.

One of Antony's bodyguards had taken his bloodied sword to Octavian as proof of his demise. When Octavian heard of the suicide, he wept since they were related by marriage and had been colleagues in power as well as comrades in arms. He then sent Proculeius to capture Cleopatra alive because he feared she might destroy her treasury before killing herself. Cleopatra refused to surrender to him, and Proculeius, while urging her to trust Caesar, carefully surveyed the outlay of the monument. After reporting to Octavian, he sent Gallus to talk to Cleopatra and keep her occupied. Then he placed a ladder beneath the very window through which Antony had been raised and entered the tomb. He grabbed the queen who tried in vain to stab herself with a small dagger.

Octavian generously allowed her to give Antony a royal funeral. She became ill from an infection from the wounds she had inflicted upon her breasts. She seized this opportunity to die, refusing all food and medication. Finally, Octavian threatened her children's lives so she consented to medical attention.

Octavian visited the queen who was living an austere existence. Dressed only in a tunic and lying on a pallet, she greeted her conqueror. She tried to justify her actions by saying that fear had prompted her to support Antony. Octavian scoffed at her excuses, so she changed tactics and began to beg for her life. She gave him a list of her assets and wealth, but one of her servants told the general she was hoarding some of her possessions. She immediately leapt to her feet and beat at the slave's face. Then she explained to

Octavius Caesar that she kept these small trinkets not for herself but as a bribe for Octavia or his wife Livia so they might persuade him to be more merciful. Octavian was pleased with her speech and was convinced she wanted to live, but she had deceived him.

As Cleopatra continued to mourn Antony, she bathed and enjoyed an exquisite meal. Afterward an Egyptian peasant came carrying a basket. When the Roman guards asked what was inside, the peasant opened it and revealed the contents were large figs. The Romans marveled at their size, and the bearer suggested they eat one allaying all their fears that something was amiss. Cleopatra received the peasant's gift graciously and during dinner wrote a personal letter to Octavian asking that she be buried beside Antony. After dismissing all the servants except two faithful women, she closed the doors. When the guards reopened them, they found her lying dead on her couch dressed in her royal costume. The two maids were also dead.

Some accounts say that the asp was hidden in the leaves in the fig basket. She induced the snake to bite her arm. Others swear that the asp was shut inside a pitcher and that Cleopatra had to provoke it into biting her arm. There is another version that she kept poison hidden inside a hollow comb in her hair, yet there were no visible signs on her body that she ingested poison. But neither was the asp found inside the monument.

Octavian allowed her to be buried with royal splendor. Her body was laid to rest beside Antony's. She was 39 years old and had been queen for 22 years. Antony was 53 and had sired seven children by his four wives. His eldest son, Antyllus, was executed by Octavian, as was Caesarion, Julius Caesar's son by Cleopatra. The rest of his children were raised by his faithful wife Octavia. ■

# TEACHER IDEAS

## Discussion Questions

1. Why did the chefs prepare more than one meal for Antony and Cleopatra?

2. Who was Antony's fourth wife, and what was her relationship to Octavian?

3. Why did Cleopatra and Antony roam the streets at night?

4. What excuse to Octavian did Cleopatra offer for hoarding her wealth?

5. How did Antony's ships differ from Octavian's?

6. How did Cleopatra prevent Antony from seeing his wife?

7. How did Antony's troops fare against the Parthians?

8. What were the names of Cleopatra and Antony's children?

9. How did Octavian capitalize on Antony's treatment of his sister? Do you think he urged her journey to Athens?

10. Plutarch includes several anecdotes about Antony. Using specific examples from the text, how would you describe Antony's personality and character?

## History Lesson: Principate of Augustus

After the defeat of Antony at the battle of Actium, Octavian stood alone as the inheritor of Julius Caesar's position. He shrewdly realized that Caesar's downfall resulted from his demand for absolute power by grant of a life dictatorship. No Roman, as a true lover of the values of the Republican constitution, would agree to a despot. The senate, created by Romulus, held a sacred position in the hearts and minds of all Romans. The election of the consuls and tribunes and all other magistrates was sacrosanct. Should Octavian try to eliminate these positions, he stood to lose everything as did his uncle Julius. Knowing this, with shrewd determination and clever manipulation he began to accomplish his desires—to be the sole authority of Rome, but in a manner acceptable to the Roman people.

Until 23 B.C., he was selected consul in the yearly elections, but then in a calculated move, Octavian resigned and opened the position to all eligible candidates. He did not, however, lose power. Instead of being consul, he began a 10-year term as the *proconsul* of Gaul, Spain, and Syria, a seemingly innocuous position. In truth, most of the Roman legions were stationed in these three districts and as proconsul, *Augustus*[3] was in charge of them, gaining crucial military backing.

At the same time, Augustus became Tribune of the Plebs for life. This position granted him the power to convene the senate and enact legislation in the assemblies. He could veto all other magistrates' initiations. More importantly, this office made him the defender of the people and lent a democratic air to his newly acquired powers. In 12 B.C., his quest for supreme authority was completed when he became Pontifex Maximus, the chief priest who presided over matters of the state religion and controlled all judicial proceedings. Octavian had truly metamorphosed into Emperor Augustus. He was *Princeps*, the first citizen of the state, a position whose authority rested in the consent of the people by his election to various magisterial positions.

---

[3]A title meaning "exalted one" conferred on Octavian by the senate in 27 B.C.

Augustus wrote a summary of his accomplishments, which were inscribed in stone and placed in his mausoleum in Rome.[4] He describes in his own words his political maneuverings:

> The dictatorship was offered to me during the consulship of M. Marcellus and L. Arruntus (22 B.C.) by the senate and people, but I refused to accept. During a critical grain shortage, I supervised the distribution of this commodity and saved the city from panic and danger within a few days. The consulship, too, was offered to me, but I refused. I was asked three times (19, 18, and 11 B.C.) to be the sole authority over the laws and morals of the state, but I refused to accept an offer which opposed the traditions of our ancestry. I carried out all measures which the senate wanted by right of my tribunican power aided by a colleague granted by the senate.[5]

The Roman Empire was born under the principate of Augustus. He was an administrative genius who created a civil service capable of running such a vast and diverse domain. He breathed life into the government that extended its sphere of influence for another 400 years. He brought peace to Rome that created a climate for all the arts to flourish. A unique man, Octavian lived until A.D. 14 and left a legacy that still continues today.

## SUGGESTED TOPICS FOR FURTHER RESEARCH

1. Golden Age of Roman Literature

2. Pax Romana

3. Horace, his life and works

4. Ptolemy of Egypt

5. Pantheon

6. Alexander the Great's conquest of Egypt

### Language Arts

## VOCABULARY BUILDING

Prefix:

- *tele* from Greek verb *tele*, meaning "far off"

1. Define words:
   - telecast
   - television
   - telescope
   - telephoto
   - telekinesis
   - telephone
   - telegraph
   - telemetry
   - telethon
   - telepathy

---

[4]This is lost, but other copies have survived, including one on a temple wall in Ankara.

[5]Augustus, *Res Gestae* 5-6.

2.  Using the words listed above, find the base and its meaning. For example, *scope* means "watcher."

3.  Modern scientists often use Greek and Latin words when naming a new discovery (e.g., *Telescopium* is a constellation in the Southern Hemisphere). Using the prefix *tele* coin five words of your own and explain their meaning.

## POETRY WRITING

During the peace of Augustus, the arts flourished. One of the greatest poets of that time was Quintus Horatius Flaccus (Horace). In his *Odes*, Horace wrote a poem on the death of Cleopatra, included here in prose form. Read this version and turn it back into a poem, using rhyme or free verse. You need not include every detail of Horace's poem, but the more the better.

Now is the time, my comrades, for us to dance and drink and enjoy the feasts of the gods. Before, it would not have been right to fetch the rare wine from its cellar while that foreign queen prepared to destroy Rome and bring death to our power. She was corrupt, along with her degenerate followers, and drunk with the belief in her eventual success. But when, finally, only one of her ships remained, this knowledge dampened her bliss. Caesar (Augustus) turned her mad audacity into trembling fear. He pursued her from the shores of Italy in the hopes of binding her in chains just like the hawk which follows the gentle dove or a hunter which follows the timid hare. She sought a nobler death and did not seek cowardly escape. With a calm visage she looked upon her palace and bravely drew the lethal snakes to her breast into which they poured their dark poison. She was very courageous with her deliberate death because she hated to be a mere woman humbled in a Roman's triumphal procession.[6]

## MOVIE WATCHING

See the movie *Cleopatra* and compare Hollywood's treatment of the relationship between Antony and Cleopatra with your knowledge of the facts.

## Cultural Lesson: Roman Marriages

Marriage was very important to the Romans who believed that the success of the state lay in the solidity of the family. Only if both parties were Roman citizens was a marriage considered legal and the children of the union legitimate. However, concessions were made when the man was a citizen but the woman was not. The children took the status of the father. Slaves did not have the right to marry though they lived together in an unsanctioned union (*contubernium*).

Marriage required the mutual consent of both partners, either by themselves or by a parent. Most patrician marriages were arranged. Both individuals had to be adults. The minimum age for girls was 12 and 14 for boys, though most Romans married much later. It was also forbidden for the two parties to be closely related.

Before the marriage there was a formal betrothal ceremony (*sponsalia*) where mutual promises to wed were issued. The man gave a gift to his intended, usually a promise ring worn on the third finger of her left hand since it was believed that a nerve ran directly from this finger to the heart.

---

[6]Horace, "The Death of Cleopatra" from *Odes* I: 37.

Once the marriage contract was signed, a date was chosen for the ceremony. The Romans believed that there were many unlucky days in the calendar that had to be avoided. Almost one-third of the year was unsuitable, but the end of June, named for Juno, the goddess of marriage, was favored for nuptials.

On the day of the wedding, the bride took special care with her attire. Her mother helped her dress in a long white tunic and a belt was tied around her waist with a special knot, the knot of Hercules, who was the guardian of wedded life. Only her husband could unloosen the belt. Her hair was parted with a spear and divided into six locks coiled together and tied with wool ribbons. An orange-red veil covered her face, and yellow shoes adorned her feet.

There were several different wedding ceremonies, but the most religious one was called the *confarreatio*. It took place in the bride's home, which was decorated with flowers, boughs, and colored ribbons. After an animal sacrifice to the gods, the bride and groom joined hands before at least 10 witnesses. Then these solemn words were spoken by the bride, "Quando tu Gaius, ego Gaia." ("Since you are Gaius, I am Gaia".) After this, the couple partook of a wheat cake (*far*), which concluded the religious portion of the wedding activities.

The bride was then taken to her new home with an elaborate procession, but first, by a false show of force, she was snatched from her parents. Flute players and torch bearers singing marriage songs led the way. Three boys attended the bride, one in front carrying a hawthorn torch, and two flanking her sides. She held a spindle and distaff as symbols of her domestic role. Anyone could join in the parade as it wandered through the streets until the wedding party came to the new couple's home. There the groom would scatter nuts to the crowd as a symbol of fertility, and the bride wound wool around the door posts and covered them with fat as a sign of plenty. She was lifted over the threshold to prevent her from tripping—a sign of bad luck. Along with the invited guests, she entered her new home and uttered again, "Ubi (Where) tu Gaius, ego Gaia." The groom offered her fire and water as representative of their domestic life together. She might throw the torch to the guests for luck. Then dinner was served to all and afterward the bride was escorted to her wedding couch placed in the atrium and decorated with flowers.

This was the most lavish of wedding rites. Another ceremony, *coemptio*, was simpler. The bride and groom merely stated their vows before five witnesses, and prayers and offerings were made to the gods. Whatever the ceremony, the status of a Roman matron was one of respect. She was the mistress of the household and teacher to her children. Her husband often consulted her advice in business matters, and she acted as his hostess. She could participate in state ceremonies, and attend public spectacles, as well as testify in court. Often, a portion of her dowry was kept for her own use and investment. The Roman couple lived together with bonds of mutual respect and concern.

In a letter to Gemnius, Pliny the Younger describes the death of a friend's wife and the once shared affection of the couple:

> Our Macrinius has suffered a severe tragedy. He lost his wife with whom he lived for 39 years without quarreling, without displeasure. What respect she gave to her husband when she herself deserved the greatest respect! Indeed, Macrinius has this great comfort that he enjoyed such devotion for such a long time, but this exacerbates his loss more. For the severity of a loss grows in proportion to the pleasure itself. I will be concerned for this dear friend until he can learn to live with his bereavement. Nothing will do better than necessity itself or length of time or the saturation of grief in ridding him of his pain. Farewell.[7]

## DISCUSSION QUESTIONS

1. What are the similarities between a modern wedding and an ancient Roman one?

2. What makes a modern wedding legal? What was necessary to legitimize a Roman marriage?

---

[7]Pliny the Younger, *Epistulae*, 8: 5.

3.   How does a modern civil marriage differ from one performed in a place of worship?

4.   Read about the wedding customs of a foreign country and share your findings with the class.

5.   What do you think is the significance of the words, "Ubi tu Gaius, ego Gaia"?

## Et Alia: Word Search

### *Clues*

*ACTIUM*
*ANTONY*
*ASP*
*AUGUSTUS*
*BRUTUS*
*CAESARION*
*CASSIUS*
*CLEOPATRA*
*CUPID*
*EGYPT*
*FLEET*
*FULVIA*
*GREECE*
*LEPIDIUS*
*NILE*
*OCTAVIA*
*PARTHIA*
*PLATO*
*PLUTARCH*
*POMPEY*
*QUEEN*
*ROME*
*SYRIA*
*TOMB*

```
W I U F V E L Q K T W M U N H B N B I M F U B C
A T S D O F V W S Z P E C E E R G T D H Z S A A
X J U F X R W X P Y N A Y X S U S S R O P Q A G
Y X D U O N H P O M P E Y A M T N P M J J Q F E
N O I R A S E A C F G I A H S U T J M J G P B D
E Z P O S E V V I U L L I W T S S Y W U K L H C
O A E C K P O T A L P E H F K P H T X C I U I X
B I L T C O C D M V N O T N N F Y I B L L T O O
H D E L K C T U E I D T R P A C H G G C R A C B
E C E G S T E T S A M A A S Y R I A E R M R O A
F L L V U A S C T R R U P D V O L M C F M C B C
L E W H I V H B T J O K E E G J F R P F N H G T
Z O I B S I C M E X M K J T E E L F Q P T O U M
J P G N S A H O D I E L I N F T O G Y N O T N A
K A K A A D N T H M O Y N P J I R S M S H S G I
M T A N C E F G B L A U G U S T U S G U Q Q I A
O R F B D B R P N E E U Q H R Q D C U P I D O G
P A E C L C V L M N O E L D K N A V G J D T N G
```

# RESOURCES

Appian. *Roman History*, 4 vols. Loeb Classical Library, 1986.

Balsdon, J.P.V.D. *Roman Women*. Westport, Conn.: Greenwood Press, 1962.

Brunt, P.A., and J.M. Moore, eds., *Res Gestae Divi Augusti*. New York: Oxford University Press, 1967.

Grant, Michael. "Augustus," *Encyclopaedia Britannica*, 1988 ed., vol. 14, 390-94.

_____. *From Alexander to Cleopatra*. London: Weidenfeld and Nicolson, 1982.

Graves, Robert, trans., *Twelve Caesars of Suetonius*. Great Britain: Penguin Classics, 1957.

Horace. *Odes and Epodes*. Loeb Classical Library, 1986.

_____. *Satires, Epistles and Ars Poetica*. Loeb Classical Library, 1986.

Johnston, Mary. *Roman Life*. Chicago: Scott, Foresman, 1957.

Plutarch. *Parallel Lives*. Loeb Classical Library, 1988.

Pomeroy, Sarah B. *Goddesses, Whores, Wives, and Slaves: Women in Classical Antiquity*. New York: Schocken Books, 1975.

# X

# Matricide
## (A.D. 59)

## INTRODUCTION

In the glorious history of the Romans, one emperor stands out, not for his greatness, but for his wickedness and depravity. Nero, the great-great-grandson of Augustus and Mark Antony, ascended to the throne of Rome in A.D. 54 at the age of 17. In A.D. 49, his mother, Agrippina, married Emperor Claudius who had two children, Octavia and Brittanicus, by a previous marriage.

Young and inexperienced, Nero relied heavily on the advice of Burrus, the praetorian captain, and his tutor, Seneca, the philosopher (see chapters 6 and 15). The first five years of his principate were distinguished by his acts of charity and his careful administration of matters of state. He married Claudius's daughter, Octavia, and seemed destined to become a well-liked and effective leader. However, all this suddenly changed. Nero wearied of his mother's domination and at the same time became involved with a woman named Poppaea. She threatened to leave him if Agrippina were not removed, and so he plotted to rid himself of maternal control.

Nero always imagined himself an artist. He began to appear on stage, an act that shocked most dignified Romans. Poppaea encouraged these activities because the less interest Nero paid to the state, the more he paid to her, increasing her influence. Octavia was banished, then murdered, and Poppaea became empress.

In A.D. 65, a group of nobles tried unsuccessfully to assassinate Nero. Among the conspirators was his old teacher, Seneca, whom the Emperor sentenced to death. Shortly after this, Nero visited Greece to indulge himself in his creative pursuits. During his 15-month absence, several legions revolted, but he refused to respond. His reluctance forced the army to proclaim Galba emperor, and the senate condemned the last descendent of Augustus as an enemy of the state.

The following story comes from the historian Tacitus (A.D. 55-117), one of the greatest Roman writers. He came from a noble senatorial family and served a term as consul (A.D. 97) and as governor of Asia (A.D. 112). His first historical works were a biography of his father-in-law (see chapter 8) and a description of the Germans (see chapter 7). Then he wrote the *Histories*, consisting of 14 books (of which only books 1-4 and part of 5 remain). The *Annals* discuss the period of history from the death of Augustus to the death of Nero though some books are missing—notably those covering the rule of Caligula, one-half of Claudius's principate, and a few years from Tiberius and Nero.

Tacitus tries to be as accurate as possible when collecting data for his history, but the objectivity of modern historians is not present. He says that he will write *sine ira et studio* (without anger or prejudice), but he clearly has certain designs for his work, namely to point out the immorality of vice and extol the virtues of goodness. The next story, describing Nero's plot to murder his mother, definitely belongs to the former.

## Matricide: Nero and Agrippina[1]

■ Nero deliberated for some time about how to restrain his meddlesome mother, Agrippina. Finally, he decided to take drastic measures and murder her. He reflected on the best way to accomplish this: should he administer poison, or have her assassinated, or use some other dastardly means? At first, poison seemed suitable. However, if he slipped the poison into her food while she was dining at his palace table, it would seem suspicious. After all, Nero had killed his step-brother Brittanicus in this way only four years before. It seemed possible to bribe one of his mother's own servants and have him administer the lethal dose, but on further consideration, this idea, too, seemed impractical because the slaves were loyal to Agrippina. The final argument against dispensing poison was that Nero knew that his mother, a suspicious woman, had been taking small doses of poison for some time to immunize herself. What other choices were feasible? Stabbing was impossible to conceal. The people of Rome would not tolerate matricide, and Nero would lose his position as emperor.

Finally, an ex-slave, Anicetus, Nero's ex-tutor, devised a clever plan. Anicetus, who also detested Agrippina, was presently in charge of the imperial fleet at Misenum. His scheme was to build an elaborate ship that Nero would give as a gift to Agrippina. The top part of the ship would have a loose fitting, and as the ship moved with the waves, the roof would collapse and fling Agrippina into the sea. She would drown, and Nero would then be rid of her. The drowning would be considered an accident because nothing was as unpredictable as the sea, and no one would suspect Nero's involvement. He could give his deceased mother a temple, altars, and other objects to display his filial devotion. Nero was delighted with this idea and promptly ordered Anicetus to construct the death boat.

At this time, Nero visited the festival of Minerva at Baiae, a town on the seacoast of Campania. He lured his mother there, apologizing for his previous behavior of disrespect. Agrippina, unsuspectingly, accepted his efforts at reconciliation and agreed to come to his vacation villa. When she arrived, Nero warmly embraced her and showed her a beautiful ornate ship docked by the shore—his gift to his honorable mother. He then invited her to a banquet that night so that the darkness would help conceal his crime.

During dinner, a traitor appeared who revealed Nero's plot to Agrippina. In shock, she returned to the town, but Nero followed her and lessened her fears with effusive attentiveness. They talked a long while, and she became convinced of his sincere devotion. As she was leaving, Nero clung to her with his heart and eyes, either as a ploy or because this was to be their last moment together. However, he did not vacillate from his heinous plan.

The stars shone brilliantly that night over a tranquil sea as if the gods were trying to thwart the crime. The ship set out with Agrippina aboard, two slaves accompanying her. Creperius Gallus stood near the helm, and the other slave, Acerronia, lay at her mistress's feet. The two women were talking about Nero when suddenly the heavy roof collapsed.

Creperius was crushed and died immediately, but Agrippina and Acerronia were protected by the strong sides of the couch that prevented the roof from falling directly on them. The ship, which was supposed to break apart, remained intact. Confusion reigned! The seamen involved in the attack tried to throw their weight to one side to capsize the boat while at the same time other crew members cast their weight to rebalance it. Acerronia, rather foolishly, began to shout that she was Agrippina, and that someone should help her, the emperor's mother. Instead, the oarsmen took up poles and oars and bludgeoned her to death. Agrippina wisely remained quiet throughout the chaos and swam silently away from the deadly scene. Her shoulder was slightly wounded, but she managed to reach a small fishing fleet whose kind sailors carried her to safety and her own villa at Lake Lucrine.

---

[1]Tacitus, *Annals* XIV: 3.

Once there, Agrippina began to reflect on the night's events. She correctly surmised that the wreck could not have occurred by chance since there were no strong winds nor did the boat strike a rock. She reasoned that the roof's collapsing could only have been engineered by someone and that the person must have been her son. Nero was the one who had urged her to come to Baiae and gave her the barge, and Acerronia's unfortunate death was further proof of Nero's guilt.

Her dilemma now was what to do because her life was in danger. She decided to pretend that the wreck was an accident and sent a freedman, Agerinus, with a message to her son. She wrote that she had just escaped a serious calamity by the kindness of the gods and Nero's good fortune. Furthermore, she continued, despite his concern for his mother, Nero should not come to see her; she needed rest and quiet. Agrippina then retired to her room and treated her wound while she awaited Agerinus's return and Nero's reaction.

Meanwhile, Nero was anxiously waiting for the news of her demise. Instead, he learned of the fiasco and that Agrippina had escaped with only a slight wound. This frightened the Emperor for he knew she must suspect his involvement with the murder plot. He feared she might arm her slaves for attack or incite the state's soldiers to revolt. She might even bring criminal charges against him for the shipwreck and murders before the senate of Rome. In a panic, Nero summoned his advisors and apprised them of the situation. They were incredulous at his daring and remained silent at first. Eventually, however, they conceded that Anicetus, the author of the scheme, should complete the task. Nero agreed, and Anicetus left to recruit men to help him.

While all this was taking place, Agrippina's messenger, Agerinus, arrived to speak to Nero. He was led to the Emperor, but before he could relay his message, Nero threw a sword at his own feet and proclaimed it was Agerinus's sword and that the man was an assassin hired by his mother. Nero had Agerinus immediately bound in chains and then killed, publicly announcing that the freedman had committed suicide.

At Lake Lucrine, Agrippina anxiously awaited her messenger's return. Outside her villa, many citizens had gathered to express their concern when they heard of her "accident." They filled the shore and wailed with grief at her misfortune, giving prayers on her behalf. Once the people realized she was safe, they began to rejoice and shout with delight until an angry band of soldiers arrived led by Anicetus.

His garrison surrounded the villa, and, after breaking down the doors, seized Agrippina's servants and dragged them away. The soldiers rushed inside and no one was spared. A few faithful attendants remained to barricade Agrippina's bedroom door, but they were immediately shoved aside. Inside, Agrippina waited with one female slave. They had heard the noise when the soldiers broke into the house, and now an ominous silence pervaded the place. The frightened handmaiden began to leave when Agrippina angrily shouted, "You also desert me!" The door opened, and she spied Anicetus and his henchmen, among whom were the ship's captain, Herculeius, and a centurion, Obaritus. Panic struck Agrippina, but she asked calmly if they had come to inquire about her health; she was much better, she assured them. She continued that if they were there for some evil purpose, she could not imagine that Nero would be responsible.

Undaunted at her bravado, the assassins surrounded her couch. Herculeius assaulted her head with a stick, and then Obaritus unsheathed his sword to finish the deed. She beseeched them, "Strike my belly," and immediately they stabbed her to death. That was the end of Agrippina, a woman greedy for power whose own son took her life.

For many years before her death, Agrippina had believed she would be murdered. She had once consulted astrologers who predicted that Nero would be emperor but kill his own mother. She supposedly replied, "Let him kill me, as long as he becomes emperor." Her wish was granted. On the night of her murder, her body was cremated, and a small funeral ceremony was conducted. As long as Nero ruled, her remains were not allowed to be buried. After his own death in A.D. 68, Agrippina's servants constructed a small tomb for her remains near the road at Misenum. ∎

# TEACHER IDEAS

## Discussion Questions

1. How did the citizens of Rome react to Agrippina's "accident"?

2. Why did the collapsing roof not crush Agrippina immediately?

3. Why does Nero reject poison as a method to murder his mother?

4. What error did Acerronia make that accelerated her demise?

5. Who was the creator of the ship, and what was his relationship to Nero?

6. How does Nero explain the death of Agerinus?

7. How does Agrippina die, and where was she buried?

8. How does Nero assuage his mother's suspicions?

9. What do you think Agrippina had in mind when she said, "Strike my belly"?

10. Did Agrippina seal her own fate when she replied to the astrologers who predicted that her son would become emperor and commit matricide, "Let him kill me, as long as he becomes emperor"? For whose benefit—her own or that of her son—do you think she readily embraced this prophecy?

## History Lesson: Three Emperors—Tiberius, Caligula, and Claudius

### Tiberius (A.D. 14-37)

Augustus's first wife bore him a daughter who had three sons, Augustus's only direct heirs. In A.D. 2, one grandson died of a fever, and two years later, the other succumbed to a battle wound; the third was banished for immoral behavior. With no heirs, Augustus eventually adopted his stepson, Tiberius. Under Augustus's guidance, Tiberius held many political and military offices, thereby gaining invaluable experience. At age 22, he led his first military command and became tribune for life one year before Augustus's death (A.D. 14). He was the natural heir to the principate, and the senate gladly confirmed Tiberius's position as such.

Tiberius was a conservative and old-fashioned Roman, dedicated to upholding the old traditions. He upheld the rights of the senate and deferred to its advice in matters of state. He transferred the election of the magistrates from the assemblies to the senate, thereby making it the only true legislative body still remaining. An efficient administrator, Tiberius's careful spending of funds added to the solvency of the treasury.

Tiberius's problems arose within his own household. According to the Roman biographer Suetonius (who enjoyed describing the lurid details of palace intrigues), Sejanus, prefect of the Praetorian Guard, wished to further his own ambitions but found his plans stalled by Drusus, Tiberius's son. Drusus suspected that Sejanus's loyalty was not to the Emperor but to himself. Fearing he would lose his position, Sejanus seduced Drusus's wife and convinced her to poison her husband (A.D. 23). Distraught over his son's sudden death and tired of palace intrigue, Tiberius withdrew to his home in Capri. In his absence, Sejanus (whose disloyalty Tiberius did not yet suspect) gained more control. Finally, however, his role in Drusus's death was revealed to the

Emperor, and Tiberius assumed control of the principate again, though he refused to return to Rome, remaining in Capri until his death in A.D. 37.

### Caligula (A.D. 37-41)

Tiberius, robbed of his rightful son with the murder of Drusus, was forced to adopt his grand-nephew Gaius and make him co-beneficiary of his private fortune. In A.D. 37, Gaius was only 25 years old, but the senate conferred the rights and privileges of the principate upon him with no reservation. Gaius had grown up with the soldiers of his father's army who named him *Caligula* (Little boot). Though young, he seemed genuinely interested in his duties and began his short rule on a positive note. He ended the censorship of books and banished the government informants from Rome.

But suddenly, Caligula seemed to lose all sense of reason. He acted irrationally and indulged himself in any dissipated activity he could imagine. He spent lavishly and executed wealthy knights and senators in order to confiscate their property. He imagined himself a god and was often found talking with his "brother" Jupiter. The man had gone mad. Statues of the great men of the Republic were destroyed and the works of Virgil and Livy removed from the libraries. Finally, the Praetorian Guard took matters into its own hands and murdered the 30-year-old Gaius along with his wife and daughter. Caligula had only been in power for four years, but his profligate ways left an indelible black mark upon the office of the principate.

### Claudius (A.D. 41-54)

Caligula left no children, and it seemed that the Romans would not have anyone to take over the reins of power. However, while the Praetorian Guards were hunting down Gaius's immediate family, they found his long-lost uncle, Claudius, hiding in the palace. Claudius was the grandson of Octavia and Mark Antony. Already 50 years old, he suffered from a paralysis that left him crippled and afflicted with a speech impediment. He had been neglected by the imperial family who assumed he would never have a political career. Claudius, a brilliant man, was able to indulge himself in his passion for learning. He had written many works on history and other erudite subjects. His treatment of the Etruscans covered 20 volumes and his work on Rome, 41 volumes. Unfortunately, all have been lost. This bookish man was now hailed as Emperor by the Praetorian Guard.

**Scroll**

At first, the senate was skeptical about Claudius's ability to lead the Empire, but this mature scholar had learned much from books and now proceeded to put his knowledge to good use. Under Claudius's guidance, his able generals extended the boundaries of the Empire including the annexation of Britain. Internal affairs of state were also handled well. He improved the judicial system and expanded the duties of the civil service. He helped to erect the finest aqueduct (the Aqua Claudia) in Rome through personal financial contributions and also built the Via Claudia, a 350-mile road that linked northern Italy to Germany. He extended Roman citizenship to the people of Gaul (his birthplace) and gave the Jews the right to worship.

Unfortunately, Claudius was a poor judge of women, and the exploits of his wives are notorious. His third wife, Messalina, was a greedy, jealous woman who, according to Suetonius, caused the death of 300 knights and 35 senators. Even Tacitus repeats the gossip that Messalina dared to "marry" the noble C. Selius in the hopes that they would take control together. When Claudius heard of this escapade, he ordered them both killed. He then made the fatal mistake of marrying his niece, Agrippina, the mother of Domitius Ahenobarbarus (Nero). Claudius already had a son, Brittanicus, but Agrippina convinced him to adopt Nero, as well; then she proceeded to poison her husband with a dish of mushrooms (A.D. 54). This learned and capable princeps died the victim of his wife's greed. She was later to discover her son to be a worthy opponent to her clever tricks.

## SUGGESTED TOPICS FOR FURTHER RESEARCH

1.  year of the four emperors (A.D. 68-69)

2.  the role of ex-slaves (freedmen) under the Empire

3.  life of Julia, Augustus's daughter

4.  Vipsania, Tiberius's wife

5.  proconsulship

6.  Suetonius

## Language Arts

### VOCABULARY BUILDING: More Words from Greek Mythology

**Achilles's heel:** A small but significant weakness, a vulnerable spot. Achilles was the son of the sea nymph Thetis who tried to change the course of fate when she learned that her son would die in battle. To make her son immune from injury, Thetis dipped the baby into the river Styx in Hades. However, Thetis held her son by his ankle, and because she forgot to dip this spot in the river, Achilles was vulnerable there. During the Trojan War, an arrow was shot into Achilles's heel, and he died.

**Adonis:** A young man of great physical beauty. When Adonis was born, he was so beautiful that Aphrodite wanted the child for herself. She gave him to her friend Persephone, the goddess of the underworld, for safekeeping, but this goddess also desired the boy. They appealed to Zeus to settle their dispute. As a compromise, he declared that Adonis would spend one-third of the year with Persephone, one-third with Aphrodite, and one-third wherever he wished. While hunting, Adonis was gored by a boar and died.

**Amazon:** A tall athletic woman. According to Greek mythology, the Amazons were a tribe of women warriors who had no relations with men except those necessary to continue their species. All male children were killed at birth. Their left breasts were removed to make holding a bow easier. Achilles defeated them in battle during the Trojan War.

**Atlas:** A collection of maps. After the war between the Titans and the Olympians, Zeus punished the Titan Atlas by forcing him to carry the world and heavens upon his shoulders. Once, while searching for the golden apples, the hero Hercules asked Atlas for help. Atlas agreed to fetch the fruit if Hercules would hold the world until he returned. When Atlas came back, however, he refused to take the tremendous burden. Using his wit, Hercules asked if Atlas would hold the earth and sky for just a moment so that he could put a pad over his body as a cushion. Atlas agreed, and Hercules picked up the apples and sped away.

**Labyrinth:** A maze, having intricate passages. According to legend, Minos, the king of Crete, refused to sacrifice a bull to Poseidon. As punishment, Poseidon forced Pasiphae, Minos's wife, to have an unnatural passion for the animal. The minotaur, half man and half bull, was born from this unnatural union. King Minos confined the beast to the labyrinth so he could not escape and every nine years sacrificed seven Athenian boys and seven girls to this monster. Theseus, the prince of Athens, volunteered to join this group. Minos's daughter, Ariadne, fell in love with Theseus and revealed to him the secret of the labyrinth. He need only to take a ball of twine to unravel as he went through the maze, kill the monster, and return by following the string.

**Narcissism:** An excessive admiration of oneself. Narcissus was so handsome that all women fell in love with him, but he would not reciprocate their affections. He scorned every female until the goddess of retribution, Nemesis, decided to punish him for his pride. While the youth was hunting, he came to a pool to drink some water, saw his own reflection, and fell in love with himself. While reaching down to touch the water, he fell in and drowned.

## WORD USE AND RECOGNITION

Locate an instance (in newspapers or magazines) of the use of these words or names or pictures of the mythological characters and bring them to class.

## ESSAY WRITING

Reread Livy's preface to *Ab Urbe Condita* (see chapter 1), paying particular attention to Livy's purpose in writing history. Tacitus, born 38 years after Livy's death, was undoubtedly familiar with the latter's work. Tacitus approached history from very much the same perspective as his predecessor. Write a one-page essay that explores this idea. What is Tacitus hoping to achieve by retelling the story of Nero and Agrippina? What is his moral objective?

## MOVIE WATCHING

See the movie *Quo Vadis* and compare Hollywood's portrayal of Nero to that of Tacitus's.

## Cultural Lesson: The Influence of Latin on the Development of English

The development of the English language took place over many millennia. It is believed that many modern tongues descended from one common ancestor—the Indo-European language. The people who spoke this prehistoric language (3000 B.C.) probably lived in what is now north central Europe. As people migrated from this location, they carried their language with them. Centuries of change and adaptation shaped the unique qualities of each Indo-European tongue. A look at the following chart illustrates the similarity of Indo-European-based words:

| English | Latin | Greek | Spanish | German | French | Dutch | Sanskrit | Persian |
|---------|-------|-------|---------|--------|--------|-------|----------|---------|
| mother | mater | meter | madre | mutter | mere | moeder | matr | madar |

Having a common ancestor is not the only relationship between languages. Societies constantly borrow words from others, and this is true of English as well. Little is known about the prehistoric inhabitants of the British Isles, but in about 1000 B.C., the Celts arrived on these islands bringing the language from which modern Welsh and Irish descended.

Then the Romans occupied this area for almost 400 years (A.D. 43-410). Though the majority of people continued to use the Celtic tongue in everyday speech, Latin was spoken by Roman officials. Cities and towns still carry their Latin names from this period (e.g., Lancaster, Stratford, London).

### Old English Period (A.D. 450-1150)

In A.D. 449, the Britains were invaded by the Picts and Scots and appealed to Germanic mercenaries to help expel the aggressors. The Germans liked the area so much that they stayed and supplanted the original Celts. Large migrations into England began with the Jutes in A.D. 449, the Saxons in A.D. 477, and the Angles in A.D. 547. Their language, called *Anglo-Saxon*, became the basis for modern English. Their own language had already been greatly influenced by the Roman occupation in their homeland, so when they settled the British Isles, they brought many Latin-derived words with them (e.g., "wall" from *vallum*).

In A.D. 601, Pope Gregory sent missionaries to Britain led by St. Augustine who was to become the first archbishop of Canterbury. These clergymen, in establishing their church, also brought the Latin language to England.

### Middle English Period (A.D. 1150-1500)

The most important influence on the English language came in A.D. 1066 when William of Normandy, a French aristocrat, invaded England. He defeated King Harold at the Battle of Hastings and established French as the language of the courts and ruling class. During that period, three languages existed side by side: Anglo-Saxon, the language of the conquered people, Norman French or Gallic-Latin, the language of the courts and government, and Latin, the language of the church. Not until A.D. 1363 did Parliament adopt Anglo-Saxon as the language of the government. By then, many Gallic-Latin words had crept into English.

### Modern English Period (1500-present)

In the fourteenth century, the Italian poet, Petrarch, became interested in reading and studying classical writers. Works that had lain dormant for years once more became popular. A renaissance of learning began and spread throughout Europe. The infusion of Latin words into the English language at this time was enormous.

English words have come from many different sources. Only about one-fourth are actually Anglo-Saxon. Three-fourths of all words found in an English dictionary are of Greek or Latin origin, and we continue to coin words from these "dead" languages, especially in the area of science and technology (e.g., *nuclear*, *vitamin*, and *television*).

## DERIVATION OF WORDS

Use your dictionary and find out the language from which the following words are derived:

| | |
|---|---|
| assassin | pretzel |
| nominate | crescent |
| trousers | cookie |
| policy | junction |
| pajama | bamboo |
| vanquish | spirit |
| dungaree | tycoon |
| vivid | audience |
| ranch | prairie |
| catsup | monarch |
| hamburger | revolve |
| mortal | rat |
| lava | tea |

# RESOURCES

Ayers, Donald. *English Words from Latin and Greek Elements*. Tucson: University of Arizona Press, 1982.

Fortner, Bertha C. *Chief Sources of Our English Language*, #484. Miami, Ohio: American Classical League, n.d.

Graves, Robert. *I, Claudius*. New York: Random House, 1989.
This is a historical novel about Claudius and his family.

Momigliano, Arnaldo D. "Claudius," *Encyclopaedia Britannica*, 1988 ed., vol. 3, 359-60.

Onions, C.T., ed. *Oxford Dictionary of English Etymology*. Oxford, England: Oxford University Press, 1966.

Pohl, Frederik. "Tiberius," *Encyclopaedia Britannica*, 1988 ed., vol. 11, 754-55.

Pyles, Thomas. *Origins and Development of the English Language*. New York: Harcourt Brace and World, 1964.

*Quo Vadis*. Culver City, Calif.: Metro Goldwyn Mayer/United Artists, 1979. Video (135 minutes).

Tacitus. *The Annals of Imperial Rome*, trans. Michael Grant. Middlesex, England: Penguin Classics, 1956.

*Webster's Illustrated Encyclopedic Dictionary*. Montreal: Tormont Publications, 1990.

# XI

# The Great Fire of Rome
## (A.D. 64)

### INTRODUCTION

The ancient Italians who founded Rome chose a truly advantageous location. Nestled between seven hills that provided natural protection against enemies, the city sits on the Tiber River, which stretches 14 miles to the Mediterranean Sea, providing easy access to trading vessels. Worn by the ages, the hills of Rome are now gentle and sloping but were somewhat steeper when the city was first founded. By the time of Nero, the city had grown to a population of well over one million inhabitants and stretched far beyond the originally settled hills.

In 8 B.C., Augustus had divided the city into 14 districts, or wards, each with its own individual fire and police protection. Fire was a continual and monumental problem for these Romans. The city had grown rapidly, and the streets were narrow and haphazardly arranged. Tall buildings, whose multiple stories were reinforced with wooden beams, loomed everywhere. Running water was not available to the upper floors, and hazardous materials, such as coal in braziers used as portable heaters and oil lamps were a necessity in ancient homes.

After the Great Fire of A.D. 64, Nero, as Tacitus mentions in the following story, attempted to build a safer city but with little success. Rome was never completely secure, and many conflagrations continued to plague the inhabitants. The fire during Nero's reign eventually contributed to his downfall. He enacted heavy taxes on the population to fund his building program, precipitating a revolt in A.D. 68. The Emperor fled Rome, and with the help of a friend, committed suicide by falling upon his own sword. Rome finally was rid of this depraved ruler.

Thoughout history, folklore has unjustly accused Nero of "fiddling" while Rome burned. In truth, he was not in the city when the fire broke out. Even the people of Nero's time believed that he had actually instigated this great calamity, and to stop this rumor, he blamed the Christians as perpetrators of the Great Fire. Normally, the Romans were very tolerant of foreign religions, accepting, for example, the cults of Isis from Egypt and Mithras of Persia with ease into their own pantheon of gods. They only objected to a new religion when it interfered with the State or was antisocial, such as Druidism of Britain and Gaul, which practiced human sacrifice. The early Christians were, in fact, often unjustly accused of crimes such as cannibalism and incest.

The probable period when Christianity spread to Rome was the time of Emperor Claudius (A.D. 41-54), but it was not until the fourth century A.D. that Christianity became an accepted practice of worship. Constantine (A.D. 306-337) was the first Christian emperor, and in A.D. 391 Theodosius the Great (A.D. 379-395) closed the temples of the ancient gods. The Olympic Games, held in honor of Zeus, were conducted for the last time in A.D. 394. Christianity had finally conquered Rome.

### The Great Fire of Rome[1]

■ In A.D. 64, a devastating fire, more disastrous than any conflagration the city had previously experienced, broke out in Rome. Whether this calamity occurred by chance or at the instigation of Emperor Nero is uncertain for there are supporters of both views.

The fire, which raged for over a week, began in the area of the Circus near the Palatine and Caelian hills. Around the Circus stood small shops filled with merchandise in which the flames originated. The fire grew quickly, and driven by a strong wind, immediately encircled the entire length of the Circus, which had no protective wall to obstruct the flames. The fire then ravaged the lower areas of the city and also spread to the higher hills. It managed to jump ahead of all barriers and raced through the narrow crowded streets of Rome.

People panicked in their attempt to escape from death. Some tried to rescue their belongings and family. Others hurried through the streets to seek safety. All this confusion added to the disaster. While people were seeking refuge, they became surrounded by the flames. Even when they managed to find an open spot that seemed safe, the fire struck there, too. The poor populace did not know where to turn and congested the streets and packed into the parks. Some were so distraught about losing their fortunes and family that they made no real effort to flee and therefore perished.

At the time of the fire's outbreak, Nero was vacationing on the coast of Antium and did not return to the city until his own home, as well as other mansions on the Palatine Hill were in danger. He quickly took measures to help the populace by opening the Campus Martius to the homeless crowds. He allowed public monuments to be used as temporary shelters and built asylums to house the destitute masses. Food was brought from neighboring towns, and the price of grain drastically reduced to try to feed everyone. Despite these humanitarian measures, Nero could not sway public sentiment to his favor. An unpopular rumor persisted that at the time the city was burning, Nero went to his private stage and sang about the fall of Troy, comparing the present calamity with the ancient one.

Finally on the sixth day, near the bottom of the Esquiline Hill, where the destruction of many buildings functioned as a firebreak, the fire abated. However, the fire started again near the Aemilian district and spread to the open parts of the city. Although the number of lives lost was less than at the earlier outbreak of the fire, nevertheless many temples and open colonades were ravaged. The new fire fueled the rumors about Nero's part in this disaster. People said that he wanted to see all of Rome in ashes so that he could build a new one and name it after himself.

Indeed, of the 14 districts into which Rome was divided, only four remained unscathed. Three were completely devastated, and the remaining seven suffered severe damage.

Nero profited from this terrible loss and rebuilt his palace in a grandiose style. Nearly 1 mile long, it covered most of the Palatine and Esquiline hills. His architects used jewels and gold to decorate the interior, and outside, fields were added to insure the Emperor's privacy. Wild animals grazed in the parks, and a 120-foot high gold statue of Nero himself adorned his gardens.

Nero did undertake to reconstruct the city in a safer manner. Building codes were enacted that prescribed the use of stone for walls, instead of wood. No common walls were allowed between homes. Each home was constructed separately to prevent the rapid spread of fire. The city's water supply was made more accessible, and fire extinguishing aids were mandatory for each private home. People generally approved of these new laws for their practicality. Also, the new parks added to the beauty of Rome.

-----

[1]Tacitus, *Annals* XV: 38.

Once the new building projects were underway, religious offerings were made to the gods to insure their assistance in protecting the city. However, nothing Nero did, not his prayers, nor lavish spending, could quell the rumors that he was involved in starting the fire. Consequently, he resolved to find scapegoats to assuage public sentiment. He falsely accused the religious sect of Christians of the urban arson. This group was hated by most for their heinous crimes. They took their name from Christ who, during the reign of Tiberius, was executed by the governor Pontius Pilatus. This pernicious fanaticism (Christianity) had been repressed at first but erupted again not only in Judaea where it began, but also, here in Rome where all atrocities grow and flourish.

Those who admitted to being Christians were arrested first, and once they confessed and revealed other names, more people were seized. Although they were not charged with setting the fire, they were charged with the crime of hating mankind because these Christians abstain from social gatherings and other public amusements.

Upon conviction, the sentence was death, and the state made the executions a form of public amusement. Some of the "criminals" were covered with the hides of wild animals and sent into the arena to be mauled by dogs. Others were crucified or used as human torches to light the darkness of night. Nero even allowed his own palace to be used for this incendiary spectacle. Despite their guilt for being Christians, people began to pity them because it was felt they were punished not for the public good but because of the cruelty of one man. ∎

# TEACHER IDEAS

## Discussion Questions

1. What building codes were enacted after A.D. 64?

2. Describe Nero's new palace.

3. Where did the fire start?

4. What were the relief measures Nero instituted for the Roman people?

5. How did Nero spend his time during the fire?

6. Who became Nero's scapegoats?

7. Describe the types of executions the Christians endured.

8. How many districts did the fire touch?

9. Tacitus is known for his sharp criticism of his own society. Find the line in this story that criticizes his contemporaries. What does he mean?

10. Why did the Romans accuse the Christians of hating mankind? Why do you think they felt threatened by the Christians abstaining from social gatherings?

## History Lesson: The Jewish War (A.D. 66-70) and the Siege of Masada

Judaea came under the protection of Rome in 63 B.C. but was ruled by local kings until A.D. 7. The most famous of these client-kings was Herod the Great (37-4 B.C.). He was a great builder and, during his reign, was responsible for the construction of the magnificent port city, Caesarea, named in honor of Augustus. He also fortified the natural fortress of Masada. After Herod's death, his son ruled until the Romans replaced him with a procurator, the most famous of whom was Pontius Pilate (A.D. 26-36).

Rome tolerated Judaism relatively well within Judaea and even granted certain privileges to practicing Jews. They were exempted from military service and allowed to abstain from emperor worship. However, these concessions did not satisfy this extremely religious people, who considered Roman domination intolerable because it excluded the notion of a Jewish nation. The Jewish community was divided between the pro-Roman Sadducees, who held political offices and enjoyed an elevated social status, and the Pharisees, the lower economic classes who were anti-Roman. These two factions fought constantly. In A.D. 66, the Roman governor added fuel to this already volatile situation by excluding the Jews of Caesarea from Roman citizenship. Riots broke out, and the Greeks of that city massacred many Jews. The situation became so serious that the Emperor Nero sent Titus Flavius Vespasianus with 50,000 troops to subdue the province.

Vespasian was waging a successful campaign when Nero's suicide forced him to return to Rome to bid for the principate. The Zealot Jews (named because of their "zeal for the Lord") took advantage of his absence and secured Jerusalem for themselves. Vespasian left his son, Titus, in charge of the Roman troops, and Titus surrounded the holy city and proceeded to starve out the inhabitants. The situation became grave, and the people resorted to cannibalism. After three months, the Romans penetrated the city walls and destroyed the Jewish stronghold. The city was looted, captives slain or sold into slavery, and the great temple of King Solomon burned to the ground.[2] Judaea ceased to exist as a separate state and became a part of the province of Syria. This also marked the end of Judaea as the religious center of Judaism until modern times.

During this war, a group of Zealots captured a Roman garrison stationed at Masada. It was to this place that a Zealot leader, Eleazar ben Ya'ir, led his followers after escaping from Jerusalem. (Masada, a natural fortress, is a large mesa 1,950 feet long and 650 feet wide that stands 1,300 feet above the Dead Sea. Sheer cliffs on all sides prevent access, and only small winding foot paths connect the plateau with the plains below.) Here, Herod had created an Eden-like oasis in the midst of the desert. His first priority had been water, and he carved 12 cisterns into the cliffs. Then he erected aqueducts that brought water from the neighboring mountains to these storage tanks. The desert climate does not produce much rain, but frequent flash floods rush down with torrential force from the high areas. Herod's engineers placed dams to stop the deluge, and then aqueducts channeled water to the Masada cisterns.

Once the water supply was assured and a double wall built around the rim as a fortification, Herod enhanced the living conditions of his retreat. His own personal villa, dubbed the "hanging palace," rested on the north face. A three-terraced structure, it contained his private bathhouse replete with warm, cold, and hot chambers, as well as an exercise court. This villa was protected from the sun and wind, and round rooms offered a panoramic view of the valley below. On the plateau above was an administrative palace also equipped with a private bath and a large kitchen, a public swimming pool, storerooms, and other buildings.

After his escape from Jerusalem, Eleazar ben Ya'ir and his band of 960 men, women, and children occupied this fortress for three years. At first, the Romans paid little attention to the Zealots of Masada, but their continued harassment of Roman property finally aroused their ire. In A.D. 72, the procurator Flavius Silva, led the Tenth Legion, plus other auxiliary troops and numerous prisoners of war, across the desert to end this rebellion.

Silva first built a siege wall around the entire mesa. He then set up eight camps along this two-mile wall to repel raiders. Realizing the impossibility of scaling the walls, Silva decided to erect a massive ramp to the summit of Masada. On the western side, a rock spur rises, making the distance from the bottom to the top only 250 feet. This is where Silva built the ramp. Earth and stones were piled up and tamped down, and wooden beams inserted to strengthen the structure.[3] Although the ramp did not stretch to the summit, it was sufficiently high to allow an enormous siege tower to be raised parallel to the defensive walls. On this tower, Silva stationed Roman soldiers, who, protected by a leather blanket, swung an enormous battering ram against the doors. In defense, the Zealots erected a wooden frame packed with dirt in front of the ram. Whenever the ram struck, it weakened the wooden wall but strengthened the inner dirt wall by compacting it. To force his entry, the general resorted to setting fire to the wooden frame. This succeeded, but darkness prevented his entering the fortress immediately.

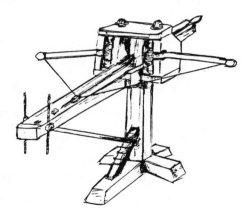

**Ballista**

On that night Eleazar ben Ya'ir persuaded his followers to take drastic action rather than become slaves of Rome. Every man agreed to kill his own family, and then ten men were chosen to kill the rest; they, in turn, dispatched each other with the last man committing suicide. When Silva and his troops entered the following morning, they found 960 people dead. Seven survivors, two women and five children, were discovered hiding in the cisterns. Their story was told to Josephus, the historian.

---

[2]Josephus's eyewitness account to the siege of Jerusalem is extant. See Resources.

[3]It is still possible to see this remarkable engineering structure today.

## SUGGESTED TOPICS FOR FURTHER RESEARCH

1. life and works of Josephus

2. Caesarea

3. Herod the Great

4. Dead Sea scrolls

5. Emperor Cults

### Language Arts

## VOCABULARY BUILDING

Bases:

- *grad* and *gress* from Latin verb *gradior, gradi, gressus sum* (to walk, step)

1. Define the following words and use each one in a sentence:

   ingress        transgress

   egress         digress

   regress

2. Find four other words derived from these stems.

3. *Grade, gradual*, and *graduate* also came from *gradior*. Explain why you think this happened.

4. Fill in each blank with a word from exercise 1 above.

   a. The adit provides an _____ into the mine but the only way to exit is through a small narrow _____.

   b. When the newborn baby arrived, his young brother's behavior _____.

   c. Let me _____ for a moment, and then I will answer your question.

   d. The preacher shouted from his pulpit, "Do not _____ the rules of God!"

## CREATIVE WRITING AND CRITICAL THINKING

Fifty years after Nero threw the Christians to the lions, the Roman attitude toward this religious group had changed little. Pliny the Younger (see chapter 13), while governor of Bithynia (A.D. 112), dealt with this sect, and wrote the following letter to Emperor Trajan for advice on how to handle the Christians:

It is my intention to refer all matters to you about which I am uncertain, for I can think of no one more qualified to give advice on important issues.

I have never attended a trial of these Christians and therefore do not know how far I should carry out my interrogations or even how to punish those who confess to being supporters of this faith. Should there be allowances for age? Should I punish those who have recanted? These are some of my questions.

So far I have followed this scheme. I personally asked whoever was accused of being a Christian if this were true. If he said "yes," I asked again, but this time I threatened him with punishment. If he still persisted, I ordered him executed.

I received an anonymous list of names accusing many people of being Christians. I rounded up these people and interrogated them. Whoever denied himself to be a Christian, I asked to swear allegiance to our gods and also to your image. (I had brought statues of the gods and of you yourself for this purpose.) They also made offerings of incense and wine to the gods and cursed Christ. All of these acts, I am assured, no true Christian would perform, so I dismissed them.

During my interrogation of these Christians I learned a little about their activities. They profess that they meet before dawn to sing songs to Christ. They pledge not to commit any crimes of wickedness, such as thievery or adultery or to prevaricate or to bear false witness. Now they have stopped meeting after your mandate forbidding secret societies.

I believed this matter worthy of your consultation because of the great numbers involved. People of all ages and classes, both men and women take part in this heresy. It has invaded not just the cities of my provinces but the villages and farms. I believe it can be stopped. Certainly your mandate seems to have had some effect. Temples once empty are beginning to fill. More buyers are purchasing sacrificial animals. I deduce from this that it is possible to persuade them to abandon this superstition and return to the right way.[4]

In reply, Pliny received the following response:

My Secundus, you have done well in examining those accused of being Christian. It is difficult to give you a universal format to follow because each case is unique. You must not search for these heretics, but if they are indicted and convicted, then they must be punished. Those who deny they are Christians and prove it by swearing to our gods should not be punished. Indeed, any information given to you without being signed must be thrown away. Hearsay has no place in our courts of law.[5]

**Letter Writing:**

How might a modern politician react to the problems associated with a subversive cult? If you were Pliny, what would you write to your superior? Then create Trajan's reply. Try to be diplomatic!

---

[4]Pliny the Younger, *Epistula* X: 96.

[5]Ibid. X: 97.

## Cultural Lesson: Common Latin Phrases Used in English

| Latin Word or Phrase | English Translation |
| --- | --- |
| ad nauseum | to disgust |
| alma mater | fostering mother |
| alter ego | another self |
| antebellum | before the war (usually Civil War) |
| bona fide | sincere, genuine |
| e pluribus unum | one out of many |
| et cetera | and so forth |
| exeunt | they go out |
| exit | he/she goes out |
| ex tempore | on the spur of the moment |
| incognito | with identity unknown |
| modus operandi | methods of working |
| pater noster | Lord's prayer |
| pax vobiscum | peace be with you |
| per annum | each year |
| per diem | for each day |
| post mortem | after death |
| prima facie | at first sight |
| sub rosa | privately (under the rose) |
| tempus fugit | time flies |
| terra firma | solid ground |
| ultimatum | final statement of terms |
| verbatim | word for word |
| vice versa | conversely |

## WORD RECOGNITION

How many of the above can you find in newspapers, books, etc.? Bring your findings to class. See who can find the most in one week's time.

## Et Alia: Emperors—Their Nicknames and Dates

Fill in the following blanks. The first one is complete.

| FULL NAME | NICKNAME | DATES |
|---|---|---|
| 1. Gaius Julius Caesar Octavianus Augustus | Augustus | 27 B.C.-A.D. 14 |
| 2. Tiberius Claudius Nero Caesar | _____ | A.D. 14-37 |
| 3. _____ | Caligula | _____ |
| 4. _____ | _____ | A.D. 41-84 |
| 5. Nero Claudius Caesar Drusus Germanicus | _____ | A.D. 54-68 |
| 6. _____ | Galba | _____ |
| 7. Marcus Salvius Otho | _____ | _____ |
| 8. Aulus Vitellius | _____ | A.D. 69 |
| 9. _____ | Vespasian | _____ |
| 10. Titus Flavius Sabinus Vespasianus | _____ | A.D. 79-81 |
| 11. _____ | Domitian | _____ |
| 12. Marcus Cocceius Nerva | Nerva | _____ |
| 13. _____ | Trajan | _____ |
| 14. Publius Aelius Hadrianus | _____ | A.D. 117-138 |
| 15. _____ | Antonius Pius | _____ |
| 16. Marcus Aurelius Antonius | _____ | _____ |
| 17. Lucius Aurelius Commodus | _____ | A.D. 180-193 |
| 18. Lucius Septimius Severus | _____ | _____ |
| 19. _____ | Caracalla | A.D. 211-217 |
| 20. _____ | Constantine the Great | _____ |

# RESOURCES

Asimov, Isaac. *The Roman Republic*. Boston: Houghton Mifflin, 1966.

Josephus, Flavius, *Jewish War*, ed. E. Mary Smallwood. Middlesex, England: Penguin Classics, 1984.

Kossolf, David. *The Voices of Masada*. New York: St. Martin's Press, 1973.

*Past Worlds*. Maplewood, N.J.: Hammond, 1988.
Maps of Imperial Rome are found on pp. 171 and 173.

Pearlman, Moshe. *The Zealots of Masada*. New York: Charles Scribner's Sons, 1967.

# XII

# Panaceas
## (A.D. 77)

## INTRODUCTION

Gaius Plinius Secundus, better known as Pliny the Elder, was born around A.D. 23 in northern Italy. The natural uncle and adoptive father of Pliny the Younger (whose description of the eruption of Vesuvius is presented in chapter 13), Pliny the Elder was born to a wealthy family and sent to Rome for schooling. After 10 years of army service, he practiced law and held several governmental posts. Pliny's true avocation, however, was writing, and he became a prolific author, producing a total of 102 volumes covering such erudite topics as linguistics, oratory, and history. Unfortunately, all of his works, except for his treatise on natural history were lost. Finished in A.D. 77, the treatise contains 37 books covering a variety of scientific topics including zoology, astronomy, and botany. Twelve books describe medicines and cures procured from plants or animals. Pliny compiled these remedies from numerous sources, and his wealth of knowledge reveals his scholarly personality. Most of the information he imparts, however, is without basis in scientific fact. Although Pliny's prescriptions and palliatives may be amusing now, they do suggest a complex knowledge of the human anatomy and a sincere desire to help alleviate the aches and pains of humankind.

In the early days of republican Rome, the medical profession did not exist. Ailments were treated by female healers who primarily used herbs and superstitious amulets. A patient's recovery often depended on animal sacrifices and religious rites. By the second century B.C., many Greeks had come to Rome, and among them were trained physicians. Greek schools of medicine established by priests, called *Asclepiadae*, dedicated to the god of medicine Asclepius, son of Apollo, had existed for centuries. The seat of worship for Asclepius was the Greek island of Cos, the birthplace (480 B.C.) of Hippocrates, the father of the medical profession.

By the time of Pliny the Elder, physicians specialized. There were *medici*, general practitioners, *medici a dentibus*, dentists, and *cherugi*, surgeons. The Greeks learned surgery, the most scientific of the medical specialties, from the Egyptians. Many complex operations were performed, for example, tracheotomies, amputations, and internal surgery—all, incidentally, without the aid of anesthetics. Roman surgeons worked in the arena to treat wounded gladiators and traveled with the armies.

The practice of medicine was never held in high regard by the Romans. Pliny described most physicians as parasites who capitalized on the misfortune of others: "The only person who can kill without fear of punishment is a doctor."[1] The following chapter describes some of the medicines and cures Pliny recommended to his Roman brothers and sisters. As should be readily apparent from their descriptions, Pliny's prescriptions are not medically indicated. Do *not* try any of them.

---

[1]Pliny the Elder, *Natural History* XXIX: 17-25.

Panaceas

# ■ Cucumbers[2]

The cucumber, especially the wild variety, can be used for numerous prophylactic aids. The medicine is extracted from the pulp of the cucumber after the juice is squeezed from the seeds. It is important to allow the vegetable to cure for an entire day before cutting, and only a reed carving tool should be used. This drug lasts a long time, up to 200 years (and becomes more potent with age). This salve restores the natural color to the skin damaged by scarring. Dried with resin, it cures skin rashes, itchiness, and diminishes the swelling of ear tumors. The seed of the cucumber stored in ash can be dried to a paste that relieves eye pain, and a juice extracted from the leaves combined with vinegar will restore hearing to deaf ears. Its smell alone revives a fainting person.

## Turnips[3]

The turnip is a powerful drug. Cooked and mashed, turnips can be put on the hands and feet to help restore circulation to frozen extremities. The seed of the turnip, when drunk with wine, is an antidote to poisons. It may also be applied to the face to create smooth skin. The Greek Democritus suggests eliminating turnips from one's regular diet since it causes flatulence, but others praise its effect as an aphrodisiac.

## Onions[4]

Just the smell of onions, which causes the eyes to water, can relieve dimness of vision. In fact, onion juice applied directly to the eyes is helpful. Also, it acts as a sleeping potion, and when chewed with bread, cures mouth sores. A salve made from green onions, wine, and honey is used on dog bites, but be sure to remove the plaster after three days. Ash and barley flour combined with onions and rubbed on the body eliminates genital sores.

## Leeks[5]

Nose bleeds can be treated by cutting up a leek and stuffing it up the affected nostril. A drink of leek and mother's milk stops hemorrhaging associated with miscarriages. Leeks cure coughs, and their leaves help burns, eye sores, and pimples. A potion of two spoonsful of leek juice and one of honey stirred into mother's milk and poured into one's nose will alleviate headaches.

## Fruits[6]

Plums aid constipation, and the leaves from the tree cooked with wine help problems associated with tonsils and the gums. A peach is even more useful. The fruit itself is harmless. The leaves pounded into a salve stop bleeding, and the pits combined with oil and vinegar assuage headaches. A raw pear is injurious to one's health, but cooked, it is good for stomachaches and acts as an antidote against poisonous mushrooms.

---

[2]Pliny the Elder, *Natural History* XX: 2.

[3]Ibid. XX: 9.

[4]Ibid. XX: 20.

[5]Ibid. XX: 21.

[6]Ibid. XXIII: 62, 66, and 67.

### Animals[7]

Many animal products are also therapeutic. Dried camel's brain added to vinegar is used in the treatment of epilepsy, dried camel gall bladder with honey loosens the bowels, and camel dung with ash curls the hair. If you can touch an elephant's trunk, especially right after it has sneezed, your headaches will disappear. Ivory chips from the tusks combined with honey remove dark splotches on the skin.

### Aphrodisiacs[8]

Several potent aphrodisiacs are manufactured from animal sources. The bladder of a boar when worn around the neck arouses the sexual appetite. Also, a drink concocted from pigs' marrow or the dried testicles of a horse works well. If a man's sexual drive needs to be arrested, try mouse dung rubbed directly on the male member.

### Urine[9]

Urine is the greatest panacea of all, but it is always best to use one's own for medicinal purposes. It helps sores, wounds, burns, animal bites, itchiness, dandruff, and even genital sores.

### Milk[10]

The most nutritious and healthy milk comes from human mothers. The next valuable milk belongs to the goat, and the sweetest is from the camel. Goat's milk does not upset the stomach, and cow's milk prevents constipation. All milk can be used to treat internal ulcers of the kidneys, bladder, stomach, and lungs, but fresh cheese made from milk is more useful for stomach pains. Cheese mixed with honey diminishes the black and blue color from bruises, and soft cheese checks diarrhea.

### Fat[11]

Another common remedy derived from animals and highly praised is fat, especially pig's fat. Even now, newlywed brides, when entering their new home, touch the door posts with fat for good luck. Some doctors mix pig's fat with that of a goose or a bull and prescribe it for gout in the feet. Boiled down, fat can be used to help consumptive coughing. Women use fat from nonparturient sows as a cosmetic. Mixed with white lead it makes scars colorless, and with lime it is applied to tumors and lumps of the breasts.

---

[7]Ibid. XXVIII: 24-26.

[8]Ibid. XXVII: 80.

[9]Ibid. XXVIII: 18.

[10]Ibid. XXVIII: 33.

[11]Ibid. XXVIII: 37.

## Panaceas for the Complexion[12]

Asses' milk helps the complexion of the face. It can remove wrinkles as well as make the skin softer and whiter. Some women bathe in milk several times a day to give the entire body a smoother appearance. (I have heard this custom was begun by Nero's wife Poppaea who would bathe in milk seven times a day.) If there are pimples or sores on one's face, spread butter on them, and what is more beneficial is to add lead to the butter pack. Bull's dung helps give cheeks a healthy red tint, but crocodile dung is more effective—always wash and rinse the face with cold water when employing this cosmetic.

## Mineral Springs[13]

Throughout the Roman Empire there are natural hot springs where anyone can enjoy the waters for relaxation or medicinal purposes. Different types of spas are beneficial for different ailments. For instance, water with sulphur helps the muscles, but if one stays in the bath too long, the odor causes faintness as well as alternate chilling and sweating of the body. Alum found in hot springs aids paralysis, as does *bitumen* (mineral pitch). Many people boast about the length of time they are able to endure the heat of the waters, but this is actually harmful to the body. Only a short dip is necessary to achieve the maximum medicinal effect, and afterward, a rinse with cold water and a rubdown with oil is beneficial. Mud extracted from these springs is used in plaster packs for injuries or diseases.

## Sea Water[14]

Sea water is used in the treatment of many infirmities. Heated and rubbed on the body, it relieves joint pain and even helps set broken bones. Venomous bites of scorpions and spiders are relieved with sea water. Steamed with vinegar it alleviates headaches; swollen breasts, emaciation, and deafness all respond to sea water treatments.

A sea voyage itself betters people suffering from tuberculosis. A cruise to Egypt seems best because of the length of time needed to travel to that part of the Mediterranean. Also, the constant motion of the waves causes violent vomiting, which clears up headaches and chest and eye pains. Drinking sea water purges the body of tumors and relieves blood clots. Either take sea water in its natural state or it can be boiled and mixed with vinegar or wine if preferred. Doctors who prescribe pure sea water suggest chewing radishes to speed up the vomiting.

## Salt[15]

Civilized people simply cannot exist without salt. It is used to flavor foods, to keep corpses from rotting, and has medicinal value as well. In the old days, our ancestors called the route to the Sabines the Salarian Road (*sal* means "salt" in Latin) because salt was brought across this highway. We call witty people salts (*sales*), and even the word *salary* is derived from salt because the military troops were once given a stipend of salt as part of their pay.

---

[12]Ibid. XXVIII: 50.

[13]Ibid. XXXI: 32.

[14]Ibid. XXXI: 33.

[15]Ibid. XXXI: 39.

Salt is found in various forms all over the Empire. Lake Tarentine in southern Italy dries up in the summer sun and becomes a vast salt pool, yielding a fine grained product. Also, evaporating sea water produces salt left on the rocks of the shoreline.

In India, mountains of salt exist from which blocks are cut just like the quarrying of stone. These salt mountains continuously grow so that the kings of India glean a greater revenue from the salt trade than from gold or pearls. In Africa, there are piles of salt that resemble hills. The sun and moon harden them and even the rain cannot cause them to melt. Only iron tools cut through these petrified hills.

Now to iterate some of the therapeutic qualities of salt: it doctors snake and scorpion bites and stings from wasps and bees. Warts, pus-filled sores, blisters, ulcers, and headaches benefit from salt treatments. Added to milk, salt aids eye cataracts, or pounded into an ointment, it is used for tongue scabs. Tooth decay can be prevented by holding a cube of salt under one's tongue until it melts. (Do this every day before having breakfast.) Mix salt with wine to soften the stomach and drive out worms. Hot salt packs relieve shoulder pains, blisters, and burns. Lick salt to treat a cough, and salt enemas alleviate hip pain. Many other medicinal uses of salt exist, and so all physicians laud its benefits. It is truly a universal panacea. ■

# TEACHER IDEAS

## Discussion Questions

1. List two headache remedies.

2. What substances can be used as an aphrodisiac?

3. What fruit commonly eaten today does Pliny believe is harmful?

4. Who was the empress who bathed in milk seven times a day?

5. Seasickness is prescribed for what ailments?

6. How did the Romans obtain salt?

7. What antidotes can be used against poison?

8. What is the most valuable milk?

9. Do you think any of Pliny's cures might have helped the ailing patient? What was beneficial? What was injurious? Does your family have any "home cures" for certain ailments?

10. Pliny said, "The only person who can kill without fear of punishment is a doctor." Do you agree with this statement? Is it true today? What might be the likely consequence today to a modern physician whose patient dies unexpectedly?

## History Lesson: The Flavian Dynasty (A.D. 69-96)

With the death of Nero, the Empire was thrown into a state of confusion. For the next several months, three separate individuals controlled the principate, all of whom died prematurely. Then the commander of the Judaean forces, Vespasian, was hailed as emperor by the armies of Egypt and Syria. He marched to Rome to secure his position leaving his son Titus to subdue the Jewish rebels.

Titus Flavius Vespasianus came from an equestrian family, and, while in his thirties, he had distinguished himself during the conquest of Britain (A.D. 43). He became consul in A.D. 51, and, due to his friendship with Emperor Claudius, he was admitted to the circles of the imperial palace. However, during a tour of Greece with Emperor Nero, Vespasian made the mistake of falling asleep while Nero presented an artistic piece. Insulted by Vespasian's poor manners, Nero relegated him to relative obscurity, and he vanished from the political scene for several years but eventually held the post of Governor of Africa in A.D. 63.

His success in Judaea led to his ascension to the office of principate in which he successfully served for 10 years (A.D. 69-79), managing the affairs of Rome with expertise and becoming as popular as Augustus. When Vespasian came to power, he found the treasury empty and the frontiers in danger. He strengthened them both. More autocratic than Augustus, Vespasian shared his consulship with only one man, his son Titus.

Unlike his predecessors Caligula and Nero, Vespasian was a virtuous man of simple pleasures and without vice who worked long hours and spent wisely. The most famous piece of architecture built under his sponsorship was the Flavian amphitheater, nicknamed the Colosseum because of a huge statue of Nero that stood outside its entrance. He was much mourned by the Roman people when he died from a fever at 70 years of age.

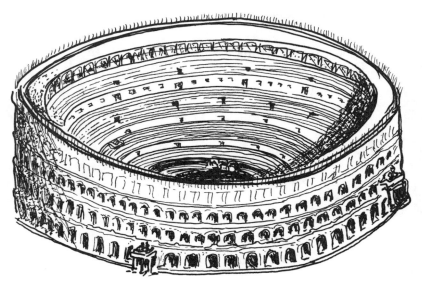

**Colosseum**

Vespasian hoped that his son Titus would succeed him. Together, they had shared the power of consul, tribune, and censor. Vespasian had also appointed Titus head of the Praetorian Guard. As a young man, Titus had grown up in Claudius's household and was a close friend of the Emperor's son, Britannicus. Present when Nero poisoned Britannicus, Titus may have ingested some of the potion himself (see chapter 10). He joined his father during the Judaic campaign and was the actual victor over Jerusalem in A.D. 70. During his short two years of office, Titus was forced to deal with several disasters—the destruction of Pompeii and Herculaneum (see chapter 13), a large fire in Rome (A.D. 80), and a virulent plague. He set up government relief organizations to help the victims of these calamities. A well-liked ruler, his only fault may have been his too lavish spending. When the Flavian amphitheater was dedicated, Titus sponsored 100 days of games at the State's expense. Only 40 years old, he succumbed to a fever in A.D. 81.

Since Titus left no heirs, the principate fell to his younger brother, Titus Flavius Domitianus, a very different person from his two predecessors. Raised by an aunt, Domitian received little attention from his father, the Emperor Vespasian. Left behind while Vespasian went on campaign, he was denied a military career. When Titus came to power, he did not share his offices with his brother Domitian who resented this exclusion. The premature death of Titus thrust him into the principate's chair without any military or political background or experience. Desirous of a personal military victory, he waged war against the Germans in A.D. 83 and was successful. He kept his armies happy by increasing their pay and thus insuring their loyalty. On the homefront, in the political arena of Rome, he was not so fortunate. Domitian rarely convened the senate and always voted first to exclude any opposition. He silenced this august body and in so doing incurred the wrath of the senators. Domitian insisted that everyone address him as *dominus et deus* (master and god), an affront to all Romans who considered it sacrilegious for an emperor to be pronounced a god during his lifetime.

In A.D. 89, the governor of Germany led an unsuccessful revolution against him, and Domitian was ruthless in his punishment of the malcontents. His repressive behavior continued, and the years A.D. 93-96 are known as "the reign of terror." Domitian replenished his exhausted treasury by confiscating the property of wealthy individuals whom he accused (mostly unjustly) of treason. He was finally murdered by a group that included his wife and the prefect of the Guard. The Flavian dynasty, which had begun so positively, thus ended on a notorious nadir.

## SUGGESTED TOPICS FOR FURTHER RESEARCH

1. Herod Agrippa II

2. Berenice, mistress of Titus

3. Arch of Titus

4. Domitia Longina

5. Apicius, cookbook writer

6. Colosseum (Flavian amphitheater)

## Language Arts

### VOCABULARY BUILDING

Suffix:

- *phobia* from Greek noun *phobos*, meaning "panic, fear." This suffix is primarily used in the fields of medicine and psychology.

1. Define the following phobias:

   acrophobia:

   agoraphobia:

   claustrophobia:

   hydrophobia:

   necrophobia:

   monophobia:

   photophobia:

   xenophobia:

2. Write a short description of a person suffering from one of the above phobias. Read it aloud and see if your classmates can guess which one you are describing.

### CRITICAL THINKING: Satire

The Romans regarded satire as their own literary invention. As the first century A.D. writer Quintilian said, *"satura quidem tota nostra est"* ("satire is, indeed, ours alone"). The word *satire* is derived from a Latin word meaning "a dish filled with mixed fruits." Like the varied nature of the fruit, satire was a loose discipline, in both form and content, often combining prose and verse and covering a wide variety of subjects.

Satirists attempt to inspire the improvement of society through critical wit and humor. Satire is typically divided into two parts: first, the thesis, the examination of the vice or folly, and second, the recommendation for a particular virtue. Satirists use many devices to clarify their position: fables, sarcasm, invective, and proverbs are but a few.

The two greatest Roman satirists have each lent their names to a type of satire; from Horace (first century B.C.) comes Horatian satire, a light and humorous approach to criticism. Horace took great care to limit his satires to themes of a social, as opposed to a political, nature. He used humor and gaiety to describe the follies of people and a gentle approach to his corrective suggestions.

From the author Juvenal comes Juvenalian satire, which is not so kind. Juvenal's satire was bitter and very critical of the politics of Rome (though he was careful to make sure his victims were deceased). Juvenal tried to urge his audience to change, but as a true pessimist, he is convinced humans have sunk so low they cannot save themselves.

## CRITICAL THINKING

1. Read the following excerpts from Horace and Juvenal. Both describe a banquet at a wealthy man's home. Compare the tone of each. Identify examples of Horace's levity and Juvenal's bitterness.

**Horace:**

Horace: How did you enjoy your dinner yesterday at the home of the wealthy Nasidienus? I hear it started quite early—around noon.

Fundanius: I've never had a better time.

Horace: Tell me all about it. What did you eat first?

Fundanius: First, we were served a wild boar which our host was quick to point out was captured during a gentle wind to improve its flavor. Placed around this were tangy white radishes, lettuce, red radishes, and other vegetables, all delicious. After this course was removed, a well-dressed slave wiped the rich maple tables with a plush purple towel, and another male slave picked up any crumbs which had fallen on the couches and floor. Then a dark Indian servant brought us Caecilian wine and a Greek steward some Chian wine mixed with sea water. Our host exclaimed, "Should you prefer Alban, Maecenas, or Falernian wine, don't hesitate to ask, we have both."

Then more waiters came into the dining room carrying a huge tray on which were the broken limbs of a crane seasoned with salt and meal. Also they served liver from a white goose which had only been fed rich figs and the choice pieces of a hare, the legs. We also saw black birds with braised breasts and rumpless pigeons. While our host was extolling the culinary achievements of his food, we all fled before we could taste anything.[16]

\* \* \*

**Juvenal:** What a dinner! The wine was so bad that even a towel would not want to mop it up. It turned the guests into madmen; a real brawl broke out. Soon everyone was throwing goblets and you had to use your own napkin to wipe your bloody nose. Freedmen began to hurl wine jugs and the fighting grew worse.

Our host, on the other hand, did not taste this cheap wine, but sipped on a vintage fare which was bottled almost 200 years ago. He wouldn't even offer his sick friend so much as a drop from his precious brew. His personal goblet was studded with amber beads and his plate covered with Indian green stones. His guests must use plain dishes, and if you are given a fancy one by mistake, a guard sticks near your side counting every gem and watching your sharp fingernails in case you try to pick off some jewel.

I will admit that his jasper is truly magnificent because he actually used precious gems from his own finger rings to put on his cups. But we guests must quench our thirst from broken often-repaired crockery goblets.

You might think our host Vireo is just a cheap man. But actually he does this on purpose to make you miserable. You are mistaken if you think he will offer you one tasty morsel, not even some half-eaten hare, or the hind quarter of a boar, or a small piece of fowl. He is wise to tease you so. If you can endure this torture, you can endure anything![17]

2. Read a satirical piece and write a short report that identifies the two parts of the satire—the vice or folly that is criticized and the recommended virtue. Suggestions: Orwell's *Animal Farm*, Evelyn Waugh's *The Loved One*, Huxley's *Brave New World*, or Swift's "A Modest Proposal."

---

[16]Horace, *Satires* II: 8.

[17]Juvenal, *Satires* V.

3.  Find examples of contemporary satire: political cartoons, Lampoon magazines, TV shows. What social or political folly is being criticized? Would you categorize the work as Juvenalian or Horatian satire?

## Cultural Lesson: Roman Meals

Pliny the Elder thought food served a medicinal as well as a substantive role. His 12 books on panaceas reveal a very large variety of eatables the first century A.D. Roman could place on his table. This was a result of the ever-expanding Empire. Whenever the Romans conquered new territory, they brought local delectibles back to Rome, and merchants were quick to import new products to placate the expansive palates of the Roman upper classes.

The Romans rarely cooked until the evening because heating the oven was a laborious chore. Breakfast (*jentaculum*), was a light meal taken whenever the individual awoke. Schoolboys and slaves ate before dawn, but almost everyone else breakfasted around 8:00 or 9:00 A.M. A slice of bread seasoned with salt or honey and some fruit would fill the Roman stomach.

*Prandium* (lunch), was also an informal meal eaten around 11:00 A.M. or 12:00 noon. Again, bread was the main offering. This might be supplemented with some leftover cold meat, fruit, and watered wine.

After the close of business and a sojourn to the local baths, the ancient Roman was ready to eat his or her first full meal of the day. Served early, around 5:00 or 6:00 P.M., the *cena* was shared by all family members and was usually taken in the atrium though wealthy Romans had a separate formal dining room, the *triclinium* (see chapter 15). Everyone reclined on couches with his head propped on his left hand. The couch slanted toward one end and was covered with cushions to make the diner more comfortable. Children usually sat on chairs facing their elders, and small portable tables on which the food was placed were arranged in front of the eaters. The Romans had no forks, but used spoons, knives, and large picks. The meat was often carved in the kitchen into bite-size pieces to eliminate messy fingers.

The cena was divided into three parts: 1) the *gustatio*, which contained cold appetizers such as eggs, shellfish, olives, or mushrooms, accompanied by *mulsum*, a wine and honey drink; 2) the main course with a minimum of three dishes, but usually more, such as fish, fowl, meat, vegetables, breads, and watered wine;[18] and 3) a dessert of fresh or dried fruits and a variety of nuts roasted and dipped in honey (sweets were limited since the Romans had no sugar).

At a fancy dinner party many elaborate dishes would be prepared. The Romans preferred to limit their party to nine participants, placing three guests on three couches. It was not unusual for this meal to last for hours since entertainment was provided between courses. Dancing girls, acrobats, musical recitals, and poetry readings were popular. Guests carried their own napkins to a party so they could bring home gifts like flutes, balls, statues, or wooden boxes.

See figure 12.1 for a "grocery list" with some of the items available to the ancient Roman.

---

[18]The Romans considered the drinking of undiluted wine poor manners.

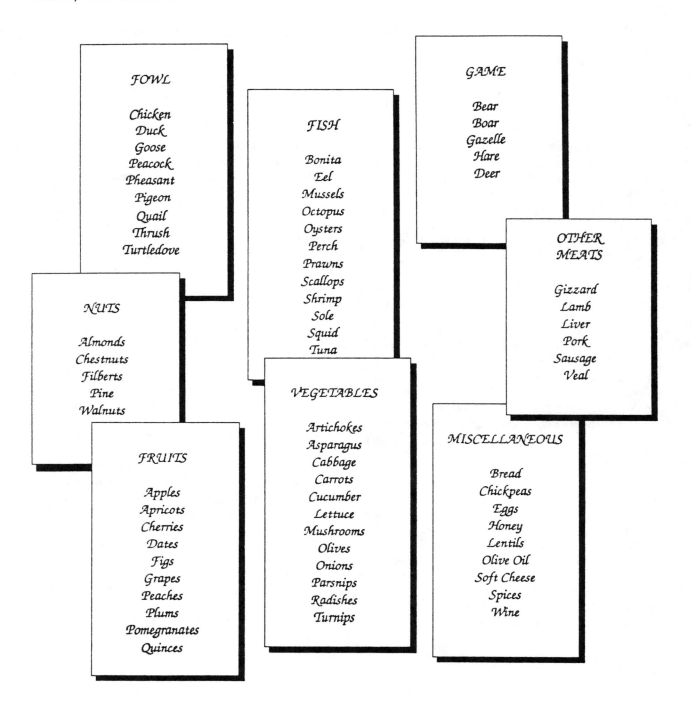

Fig. 12.1. Roman Grocery List.

**SHOPPING EXPEDITION**

In groups of two or three, create a menu for a Roman banquet using the Roman Grocery List. Include three full courses for your *cena*. Then "go shopping" (some items may not be available) and compute the cost of your meal for nine guests at today's prices. You need not buy anything, and you'll have to estimate quantities. You might include the cost of hiring some form of entertainment.

# RESOURCES

Arrowsmith, William, trans., *Satyricon by Petronius*. New York: New American Library, 1983.

Fast, Howard. *Agrippa's Daughter*. New York: Pocket Books, 1966.

Grant, Michael. *The Roman Emperors*. New York: Charles Scribner's Sons, 1985.

Greenlalgh, P. A. L. *The Year of the Emperors*. New York: Barnes and Noble, 1975.

Massie, Allan. *The Caesars*. New York: Franklin Watts, 1984.
    This book details the lives of Emperors Augustus through Domitian and Julius Caesar.

Pollard, Arthur. *Satire*. London: Methuen, 1970.

Solomon, Jon, and Julia Solomon. *Ancient Roman Feasts and Recipes*. Miami, Fla.: E. A. Seeman, 1977.

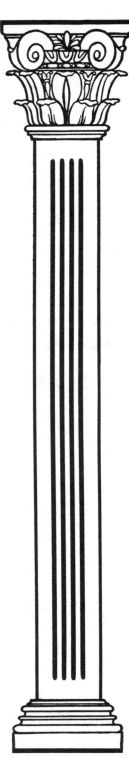

# XIII  The Eruption of Vesuvius
## (A.D. 79)

### INTRODUCTION

On August 24, A.D. 79, the volcanic mountain Vesuvius erupted and buried two ancient Roman towns, Pompeii and Herculaneum. These cities lay entombed until 1709 when an Italian well digger fell into an ancient theater interred below the earth. What marvels this man helped to reveal—an entire city frozen in time! Bread still lay in the ovens, a dog was hopelessly bound to his chain, houses and furniture remained for the archaeologist to uncover for the modern world. The eruption of Vesuvius and the eventual unearthing of Herculaneum and Pompeii have given much insight into the daily lives of these ancient people; to their inhabitants, however, it was a deadly disaster.

Both cities lie south of Rome on the Bay of Naples. Due to the continual shifting of the African plate against the Italian peninsula, this area is fraught with earthquakes and volcanic activity. Pompeii, a town of perhaps 20,000 inhabitants, gained its wealth from exporting wine. From the lavish villas excavated there, it appears to have been a well-frequented resort town of the ancient Roman. Herculaneum, which lies only four miles from Mt. Vesuvius, was much smaller, with a population of only 5,000 people. A fishing community, it also attracted wealthy vacationers.

What actually happened on that fateful day? Around one o'clock in the afternoon, Vesuvius exploded. For 11 hours it hurled a column of pumice 12 miles into the sky. Immediately, ash began to fall upon Pompeii at a rate of 6 inches per hour. By midnight, the column in the center of the volcano collapsed and an avalanche of gas, pumice, and rock rolled through Herculaneum and killed many of its residents. Flows of lava continued to besiege Pompeii until it, too, was finally buried by the morning of August 25. When the cataclysm was finally over, Herculaneum lay concealed beneath 66 feet of earth. The coast of Italy was altered as lava filled the sea, and many people lost their lives.

In August A.D. 79, Pliny the Younger was staying at the villa of his uncle, the author and scientist, Pliny the Elder, at the town of Misenum. Although 20 miles west of Mt. Vesuvius, Misenum was rocked by the volcanic explosion. The elder Pliny was in charge of the imperial fleet at Misenum and felt compelled to rescue friends living near the disaster. He perished during his mission at the town of Stabiae.

Later, the historian Tacitus requested Pliny the Younger to describe in writing his eyewitness account of the eruption of Mt. Vesuvius. Pliny graciously wrote two letters to Tacitus that recount his uncle's death and his own escape. Tacitus included this information in his book, the *Annals*, but unfortunately, this part of his work is not extant.

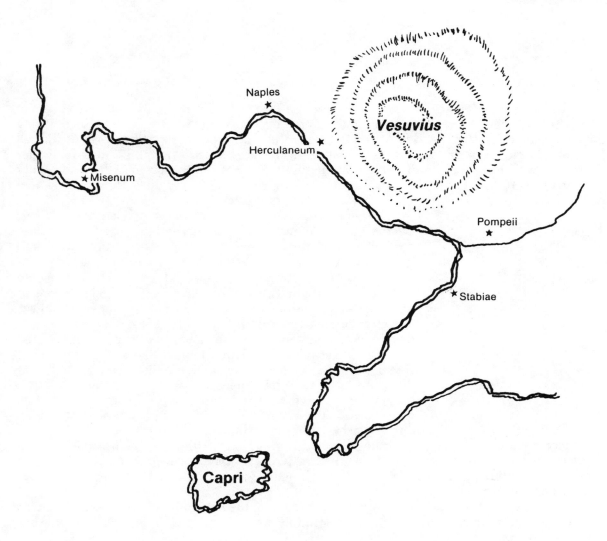

Naples
Herculaneum
Misenum
Vesuvius
Pompeii
Stabiae
Capri

**Bay of Naples**

The Eruption of Mount Vesuvius

■ Epistula I:[1]

Greetings to Tacitus from Pliny the Younger:

You have asked, Tacitus, that I describe the events of my uncle's demise so you may impart this information to posterity. I am honored by your request. Although he died during the unfortunate disaster that devastated this beautiful land, your description of his death will add to his immortality. Indeed, I believe that those men are blessed whom the gods grant either to do things that are worthy of being written about or write things that must be read. Truly they are most fortunate who are given both. Among these will be my uncle, both by his own works and by yours. For this reason I will describe that fateful day.

**Pinus Pinea**

My uncle was at Misenum in charge of the imperial fleet. On the 24th of August around the seventh hour (1:00 p.m.), my mother pointed out to him that an unusual cloud had appeared in the sky. It was very large and quite dark. Pliny the Elder was sunbathing at the time and casually took a dip in the cold waters. Then, after he ate and read awhile, he asked someone to bring his sandals and climbed a small hill so that he could see this strange phenomenon more clearly. He could not tell then from which mountain the cloud came, but later, we discovered it was Mt. Vesuvius. The cloud looked like a pine tree, for it rose up into the sky from a long column like a trunk. On top of this shaft, similar to branches, the vapor spread out laterally. Maybe a gust of wind carried it aloft or it diffused because of its own weight. It was partially white and gray as if it contained dirt and ashes.

Since my uncle was a curious man, he decided to investigate this marvel more closely. He ordered a small boat to be made ready for the trip across the bay. He even asked me if I wanted to go with him, but I declined, saying I had too much studying to do, and that he, my teacher, had assigned all that work.

As he was leaving, a messenger arrived from Retina, the wife of his friend Bassus. She was terrified by the imminent danger in which her family was caught because her villa lay near the volcano and escape was only possible by ship. She begged Pliny to rescue her household.

My uncle then quickly changed his plans. Instead of a small boat, he ordered a large galley to be launched so he could rescue not only Retina but other vacationers on the eastern shore. He hurried straightway toward the danger from which most everyone else was fleeing. What is more remarkable is that he exhibited no fear and even dictated notes on his scientific observations of this natural disaster.

Hot dense ash began to fall on the ship as my uncle and the sailors approached the land. Even pumice stones, which were black and burning, rained upon the rescue party; large rocks with fire hurled downward from the sky. Suddenly, the sea itself seemed to be pulled outward as the debris from the mountain filled up the shoreline. Pliny hesitated a bit considering whether they should all turn back. The pilot urged him to stop this foolishness, but Pliny replied, "Fortune helps the brave. Seek Stabiae." My uncle's friend Pomponianus lived there, and although the danger was not yet imminent, the volcanic flow was clearly in sight and moving closer. After a short sail, the boat landed at Stabiae, and Pomponianus greeted my uncle. He consoled the frightened Pomponianus and urged him to stop worrying. Nonchalantly, he asked if he could take a bath and have a light meal. Pliny seemed quite cheerful or what is more outstanding, pretended to be cheerful in the midst of this great calamity.

---

[1]Pliny the Younger, *Annals* VI: 16.

Meanwhile, near Mt. Vesuvius, one could see many glaring fires, the brightness and clarity of which were augmented by the darkness of night. My uncle kept saying, to lessen his comrade's fears, that the fires were merely those left behind by frightened farmers who abandoned their homes. Then he went to sleep and slept very soundly. His friends, who were keeping watch, could hear his loud snoring, which was most resonant because he was such a heavy man. During the night, the courtyard in Pomponianus's home began to fill up with so much ash and pumice that it looked as if Pliny the Elder might be trapped inside the bedroom.

The men aroused Pliny, and together they conferred about whether it would be safer to stay inside the house or to wander about in the open air. The house had been shaking so violently with huge tremors that it seemed to be moving from its own foundation. It was not safe to remain inside. On the other hand, outside, burning pumice continued to fall. They chose the latter course and took pillows and bound them to their heads with linen to protect themselves from the flying debris.

Despite the fact that it was daylight elsewhere, the sky seemed black and more dense than most nights. The people carried torches to light their way as they hurried to the shore to make an escape. The sea still swelled with high waves, and no exit was possible. Exhausted, my uncle was forced to lie down on an old discarded sail, and he drank quantities of cold water. The oppressive smell of sulfur and ever-present flames turned most to flight. My uncle struggled to get up with the help of two slaves but immediately collapsed. I think this was the result of his breath being clogged with dense vapors and his stomach being constricted.

When daylight finally returned, three days after my mother and I had seen my uncle last, our slaves found his body on the beach. He was unharmed and fully clothed. He looked as if he were sleeping, though he was, of course, dead.

My mother and I were still at Misenum during my uncle's rescue attempt, but I will not burden you with these details. I will add one more item—that I have written only about what I was personally involved in or what information I heard immediately afterward from his companions. Take what is most useful to you. Farewell.

Epistula II:[2]

To Tacitus from Pliny the Younger:

You have recently written to me and said that my previous letter concerning my uncle's death sparked your interest to learn more about my reactions and fears on that disastrous day of August 24th. Therefore, I will oblige your request and describe the events at Misenum.

After my uncle left on his rescue mission, I labored over my studies. Then I took a bath and had dinner. For many days there had been frequent earth tremors, but this was not unusual for the area. That night, however, the shocks were so strong that we thought the buildings might topple. While I was trying to sleep, my mother, afraid for our lives, burst into my bedroom. We went outside the house into the courtyard, which faced the sea, and sat there for awhile. It may have been bravery or just plain stupidity (I was only 18 at the time), but I decided to read a book of Livy despite the gravity of the situation.

All of a sudden, a Spanish friend of my uncle's appeared on the scene and interrupted our reverie. When he saw that I was just reading a book and my mother was relaxing in a chair, he began to challenge our casual behavior. I ignored his pleas for flight and continued to enjoy my text.

---

[2]Pliny the Younger, *Annals* VI: 20.

Finally dawn approached, but it was still quite dark since the sun was obscured by a black fog. Concerned that the roof of our house might collapse, my mother and I decided to leave Misenum, if possible. We walked out to the street and were immediately surrounded by a large crowd following our lead.

We noticed many amazing phenomena while attempting to make our escape. We had ordered a carriage to carry us out of town, but the earth was heaving up and down so dramatically that the vehicle could not stay in one spot. Moreover, the waters of the sea had been sucked out away from the shore and many fish were lying dead, stranded on the sand. Even the sky was ominous for it was lighted with flames similar to, but much greater than, lightning flashes.

Then that same man from Spain began to berate us for our tardiness in leaving. He said, "If your brother, your uncle lives, he would want you to be safe. If he has perished, he would want you to survive. Why then do you prolong your escape?" My mother and I replied that unless we were certain of Pliny the Elder's safety, we could not leave. The Spaniard finally gave up and hurriedly ran from the danger.

Soon thereafter, a dark cloud enveloped the land and covered the sea. We could not see Capri or the promontory of Misenum. My mother begged, urged, and even ordered me to flee. She insisted that I escape since I was young. She, on the other hand, was too heavy with age and weight to run, and she would die happy knowing I was safe. I answered that I would not leave her, and so I grabbed her hand and pulled her along. She followed with difficulty and chided herself for delaying my progress.

Ash, though less dense, continued to rain upon us, and as I looked back I saw a huge billow of fog threatening to envelop everything. Afraid that we might be trampled by the crowd, I led my mother to the side of the road. We sat down, and immediately, total darkness descended. It was as if someone had turned off a light in a room. You could hear women and children screaming and crying. People were trying to find their families by the sound of their voices, because one could not see through the impenetrable darkness. Many prayed to the gods for death. Others thought that the gods had deserted them, and this was the last day of the world.

Many persons added to the true dangers with fabricated terrors. They declared that many buildings at Misenum had collapsed and the town was burning. Gradually the sky became lighter, but we thought it was only the reflection of fire. Much heavier ash began to fall, and we repeatedly had to shake it off so we would not suffocate. I might be able to boast to you, Tacitus, that not a groan escaped my lips, but it was only because I was too numb with fear.

Finally, the fog became thinner and the clouds lifted. Soon true daylight appeared, and the sun shone in the sky. It was a pale lurid color like during an eclipse. Everything around us was changed. The land was covered with deep ash, which looked like snow. My mother and I returned to our home at Misenum. We were still afraid since the earthquakes persisted but had no thought of leaving until we could learn of news of my uncle.

That is all I remember, Tacitus. Take my personal story and turn it into history. Farewell. ∎

# TEACHER IDEAS

## Discussion Questions

1.  What was the date of the eruption of Mt. Vesuvius?

2.  Name the two towns destroyed by this eruption.

3.  What caused Pliny the Elder's death?

4.  Describe the elder Pliny's reaction to the dangers he faced.

5.  What unusual phenomena did Pliny the Younger observe at Misenum as a result of the volcanic eruption?

6.  According to Pliny, how did many of the ancient Romans behave in the face of this disaster?

7.  What did Pliny the Elder use to protect his head from the falling debris?

8.  Who urged Pliny and his mother to leave their villa?

9.  In Epistula I, Pliny the Younger states that he believes that "those men are blessed whom the gods grant either to do things that are worthy of being written about or write things that must be read. Truly they are most fortunate who are given both." What does he mean by these words? Can you give an example of an individual who fulfills both of Pliny's requirements (e.g., Winston Churchill)?

10. In these two letters to the historian Tacitus, Pliny the Younger reveals much of his own personality. What do you think this ancient Roman was like? Give specific examples from the text. For example, his refusal to go with his uncle because he had work to finish suggests that he was disciplined and studious.

## History Lesson: The Praetorian Guard

Throughout the history of Imperial Rome, one small group of soldiers held almost as much power as the emperor himself: the Praetorian Guard, the personal bodyguard of the Emperor and his family. During the Republic, a separate corps was always assigned to guard the headquarters of generals during wartime. Augustus expanded the duties of this elite group and awarded them special privileges.

Begun in 27 B.C., the praetorian soldiers were nine cohorts strong (each cohort consisted of 1,000 men) commanded by two prefects. Praetorian guards were paid three times the pay of an ordinary legionaire, and their time of service shortened from the normal 20-year term to 16 years. The force was billeted outside the city limits to avoid any conflict with the old republican custom of forbidding troops within the city of Rome itself, a prohibition intended to prevent a military dictatorship and affirm the power of the senate and people of Rome as superior to the army.

Tiberius, Augustus's successor, made the near fatal mistake of giving control of these troops to a single man. After Tiberius left Rome for Capri, his prefect Sejanus (see chapter 10) took command and moved the Guard, previously housed in several stations, to a single barracks just outside the Viminal Gate. Sejanus could summon these troops at any time, and because no other military force was allowed in the city, his power was left unchecked.

The Praetorian Guard was instrumental in determining who would be emperor. After assassinating Caligula, the Guard located his uncle Claudius (see chapter 10) and elevated him to the throne. Claudius thanked them by giving all the soldiers a generous monetary gift to insure their loyalty. In the chaotic year of A.D. 68-69 (the "year of the four emperors," see chapter 12) when four military men became the principate, the Guard was instrumental in their ascensions.

After deposing Emperor Commodus in A.D. 192, the Guard placed Pertinax on the throne, but he lasted less than a year. He tried to curtail the Guard's power, an attempt that cost him his life. Dio Cassius, in his history of Rome described how Didius Julianus, upon hearing of Pertinax's death, ran immediately to the Praetorian Guard barracks. He stood outside the gates and shouted to the soldiers that he would pay them to put him in power. An actual bidding war then ensued between Julianus and another contender, the former winning at a cost of 25,000 sestertii per soldier. Later emperors were wise to subdue the power of this elite troop, which was eventually disbanded by Constantine I.

## SUGGESTED TOPICS FOR FURTHER RESEARCH

1. Dio Cassius

2. Commodus

3. Constantine I

4. Festival of Vulcanalia

5. Nereids

### Language Arts

## VOCABULARY BUILDING

Bases:

- *spec, spic, spect* from Latin verb *specto*, meaning "to look at, watch"

1. Define the following words and use each in a sentence:

   spectacle      prospect

   retrospect      conspicuous

   suspicion

2. Which of the previous words are nouns? Which are adjectives?

3. Fill in the blanks with the words from the exercise above.

   a. She made a terrible _____ of herself and embarrassed her mother.

   b. The detective's _____ that the cat burglar was John Doe proved correct.

   c. The _____ of having to climb another 1,000 feet discouraged the hiker.

   d. In _____, I should not have bought that plaid jacket.

   e. He wore a _____ red and purple tie.

4. Find four more words that are derived from *specto*.

## SIMILES

A simile is a figure of speech in which a similarity between two objects is directly expressed. Most similes are introduced by the words *like* or *as*. Identify at least four similes from Pliny's two letters (there are five).

## CREATIVE WRITING

The historian Tacitus requested information from Pliny so he could include a description of the eruption of Vesuvius in his *Histories*. Tacitus's work has not survived.

1. Carefully reread the two accounts and then recreate Tacitus's historical narrative.

2. Write a letter from Tacitus answering either letter of Pliny the Younger.

3. Team activity: Videotape an imaginary television evening news report from August 24, A.D. 79.

4. Team activity: Rewrite the events into a one-act play using four characters: Pliny the Younger, Pliny the Elder, the mother/sister, and one slave. Present the play to the class.

## ETYMOLOGY OF WORDS

### Myth of Vulcan

Vulcan was the son of Jupiter, king of the gods, and his wife Juno. Of all the immortals, only Vulcan lacked pulchritude. In some stories, Jupiter was so angered by his ugliness that he threw Vulcan from Olympus. Vulcan fell for an entire day and eventually landed on the Greek island of Lemnos. In another version, it was his mother Juno who hurled him from Olympus, and Vulcan fell into the sea where he was rescued by the nereids.

Vulcan was the god of earthly fire—that which originated from within the earth, as opposed to lightning and man-made fires. He later developed into the god of those crafts that required the use of fire, for example, pottery and metal smithing. Vulcan's workshops were inside volcanic mountains. Whenever he was working on a creation, the volcano spurted fire and smoke.

The story of Vulcan having his forge beneath the mountains evolved to explain the phenomenon of volcanoes. Other theories were that volcanoes were the entrances of Hell or that the 100-headed monster Typhon moved beneath the earth and caused the eruptions.

## WORD SOURCES

1. Write a myth to explain a natural event, for example, Halley's comet.

2. Read more myths of Vulcan (Greek name, *Hephaestus*) in Homer's *Iliad* (1:586 ff) and *Odyssey* (VIII:266 ff).

3. Compare the Greek myths that explain volcanic activity with Polynesian stories of the goddess Pele.

4. Using a dictionary, find the meanings of *vulcanism, volcanism, vulcanology, vulcanize,* and *volcano*. Why are these terms derived from the god Vulcan?

## Cultural Lesson: Familiar Latin Quotations

| QUOTATION | DEFINITION | AUTHOR |
|---|---|---|
| Mens sana in corpore sano. | A sound mind and a sound body. | Juvenal |
| Carpe diem. | Seize the day (opportunity). | Horace |
| Alea iacta est. | The die is cast. | Julius Caesar |
| Errare humanum est. | To err is human. | Seneca |
| Fortes fortuna adiuvat. | Fortune helps the brave. | Terence |
| In hoc signo vinces. | In this sign (cross) you will conquer. | Constantine |
| In medias res. | Into the midst of things. | Horace |
| Amor omnia vincit. | Love conquers all. | Virgil |
| Vita brevis, ars longa. | Life is short, art is long. | Hippocrates |
| Timeo Danaos et dona ferentes. | I fear the Greeks bearing gifts. | Virgil |
| Pares cum paribus facillime congregantur. | Birds of a feather flock together. | Cicero |
| Veni Vidi Vici. | I came, I saw, I conquered. | Julius Caesar |
| Ex nihilo nihil fit. | Nothing comes from nothing. | Lucretius |

## FAMILIAR LATIN QUOTATIONS

List when each author of the above quotations lived, his occupation(s), and his published work(s).

## Et Alia: Volcanoes

In simplest terms, a volcano is a vent between the molten rock of the earth's interior and the earth's surface. Volcanoes vary in size and shape. There is a series of volcanoes located in the Mediterranean area, a few of which are Etna, Santorini, Stromboli, and Vesuvius. Prior to A.D. 79, Vesuvius had been inactive, and the ancient Romans were ignorant of the danger near which they lived. Since the first century disaster, Vesuvius has erupted many times.

## SCIENTIFIC RESEARCH

Choose three of the following topics and present your findings to the class:

1.  How volcanoes are formed.

2.  The parts of a volcano (i.e., caldera, cone, etc.) and its elements (i.e., gases, silica content, etc.).

3.  The types of eruptions and how they differ (i.e., Plinian, Strombolian, Steam, and Hawaiian).

4.  Why earthquakes are closely associated with volcanic activity.

5. The difference between extinct, active, and dormant volcanoes.

6. The importance of tectonic plate activity and the formation of volcanoes.

7. The explosion of Santorini in 1450 B.C. on the island of Thera.

8. Research the world's newest island, Sursey (off the coast of Iceland). It has been preserved and kept pristine so that scientists can monitor the growth of life on this piece of land.

9. Draw pictures of different types of volcanoes (Plinian, Strombolian, Steam, and Hawaiian).

## MOVIE WATCHING

View the National Geographic videotape, *Claimed by Vesuvius* (see Resources). It offers excellent information on volcanic activity in the Mediterranean and the archaeological finds of Pompeii and Herculaneum.

# RESOURCES

*Claimed by Vesuvius*. National Geographic Vestron Video, 1987. Video.

Erickson, John. *Volcanoes and Earthquakes*. Blue Ridge Summitt, Pa.: Tab Books, 1988.

Gore, Rick, "The Dead Do Tell Tales at Vesuvius," *National Geographic* 165 (May 1984), 557-613.

Grant, Michael. *Cities of Vesuvius*. New York: Penguin Books, 1971.

_____. *Myths of the Greeks and Romans*. New York: New American Library, 1989.

Hamilton, Edith. *Mythology*. New York: New American Library, 1940.

Hills, C. A. R. *The Destruction of Pompeii and Herculaneum*. London: Dryad Press, 1987.

*Past Worlds*. Maplewood, N.J.: Hammond, 1988.
    Refer to pp. 176-77 model of Pompeii and Mt. Vesuvius.

Rose, H. J. *A Handbook of Mythology*. New York: Dutton, 1959.

Vogt, Gregory. *Volcanic Eruptions*. New York: Franklin Watts, 1989.

*Volcano*. Alexandria, Va.: Time-Life Books, 1982.

Wood, Robert Muir. *Earthquakes and Volcanoes*. New York: Weiderfield and Nicolson, 1987.

# XIV

# Three Eerie Tales

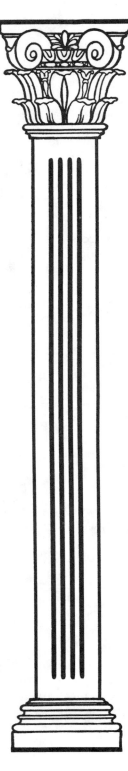

## INTRODUCTION

The ancient Roman, whether of the upper or lower class, firmly believed in the supernatural and the strength of magic. Ghosts were not imaginary apparitions but forces with which to reckon. After Julius Caesar's murder, there were reports that ghosts were seen on the streets of Rome as a warning to his assassins.

The powers of witches, especially in the realm of love, were greatly feared. Witches could control nature and even bring to earth the moon and sky. They were adept at transformations, turning humans into stone or themselves into nubile young women intent upon ensnaring an unsuspecting man.

The Latin word for witch, *strigia*, is derived from the Greek word for screech owl and imitative of the sound witches make when they are intent on doing evil. Like our modern witches, ancients imagined these hags to be old, unattractive crones with bare feet and scraggly loosened hair. Witches concocted magic potions, and when human blood was needed, sucked it from children.

Magic pervaded the daily life of all Romans. It was common practice for them to wear a prophylactic amulet that was thought to be endowed with a power to protect its owner. It could be made from minerals or precious stones, but most often an amulet came from an animal. The eye of a lizard warded off eye pain, and a wolf's tooth prevented teething problems.

Following are three of the very few Latin stories about sorcery that exist. The first, about a haunted house, comes from a letter written by Gaius Plinius (A.D. 61-114), Pliny the Younger, to his friend Sura. Pliny came from a wealthy family, was educated in Rome, and began his legal career at the young age of 18. He was adopted officially by his uncle, the naturalist Pliny the Elder (see chapter 12), and though married three times, he had no children. The younger Pliny was a patriotic citizen who served under Emperor Trajan in several political offices. In A.D. 100, he became consul, in A.D. 103, augur, and in A.D. 111-112, served as governor of Bithynia.

Pliny published his personal correspondence in a collection of nine books. These delightful letters reveal much about ancient Roman life. After his death, a tenth book was issued that contained his letters to the Emperor. Pliny also wrote orations, but only the *Panegyric*, dedicated to Trajan, has survived.

The final two stories are excerpts from the *Satyricon* created by one of the most enigmatic of Roman writers, Gaius Petronius. Little is known about this man, and there is no conclusive proof that he wrote the *Satyricon* though most classicists agree that the Petronius mentioned in Tactitus's *Annals* is the author of this unusual story. Tacitus described Petronius in this manner:

> A few words must be spoken about Petronius for he spent his days in slumber and his nights in official duties and pleasure. Because of his debaucheries, he joined Nero's small inner circle as the *arbiter elegentiae* (judge of good taste), and Nero considered nothing tasteful unless Petronius had approved of it. Finally, Petronius incurred the wrath of Nero's advisor, who indicted Petronius on false charges of treason. Realizing that the end was near, Petronius decided to commit suicide. He opened his veins and rebound them whenever he desired. He carried on a lengthy conversation with his friends, not about serious matters, and listened to poetry and light verse. He gave some of his servants presents, and others, beatings. He even had dinner and slept a little. Before he finally succumbed to his wounds and died (A.D. 65), he wrote a missive to Nero describing all the Emperor's past peccadillos.[1]

Unfortunately, only fragments from two chapters exist of the book Petronius authored. One of the longest sections describes the garish banquet of the *nouveau riche* freedman Trimalchio. It is a delightful piece filled with humor and spice, and it is during this lavish meal that two guests tell the stories of a witch and a werewolf.

---

[1]Tacitus, *Annals*, 16, 17-20.

## A Ghostly House[2]

■ Let me tell you an eerie story I have heard about an unusual house in the city of Athens. This home was spacious and elegant, but no one wished to live in it because of the peculiar happenings that occurred there every night. When it became dark and everything was quiet and still, the house echoed with the clattering of iron chains. At first, the noise seemed to be far away but rapidly grew closer until finally a ghost appeared. It was an apparition of a gaunt old man whose filthy beard and hair reached almost to the floor. His feet were bound in iron shackles, and his hands were confined in chains that he shook constantly.

Because of this strange spirit, everyone who tried to live there spent his nights in frightened wakefulness. Even in the daytime, the memory of the ghost drove the inhabitants to madness. Finally, the house was deserted by the living and left to the ghost to wander throughout its empty rooms. Nevertheless, the house was advertised for sale or rent in case some poor ignorant person might wish to occupy it.

Now, one day a philosopher named Athenodorus came to Athens and read the notice about the house. Suspicious of the low price, he learned from friends the true reason for the bargain—the house was haunted. Instead of being reluctant, Athenodorus was all the more eager to rent the place and quickly moved into his new home.

As soon as it became dark, he ordered his servants to make up his bed in the entrance hall. He then asked for a tablet, a pen, and a lamp and sent everyone away. He immediately began to write, thinking that if he were busy, his mind would not imagine sights and sounds. All seemed quiet and peaceful at first, but then he heard the ominous noise of rattling chains. Athenodorus did not even lift his eyes nor put down his pen but kept his mind on his appointed task and listened intently with his ears. The noise grew louder and louder as the ghost came closer to his room. It wavered on the threshold and then ventured inside the room itself. Nonchalantly, Athenodorus looked up and gazed upon the face of the lifeless old man. The ghost stood perfectly still but motioned with its finger as if it were beckoning the philosopher to follow. Athenodorus, in reply, held up his hand indicating to the ghost that it should wait. Again, he concentrated on his manuscript, but the phantom, agitated by the delay, furiously shook the chains over Athenodorus's head. Immediately, the brave man looked up, and as the ghost was still motioning for him to follow, he picked up the lamp and obeyed the command. Together they walked into the garden where the ghost suddenly disappeared.

Athenodorus plucked some grass and twigs and laid them on the spot where the ghost had vanished; then he returned inside for a tranquil night's sleep. The next day, the brave philosopher went to the authorities, and after telling his story of the previous night's activities, suggested that they dig up the place he had marked. The magistrates complied and discovered a pile of bones interred in the earth still bound in chains though no flesh remained because the corpse had been in the ground so long. The public officials promptly collected the bones and buried them with proper accord. After that, the house was completely purged of its ghostly occupant. ■

---

[2]Pliny the Younger, *Epistulae* VII: 27.

## The Tale of the Werewolf[3]

■ When I was still a slave, our house was located on a narrow little street. At that time, with the help of the gods, I fell in love with a girl named Melissa, the wife of the innkeeper, Terentius. She was a tempting little morsel, and I swear I loved her not only because of her physical prowess in bed, but because she had a most pleasant disposition. She generously gave me everything she had: if she earned a penny, she offered me half. Oh, what a delightful young lady!

Old Terentius finally died, and so I decided to hurry to Melissa's side and console her. I could not wait to see her and enjoy her passionate embraces. My master had journeyed to Capua on business, and taking advantage of his absence, I planned to leave immediately.

I invited a friend to accompany me since Melissa lived about five miles away. The man was a soldier, strong as hell, a good companion for a late night's sojurn. We trotted off as soon as night fell while a full moon shone as brightly as the noon-day sun. After awhile we tired from our walk and rested beside the road in a graveyard. I sat down and began to sing to while away the time when I noticed my companion was taking off all his clothes.

My heart was in my throat as I watched him urinate over his garments. Then, suddenly, he metamorphosed into a wolf and ran howling into the forest. I swear I am telling the absolute truth. Though frightened, I approached his clothing and found they had petrified into stone. Regaining my courage, I unsheathed my sword and brandished it in front of me, cutting at the empty shadows as I ran full speed ahead.

Pale as a ghost and with the sweat of fear rolling down my crotch, I finally arrived at Melissa's. I nearly fainted into my lover's arms. She was quite surprised to see me at such a late hour and then relayed a most peculiar happening. She said, "If you had dropped in a little sooner, you could have helped us. A wolf attacked our sheep and made a real bloody mess, but one of the slaves managed to pierce his neck with a spear."

I couldn't believe what I was hearing. My eyes nearly popped out of my head. I spent a restless night there and at dawn headed back home. When I reached the graveyard, I looked for the petrified clothes, but found nothing except a pool of blood. At home, that same soldier was lying prostrated on the bed, being treated by a doctor for the wound in his neck.

I realized then that he was a werewolf, and never again would I eat a meal with that man. Not even if you paid me. ■

---

[3]Petronius, *Satyricon* 61-62.

## The Night of the Witches[4]

■ When I was just a young lad, a favorite male slave of my master died. This boy was a real pearl, beautiful in looks and almost perfect in every way. We were all mourning this child's death, especially his bereaved mother, when suddenly the sound of witches howling struck our ears. It was a terrible screeching noise as if a dog had ensnared a rabbit in his jaws. Fearful, we all stood immobile as we listened. But one of us was not intimidated—a male slave from Cappodocia. He was quite a tall man who possessed an athlete's body and tremendous courage.

Bravely, he wrapped his left hand in a cloth and snatched up a sword in his right. Then he ran outside and stuck his rapier into the stomach of one of the witches. Inside, we heard a loud groan but did not actually see the confrontation. Soon our brave hulking slave crashed through the door and hurled himself onto a bed. His entire body had turned black and blue as if he had been flogged with many whips.

All of us trembled with fear at this occurrence but continued with our work thinking the danger had passed. Then, while the mother was embracing the body of her dead son, she screamed in shock. Her boy was missing and left in his place was a straw dummy. It had no heart, nor insides, nor anything. The witches had taken the beautiful lad and made a substitution. This was not the only unfortunate outcome of the witches' visit for the poor male slave met a terrible fate. His body never returned to its normal color, and after a few days, he went mad and died. ■

---

[4]Petronius, *Satyricon* 63.

# TEACHER IDEAS

## Discussion Questions

1. What was Athenodorus's profession?

2. How did the ghost get Athenodorus's attention?

3. Why did the ghost wander aimlessly for so many years?

4. Who accompanied the slave to his girlfriend's house?

5. What caused the slave to realize his companion was a werewolf?

6. What happened to the soldier's clothes left in the cemetery?

7. What happened to the slave who encountered the witches?

8. Why did the witches want to haunt this particular house?

9. Do you think ghosts or supernatural beings actually exist? Why?

10. Witchcraft is still practiced in some societies even today. What is its appeal? Why did it develop and why does it continue to exist?

## History Lesson: Trajan (A.D. 53-117)

Domitian's murder in A.D. 96 marked the end of the "reign of terror" and the beginning of a century of peace and prosperity under the guidance of the "Five Good Emperors."[5] Marcus Ulipus Traianus (Trajan), from southern Spain, was the first emperor who was not born in the Italian peninsula. Trajan held the traditional political offices and commanded a legion in A.D. 89 that was sent by Domitian to stop the rebellion in Germany. Nerva, Domitian's successor, ruled only two years and during that time adopted Trajan as his heir. At his death in A.D. 98, Trajan was immediately hailed as *princeps* (chief of state).

Well liked by both the army and senate, Trajan governed in a most competent manner. Trajan dedicated himself to reversing many of the injustices perpetrated by Domitian. He embraced the senate and sought their advice on state matters. He limited his consulship to six terms and allowed the senate to choose the other magistrates. He worked cooperatively with this august body not against it.[6] He instituted social programs to help the poor, notably the *alimenta* to feed hungry children. He initiated a large building program constructing many roads and aqueducts, erecting the first large bath houses at Rome, and adding a forum. He tried to alleviate the financial burden of the provinces by reducing their taxes. In the past, the provincial governors were notoriously corrupt, bent more on lining their own pockets than giving the State its due. Trajan took particular care to select each government official and sent Pliny the Younger to Bithynia, a province suffering from serious fiscal difficulties. The tenth book of Pliny's *Epistles* contains 121 letters between these two. Pliny consulted Trajan on every detail of his administration (see chapter 11) and no matter how trivial the request might seem, Trajan took care to answer, an indication of his concern for all of Rome's subjects. In the following letter to Trajan, Pliny expresses his concern about the inadequate water supply in a Bithynian town:

---

[5]Nerva, Trajan, Hadrian, Antonius Pius, and Marcus Aurelius.

[6]Though the senate never regained the power they held under the Republic.

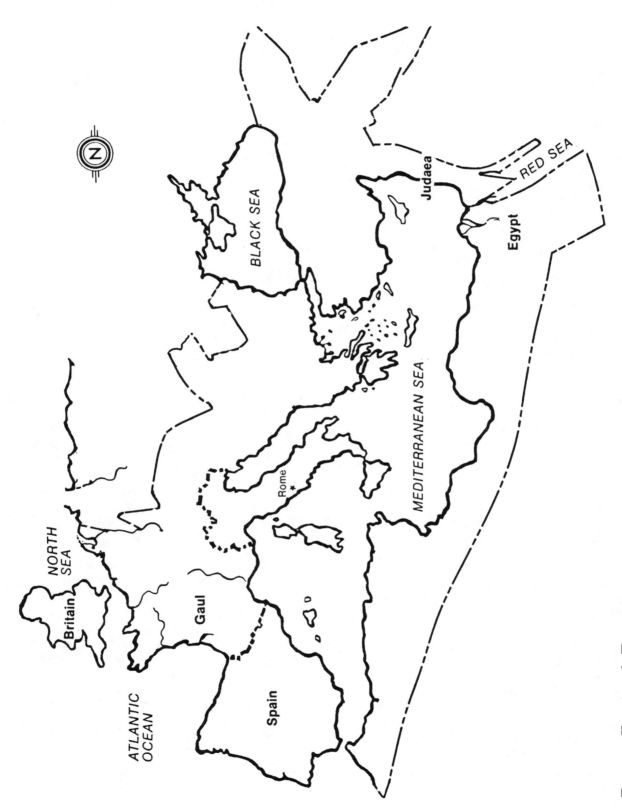

Roman Empire A.D. 114

**Pliny:** The people of Sinope, Emperor, do not have an adequate water supply. About sixteen miles away is a clean and plentiful stream, but near its mouth the ground seems somewhat marshy for about one mile. I am concerned about this and have ordered a closer inspection of the area which should not cost too much. I hope the engineers can determine whether this spot can bear the weight of an aqueduct. The financing of this project should not be difficult if you approve of this operation which will improve the health and pleasantness of this colony now bereft of water.[7]

Here is Trajan's response, illustrative of his genuine concern for the Roman people:

You may begin, my most dear Secundus, to examine whether that marshy spot is able to sustain the weight of an aqueduct. For I do not doubt that water must be brought to Sinope assuming that the colony itself can do so with its own resources, especially since this project will benefit their health and pleasure.[8]

Trajan was also determined to extend the Roman boundaries. His first campaign was waged against Dacia (modern day Rumania) commencing in A.D. 101. Once successful in this campaign, Trajan turned to the East and the Empire of Parthia, which had always troubled Rome by encroaching on her boundaries. Trajan captured Parthia's main city and sailed down the Tigris to the Persian Gulf. Despite a Parthian rally in A.D. 116, Trajan managed to install a pro-Roman king on the throne. Trajan's success was short-lived; on his return trip to Rome he died of a fever. Trajan's eastern campaign had placed a drain on the state's treasury, and his successor, Hadrian, considered it too costly to maintain troops on the border of Parthia and abandoned the area. Under Trajan's rule, the Empire expanded to what would be its greatest geographical extent.

## SUGGESTED TOPICS FOR FURTHER RESEARCH

1. the use of the arch in Roman architecture

2. Roman aqueducts

3. Trajan's column

4. Nerva

5. Forum of Trajan

### Language Arts

## VOCABULARY BUILDING

Suffixes:

- *able/ible* from Latin adjective *abilis*, meaning "suitable for, inclined to, deserving of"

---

[7]Pliny the Younger, *Epistles* XC.

[8]Ibid. XCI.

1.  Try to determine the meaning of the following words without using a dictionary.

    | | |
    |---|---|
    | readable | knowledgeable |
    | peaceable | pitiable |
    | enjoyable | legible |
    | washable | audible |
    | perishable | controllable |

2.  Choose five words from exercise 1 and use each in a sentence.

## DRAMATIC PRESENTATION

Divide the class into groups to present a skit taken from each of the three "eerie tales." More than one group can present the same skit. Characters needed for each skit are:

A Ghostly House: Athenodorus, ghost, realtor, and public official.

The Tale of the Werewolf: slave, soldier, Melissa, attacker, and doctor.

The Night of the Witches: dead boy, mother, Cappodocian, witches, and extras.

## CREATIVE WRITING

The *Satyricon*, which includes the stories of the werewolf and the witches, is a romance that is considered to be the earliest example of prose fiction. A romance differs from a novel in one central respect. In a novel, emphasis is on a well-defined plot, often at the expense of character development, but in a romance, the characters and events dominate the plot.

Write a short romance (do *not* confuse this term with modern love romances). Use the plot of one of the stories in this book. Choose one of the following:

The Sabine Women—chapter 2.

The Rape of Lucretia—chapter 3.

Scipio and the Virgin—chapter 5.

Antony and Cleopatra—chapter 9.

Matricide: Nero and Agrippina—chapter 10.

### Cultural Lesson: Roman Roads

"All roads lead to Rome" has been a familiar phrase for almost two millennia, and there is a great deal of truth to this expression. Twenty roads extended out from ancient Rome connecting the city to all corners of the Empire. The Romans built more than 250,000 miles of roads and became a mobile society. Troops were able to march long distances in a short time over these thoroughfares, and supplies could be sent to military posts no matter what their location. The official postal service used the roads to relay information. The emperor Tiberius, when he needed to reach his dying brother in a hurry, was able to travel 500 miles in 24 hours. Without these extensive road systems, Rome could not have been as successful in its conquests or colonization.

From the time the first major road (Via Appia) was built in 312 B.C., the Romans continued to lay highways across Europe, Asia, and Africa. Wherever troops went, roads were constructed, often by the soldiers themselves. All legionnaires carried spades, and when not occupied in military engagements, helped to dig the three-foot deep road beds. This wide ditch was then filled with a layer of rough stones and cemented with sand or coarse gravel; rammers packed these materials down. Next came a nine-inch layer of small stones, all less than palm size. Then, the top bed of fine gravel was laid into which the paving stones were set. These finished blocks were cut by experienced masons to fit together perfectly to prevent cracks that could admit water and cause deterioration. The surface of the road was slightly curved, sloping downward from the center toward the sides for drainage purposes. Foot paths were sometimes built parallel to the main road for pedestrians. Not all roads were of such intricate design—just the main ones designed to accommodate two-wheeled vehicles. Smaller, less traveled lanes were mostly gravel.

The construction of roads was under the jurisdiction of the censors in Republican times and run by highway commissioners during the Empire. It was a costly proposition to build so many thoroughfares, and this expense was born in a variety of ways. Often the conquered province through which the road went was forced to pay for its construction and repair. Other times, taxes were collected or tolls on bridges exacted for this purpose. Also, private donors built many of the Roman roads. Pompey built the first road across the Alps in 77 B.C., and Agrippa, the builder of the Pantheon, laid five roads across Gaul. Augustus personally financed 250 miles of repaving of the Via Flaminia.

As the roads stretched over various terrain, hills had to be cut through, rivers spanned by bridges, and valleys traversed by viaducts. The Romans erected more than 2,000 bridges, half of which were constructed in Italy. The Tiber was crossed by ten stone bridges; the oldest, Pons Fabricius (which is still standing), was built in 62 B.C. The Pont du Gard remains in France, and in Spain the Alcantara bridge stands 158 feet above the river and stretches more than 600 feet in length.

In *Gallic War*, Caesar describes how his troops erected a temporary wooden bridge across the Rhine. The knowledge of stress points and the attention to detail exemplifies the Romans' fastidious approach to construction, as described in the following excerpt:

> I decided to cross the Rhine River but thought it unsafe to use boats. Therefore, although it was most difficult to build a bridge due to the width and depth of the river and also due to the tremendous current present there, I considered it imperative to do so.
>
> This was my plan for the construction. I had timber poles 18 inches in circumference cut to the depth of the river and joined together at a distance of two feet. These were lowered into the river and hammered with mallets into the bottom—not in an upright position but inclined forward a bit. Opposite to this construction were two more timbers, also slanted to withstand the flow of the river. Two-foot beams were set on top to act as a brace and to keep these poles apart. So strong was this design that wherever the water exerted the greatest pressure, the beams stood the strongest. On top of the braces was laid a frame work of poles to form a road-like surface.
>
> Buttresses were also driven into the river downstream and used as props against the timbers. Then I had placed other piles upstream in a random pattern but close together. These were to act as defenses in case the barbarians sent tree trunks or boats to knock down our bridge.
>
> The work was completed within ten days from the time when the timber was first cut. I stationed guards on both sides of the bridge and then hurried my troops across into the territory of the Sagambri.[9]

---

[9]Caesar, Julius, *Gallic War* IV: 17.

After 124 B.C., the Romans began to erect milestones (*milaria*) along the highways. These large stones (about 8 feet tall and 20 inches in diameter weighing about 2 tons) were set 2 feet into the earth every Roman mile (5,000 feet). They served to give information to the army and travelers because they marked the distance from the city of Rome. Augustus erected the golden milestone (actually only bronze) in the Forum (Romanum), and all roads were measured from this point. However, this became unmanageable and so the principal city in each province was used instead. Not only was the distance etched into the stone, but often the name of the emperor, the builder, and the legion's name were included on the milestone.

Official way stations used by government couriers occurred about every 12 to 18 miles. Horses and mules could be changed here. The imperial postal service organized by Augustus could cover about 50 miles in 24 hours. Public inns were also built along the roads though most Romans thought them unsafe and preferred to stay at friends' homes if possible when traveling. The Romans built a road to last for 100 years without repair, but today, one can still use many of them almost 2,000 years later.

## USING AN ATLAS

The ancient Romans maintained records on all their roads, but it was a difficult situation without the aid of modern technology. Today you can find out many facts about any location in the world. With the aid of an atlas complete the following activities:

A. Using the Mileage and Driving Times Map:

1. Plot a trip from Boston to Kansas City via Chicago. How long will the trip take? How many miles must you cover?

2. Plot a trip from Boston to Kansas City via Cincinnati. How long will it take? How many miles must you cover?

3. Compare your answers in questions 1 and 2 above to that of your classmates. Who got there quicker? Why?

B. Using the U.S. Mileage Chart, find out the distance between:

1. New Orleans, Louisiana and Louisville, Kentucky

2. San Antonio, Texas and Portland, Maine

3. Hartford, Connecticut and Omaha, Nebraska

4. New York, New York and Los Angeles, California

5. Oklahoma City, Oklahoma and Des Moines, Iowa

C. Look at the map of your own state and answer the following questions:

1. What is the capital?

2. What is the largest city?

3. What is the primary north to south interstate highway?

4. What is the primary east to west interstate highway?

5. Are there any national forests or monuments? Name them.

6. What are the major bodies of water? Where are they located?

7. How many square miles are there in your state?

8. What is your state's total population?

9. What states are contiguous to yours?

# RESOURCES

Birley, Anthony, trans., *Lives of the Later Caesars*. Middlesex, England: Penguin Classics, 1976.

Grant, Michael. *The Roman Emperors*. New York: Charles Scribner's Sons, 1985.

Macaulay, David. *The City*. Boston: Houghton Mifflin, 1974.
    This book includes detailed drawings and a description of the building of a Roman town.

*Past Worlds*. Maplewood, N.J.: Hammond, 1988.
    Refer to the roads and aqueducts on p. 171.

*Road Atlas*. Boston: Rand McNally, 1991.

Von Hagen, Victor W. *The Roads That Led to Rome*. New York: World, 1967.

# XV

# Pliny's Villa

## INTRODUCTION

As Rome's population grew, so did the need for adequate housing. Most Romans could not afford a single-family dwelling (*domus*) and lived in large apartment complexes (*insulae*). Rent was high, and sanitary and safety conditions often inferior. These flats were multi-storied and poorly built by greedy speculators. Although the first floor was typically constructed of concrete, the upper stories were fabricated with wood and thus susceptible to collapse and fire. Emperor Augustus unsuccessfully tried to limit the height of these insulae to 70 feet. It was Nero, however, who imposed a building code that required the use of fireproof materials (volcanic stone) on external walls. No running water or central heating reached the upper apartments, and large families were often crammed into a single room. In A.D. 350, a survey of all buildings in Rome was completed that revealed that there were 1,782 domus and 44,171 insulae at that time, roughly one single-family house per every 26 blocks of apartments.

At the opposite spectrum from the apartment dweller was the wealthy Roman who could afford a mansion on the Palatine Hill. It is possible to get a sense of what these homes were like by examining those unearthed at Pompeii and Herculaneum. When living in the city, the ancient Romans constructed their homes to shut out the noise and commotion of the street. They might rent out a small store front to a merchant on the bottom floor of the house, but the rest of the structure was private and secluded. A small entrance hall stood before the door to separate the business from the private residence. The first room was the atrium, a courtyard with a large opening in the roof called a *compluvium* that let in light because the first floor rooms contained no windows (to shield out the activity of the busy streets). Rain also came through the compluvium and fell into a shallow pond (*impluvium*) that drained into the underground cisterns. The atrium was originally the main room of the house and served as the sitting room and kitchen. Later, it became a reception hall where the master received clients and business associates. Typically, there would be two small recesses on the side of the atrium to house busts of the family's ancestors, as well as a small room (ala) for personal papers and records.

Leading from the atrium was a door that opened onto a large garden or *peristylum*. A columned walkway surrounded the garden, and fountains, trees, and flowers were in the center. Rooms opened on to this inside garden such as the dining room and small bedrooms. The kitchen (culina) and bathroom were in the rear of the house and shared a common drain that carried waste to the public sewer system.

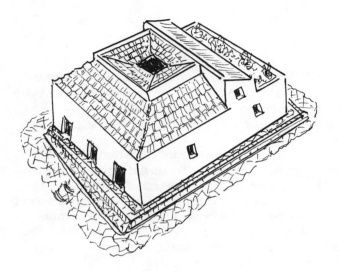

1 vestibulum
2 shop
3 atrium
4 impluvium
5 cubiculum
6 ala
7 tablinium
8 triclinium
9 culina
10 peristylum

(See English translations on page 155.)

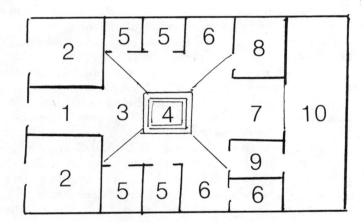

**Domus**

Many wealthy Romans might add more rooms upstairs including a *solarium*, a roof-top garden. The slaves' quarters were generally on the second floor as well as storage rooms.

The Romans decorated their homes with beautiful mosaics on the floor and painted panels on the walls. Even the ceilings were embellished with gold, ivory, or bronze. Furniture was sparse: chairs, tables, and couches were the essential items.

Wealthy Romans, tired of city life, might choose to own a second home (*villa*) in the country. Villas differed from town homes in that they did not need to shut out the noise of the city and so had windows and doors that opened to the outside. Pliny the Younger owned four villas throughout Italy and described two of them in detail to his friends. The following letter describes his villa in Laurentum.

Pliny's Villa[1]

■ To Gallus:

Let me describe my villa to you, and then, perhaps, you will escape the urbane existence of Rome and come to the country for a visit. My villa is only 17 miles from the city so that it is possible, after a hard day's work, to retire to the country for rest and relaxation. If you take the road from Laurentum, turn off at stone marker XIV, or if you journey via Ostia, take marker XI.

As soon as you enter the villa, you will find yourself in a modest atrium that opens onto a colonnade shaped like the letter *D*. In the center is a small but cheerful garden retreat; it is impervious to inclement weather because the eaves overhang from the roof to protect the site. As you walk through the colonnade, you come upon another open patio that leads to a large dining room. This chamber stretches toward the sea and has windows or doors on all sides allowing a spectacular view all around. The front end faces the water, as do the sides, and the rear looks back toward the villa and open courtyards I have just described. You can even see beyond the garden toward the woods and mountains—a splendid panorama for guests as they eat.

On the left of the dining area lie two rooms, the smaller of which has a window to let in the rising sun, and the larger room has windows to catch the afternoon light. The outer walls of this room abut the dining room and form a larger corner niche, which is always warm even in winter and which my entire household uses as an exercise court. From the yard, a round room extends that has windows on all sides to follow the sun no matter where it is in its daily course. I have a built-in cupboard there where I have stashed all my most favorite books because this circular room is the perfect place for reading.

Another large wing of the house can be reached by walking down a long hallway that leads from this library. Here are the sleeping quarters used mostly by my slaves and freedmen, furnished and decorated so elegantly that these chambers can even be enjoyed by guests when needed. I have steam heat pumped through a hollow passage on the side of the hall that warms these rooms whenever necessary.

In another wing of the house are several rooms and a second small dining area. The sun keeps these rooms well lit and warm, and the sea breezes keep them cool. Outside is another courtyard that stands before my private bath house. I have a large cold room that contains two plunging tubs, because if you want a real cool dip, you can immerse yourself in the sea. Next is the oiling room for massages and scraping, the steam room, and then a sumptuous warm room that contains a pool large enough for swimming. The bathers can look out of the windows here toward the sea and the beautiful shoreline. Directly outside stands the ball court for exercise.

At the end of the arena area is a two-storied tower that contains two rooms up and the same number below, one being a third dining room with a spectacular view. There is also another tower that has a large single room and a storeroom and cellar on the top floor and a dining room on the bottom, looking only onto a quiet garden and secluded from the noise of the sea.

The garden is carefully laid out to include a walkway all around that is bordered by a boxwood hedge. Where the roof protects the hedge, the boxwood grows lush and healthy. However, wind and sea spray are harmful to it, and in these spots I have planted rosemary instead. There is even a small copse of fig and mulberry trees in the gardens, and it is always pleasant to walk barefooted through the soft loam.

---

[1]Pliny the Younger, *Epistles* II: 17.

Another very large colonnade branches out from the villa. On one wall, windows face the sea, and on the other, windows look toward the garden. I can open these windows when the weather is calm and even when it is windy, it is possible to keep some open. The windows let in the breeze, and the air never becomes stale. An open trellis covered with sweet smelling violets stands within the colonnade whose walls capture the warmth of the sun and protect the garden from the cold north wind. Even in winter the portico glows with the early morning sun but is shaded from the afternoon light.

Toward the end of this colonnade is my favorite room—since I designed it myself—a sunroom with a spectacular view of both sea and garden. There are only two chairs and a couch in it, and when lying down, you can see the sea at your feet, the entire villa behind, and the forest to your side. All the windows afford many different views of the outdoors. There is even a small bedroom nearby that no voices, nor movement of storms, nor lightning, nor even the daylight itself can penetrate. The reason for this is that there is a secret empty passage that lies between the bedroom and the garden and absorbs all sound.

Close to this room is a furnace to heat this wing of the villa. Whenever I go to this part of the house, I seem to be far away. I especially escape during the Saturnalia while the rest of my household is enjoying the frivolity of the season. I cannot hear the shouting and noise and so do not disturb their pleasure nor they my studies.

The only drawback to the location of the villa is that there is no running water close by. We must rely on wells, which is no severe handicap because pure unsalty water lies quite near the surface of the ground. The nearby forests supply wood for fuel, and the town of Ostia has a large marketplace where all necessities can be purchased. The little village down the road has three public baths, a wonderful convenience if I happen to arrive at my villa on short notice, and my own baths are not heated.

There are many pleasant homes like mine lining the coast so that it looks almost like a little city. The sea itself does not abound with exotic fish; nevertheless, it produces sole and very good shrimp. My own villa is known for its milk and dairy products.

Do I not seem, Gallus, justified in my effusive praise of my villa? Why not come for a visit, and you can enjoy the peace and tranquility of the place. Leave the hectic city behind and relax! Farewell, your friend Gaius Plinius. ■

# TEACHER IDEAS

## Discussion Questions

1. What products did Pliny's farm produce?

2. Why does Pliny write Gallus about his villa?

3. Name two types of seafood Pliny might have eaten at his villa.

4. How did Pliny keep noise out of his small bedroom?

5. About how many miles from Rome was Pliny's villa located?

6. Why must Pliny plant rosemary hedges?

7. Why was Pliny glad that there were public baths near his villa?

8. How do the rooms stay warm?

9. Imagine yourself in this Roman villa. What do you especially like about the house? Why? Be specific. What was Pliny's favorite room? Why?

10. Pliny is no longer the 18-year-old boy at Vesuvius's A.D. 79 eruption. Though he is now an adult, do you think his personality has changed? This letter reveals much about Pliny: what he likes, his amusements, etc. Compare what you know about Pliny from this letter to the youth of chapter 13. How are they alike? How do they differ? Use examples from both chapters.

## History Lesson: Hadrian (A.D. 117-138), The Scholarly Emperor

Publius Aelius Hadrianus was born in Spain in A.D. 76. He was only 10 at the time of his father's death and became the ward of his uncle, Trajan, the future emperor. Educated in Rome, he held all the customary political offices from tribune (A.D. 105), to consul (A.D. 108), to governor of Spain (A.D. 117). Hadrian's ties to Trajan were strengthened by his marriage to the latter's grandniece, Sabina. He also accompanied the Emperor on both military campaigns against Dacia.

When Trajan died, Hadrian left Spain and arrived in Rome in A.D. 118. He was to stay in the capital only three years. Once satisfied that the government could run without him, he set off to visit every province in the Roman Empire. These travels occupied Hadrian's entire life. He always returned to Rome, but never for long. His sojourns were prompted by a keen intellectual curiosity, as well as a desire to review the state of Rome's government no matter how far away. When he discovered corrupt officials, he punished them severely.

In A.D. 122, he visited Britain and initiated the building of the great wall (now called *Hadrian's Wall*) to divide Britain from Scotland. He went to the far reaches of the known world, including Asia, Africa, Gaul, Spain, and Greece. Hadrian realized the enormous size of the Empire was a financial liability, draining the treasury, due to the military manpower required to maintain it. Therefore, he gave up the provinces newly won by Trajan and returned all land beyond the Tigris and Euphrates to Parthia.

Whenever in Rome, Hadrian plunged energetically into the problems of state. He set in motion the codification of Roman law and expanded the civil service to include the knights. A progressive law he enacted forbid the murder of a slave by his master without the benefit of a trial. He built many buildings but refused to put his name on them. Construction of his own villa, which covered seven square miles, was a 20-year project. This magnificent structure may be visited today. Hadrian brought back many ideas from his foreign travels and incorporated them into his palace.

A true scholar, Hadrian had many interests. He wrote prose and poetry. Four poems survived. He was an expert mathematician and a strong believer in astrology. He was reputed to be a wit and could recite entire books from memory. Hadrian had no sons and so adopted the 51-year-old Titus Aurelius Antonius as his heir. After an illness, this brilliant energetic man died in A.D. 138.

## SUGGESTED TOPICS FOR FURTHER RESEARCH

1. Hadrian's villa

2. Hadrian's mausoleum

3. Antonius Pius

4. baths of Diocletian

5. baths of Caracalla

## Language Arts

### VOCABULARY BUILDING

Prefixes:

- *ante* from Latin preposition *ante* meaning "before"
- *post* from Latin preposition *post* meaning "after"

Define the following words and use each in a sentence:

| | |
|---|---|
| antemeridian | antebellum |
| postmeridian | postpone |
| antedate | antecedent |
| postdate | |

### CRITICAL THINKING

1. To learn about the ancient Roman, classical scholars rely not only on archaeological finds to unravel the secrets of the past, but also on the writings of the Romans themselves. By extracting information from Roman authors, a clearer picture is formed about how the Romans lived.

    Pretend you are trying to learn about the villas of wealthy Romans by using Pliny's letter to Gallus. Then answer the following questions:

    a. What information can you glean about the architecture of this home?

    b. What do you know about the outside gardens?

    c. What amenities does this house contain?

    d. What furniture did Romans include in their homes?

    e. What might a Roman do for entertainment?

2. With this same idea in mind (deriving information from a written account), read the following description by Seneca of his life while living above a public bath house. Then answer the questions that follow.

> I live above a bathhouse, and everywhere a variety of sounds assails me. It is driving me crazy—this continual din of voices.
>
> When the muscle men are exercising, or pretending to exercise, and they use the iron weights, I can hear them groan. As often as they inhale and exhale, I hear their loud hissing and harsh panting.
>
> If that were not enough, I also must contend with the noise of the masseurs who pour their cheap oil on reclining bodies and then proceed to clap their victims' shoulders loudly. Even the ball scorer raises his voice while counting the balls.
>
> Add to this a quarrelsome thief who has been caught filching someone's purse and a sonorous bather who enjoys hearing his own voice raised in song.
>
> Other bathers leap into the pool with the earsplitting sound of the water being slapped. Moreover, there are the normal voices of the bathers gossiping and the base hair plucker who is never quiet unless he is shearing someone's armpit or answering a deafening call from a client.
>
> I can barely recite all the varieties of cries from the drink vendors, or sausage sellers, or pastry peddlers, each shouting their prices in varying tones of dissonant clamor.[2]

a. What activities take place in a bathhouse?

b. How many different types of people work there?

c. What might a Roman enjoy to eat while at the bath?

## Cultural Activity: The Baths

### Balnea et Thermae

In describing his elaborate villa, Pliny details his private bath house (*balneum*), which possessed a warm room (*tepedarium*), a cold chamber (*frigidariium*), and a massaging room (*unctorium*). It was quite common for wealthy Romans to have such opulent accommodations, but not everyone could afford a bath house. The Romans believed that insuring cleanliness was an important daily activity for all people. Consequently, public bath houses were built all over the Empire.

Early in Rome's history each household had only a small bathing chamber located near the kitchen to keep the room warm. It contained a lavatory for daily ablutions and a tub. After the Second Punic War (202 B.C.), public baths began to appear in Rome. Built by entrepreneurs, a small fee was required for admission—about one penny—though women were charged double. By 33 B.C., there were no fewer than 170 public bath houses in Rome. Many were managed by the government aediles who kept them in repair and assured their cleanliness. The Romans' love for bathing continued to grow, and records indicate that in Constantine's day (A.D. 300), the number of balnea had increased to 856 with an additional 100 *thermae* (gymnasium-bath houses) in existence.

Most Romans liked to retire from work by early afternoon, and after a light lunch, would visit the public baths for gossip and relaxation. Women and men did not bathe together but had separate accommodations or restricted hours for admittance. Children could enjoy the baths for free. The lower classes did not have their own baths and went to public facilities. Later the baths became a social gathering place for people of all classes.

---

[2]Seneca, *Epistulae Morales* LVI.

With the invention of the hypocaust, or underground heating system, the temperature of the baths was easily regulated. Most bath houses contained four basic rooms, a warm anteroom, which served as a dressing room and where the air readied the bather for the next chamber, which was the hot room (*calidarium*). Located directly over the furnace, the calidarium allowed the bathers to work up a sweat. There was a shallow pool and a large basin that contained cold water to cool the participants. Next, they might plunge into a cold bath and then end with a massage and an oil scraping. The Romans enjoyed a rub down with olive oil, scraped off with a wooden or bone tool. They would end their regime by returning to the warm antechamber for a final cleansing and thence to dress in their street clothes. The room order could be changed or rooms omitted if it pleased them.

By the time of the Empire, the balnea grew to accommodate more sophisticated tastes. No longer merely a bathing place, these new thermae were gigantic health clubs. They contained handball courts, wrestling arenas, exercise areas, libraries, restaurants, places to hear musical entertainments, and gardens. The first one was built at the time of Augustus on the Campus Martius, a large city park in Rome. Perhaps the most famous were the Baths of Caracalla, which opened in A.D. 217 and covered approximately six acres. Sixteen hundred bathers could use these baths at one time. Even larger were the Thermae of Diocletian (A.D. 300) near the Viminal Hill covering 130,000 square yards and accommodating 3,200 people. Ancient Romans could spend entire afternoons enjoying the sports activities of these public gymnasia.

## COMPARISON

Compare the activities and a floor plan of a Roman therma and a modern health club facility.

## Et Alia: Art

1. Using Pliny's description, draw a plan of his villa.

2. Construct a model of a Roman house using a shoe box. Discard the top. Inside, divide the "house" into appropriate rooms. Be creative! Cut out doors. See Resources for references containing illustrations of ancient Roman homes. Be sure to include and label the following:

   atrium: entrance hall

   impluvium: pool in atrium

   ala: storage room

   triclinium: dining room

   tablinium: passage room

   cubiculum: bedroom

   peristylum: garden

   culina: kitchen

# RESOURCES

Birley, Anthony, trans., *Lives of the Later Caesars*. Middlesex, England: Penguin Classics, 1976.

Carcopino, Jerome. *Daily Life in Ancient Rome*. New Haven, Conn.: Yale University Press, 1940.

Grant, Michael. *Cities of Vesuvius*. New York: Penguin Books, 1971.

_____. *The Roman Emperors*. New York: Charles Scribner's Sons, 1985.

Hades, Moses. *Imperial Rome*. New York: Time-Life Books, 1965.
　　Features a diagram of the Baths of Caracalla.

Kraus, Tehoder. *Pompeii and Herculaneum*. New York: Harry N. Abrams, 1975.
　　Be sure to view the illustrations on pp. 55, 56, 155, and 156.

*Past Worlds*. Maplewood, N.J.: Hammond, 1988.
　　Refer to the Roman villa featured on p. 175.

*Peoples and Places of the Past*. Washington, D.C.: National Geographic, 1988.
　　See pp. 109-15 featuring a drawing of a Roman house.

Tingay, G. I. F., and J. Badcock. *These Were the Romans*. Great Britain: Hulton Educational Publications, 1972.
　　See the illustrations on pp. 138-39.

Yourcenar, Marguerite. *Hadrian's Memoires*. New York: Farrar, Straus & Giroux, 1954.

# XVI

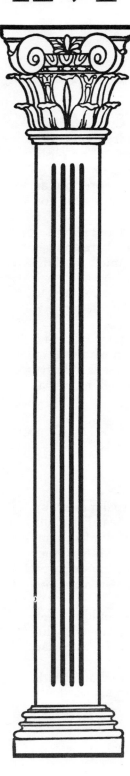

# Slavery

## INTRODUCTION

Rome's conquests in the early Republic brought slaves to the labor market, and slavery was a most lucrative business. The average Roman soldier earned only about 45 dollars a year. This meager income was supplemented by the booty and plunder the army took from the conquered lands. For generals, the sale of slaves substantially added to their purses.

In 146 B.C., when Scipio destroyed Carthage, he sold 60,000 inhabitants from this city into slavery. In 101 B.C., Marius reaped a large profit from the 140,000 Cimbri he took from northern Italy. It is estimated that Julius Caesar and Pompey sold over 1 million people of Asia Minor into slavery in the first century B.C.

The institution of slavery in ancient Rome had some unique features. Although owners had complete control over their slave's person and labor, and the slave was without legal rights, there were legal means by which a slave could gain freedom. It was common practice for an owner to pay slaves for extra services so that slaves could eventually buy their liberty, or frequently owners manumitted their slaves in their wills. Pliny the Younger released 500 slaves in this manner. As soon as their freedom was granted, slaves obtained the complete status of a Roman citizen, though they could not hold political office. Their grandchildren, however, held all the privileges of free born citizens. By the time of the Empire, the freedmen class was an important addition to the civil service class of the government.

How many slaves were there in ancient Rome? In the beginning, slaves were utilized primarily on farms and in large businesses. City dwellers rarely had more than one slave, but this situation changed dramatically by the time of Christ when there were probably 2 million slaves living in Italy alone. Then, it was not uncommon for wealthy Romans to have several hundred slaves on their household staff. The Emperor maintained as many as 20,000 slaves to attend to personal matters: to polish silver and gold plates, to tend to his city, military, and theater wardrobes, to look after his jewels, to groom his hair, to serve his food, to taste his food, to light the lamps, and to help with his bath. And the list goes on ad infinitum.

Masters could be both gentle and cruel. The following stories come from two letters written by Pliny the Younger. In the first letter, one can see the passion and concern Pliny holds for his ex-slave Zosinus, who is still a member of Pliny's household. Unfortunately, not every master was as kind, and the last story about Larcius Macedo reflects this sentiment.

Slavery

■ Epistula V:[1]

Pliny sends greeting to Valerius Paulinus:

I am greatly concerned about the poor health of my freedman, Zosinus. He is an honorable man who is very well read and can recite poetry and even history aloud with great skill and feeling. He also plays the lyre with proficiency, but his greatest accomplishment is being a comedian. I am constantly amused and delighted by his humor.

I have mentioned his fine qualities, Valerius, so that you may realize how precious an individual is Zosinus. After many years in my service, I feel a tremendous affection toward him, and I am deeply worried that he is gravely ill.

Many years ago, while he was vigorously reciting, he began to spit out blood. I immediately sent him to Egypt for treatment and rest. He seemed to recover there and has recently returned to my home. Straightway he began to exert his voice too much, and the coughing returned as well as the discharge of blood.

Because of his relapse, I am determined to send him to your farm in the country to convalesce. I have often heard you say that the air there is good for one's health and that the milk from your cows has restorative powers.

Therefore, I am asking you, as a friend, to write to the caretaker of your farm and inform him of Zosinus's arrival. Indeed, please urge your people to give him whatever he might need, at his own expense, of course. It should not be very much, for he is a thrifty man who refrains from indulging in any extravagances. I will give him as much money as he will need for his trip. Farewell.

Epistula III:[2]

Greetings to Acilius from Pliny:

I have recently heard of the murder of Larcius Macedo, a proud but cruel master, by his own slaves. He was bathing in his private baths at his country home near Formiana when, suddenly, some of his slaves invaded his sanctuary and surrounded him, preventing his escape. One attacker assaulted his throat, another smashed his face. Other slaves pounded and crushed his chest and stomach. They even struck at his private parts. Finally, when they thought he most certainly was dead, they hurled him onto the hot pavement of the bath house floor.

Immobile, Larcius showed no signs of life, maybe because he actually could not feel anything or perhaps because he wished to pretend to be dead in order to trick his assailants. The recreant slaves then carried him outside, announcing that their master had collapsed from the heat.

Other faithful slaves not involved in the attack picked him up and carried him inside his villa. His mistresses ran about in a panic, howling and shouting. Larcius suddenly opened his eyes and with a slight movement of his body proved he was still alive. Possibly, the noise and loud voices aroused him from his unconscious state, or perchance, the cool air had revived his senses.

---

[1]Letter to Valerius Paulinus from Pliny the Younger, *Epistulae* V: 19.

[2]Letter to Acilias from Pliny the Younger, *Epistulae* III: 14.

The rebellious slaves immediately fled in many directions. Most of them have already been captured, and the rest are still being sought. Larcius was resuscitated with some difficulty by the doctors. Although he managed to live only for a few days, in that time he had the opportunity to see the wicked perpetrators executed for their crimes. He could not, however, recover from the enormity of the blows he suffered and finally succumbed to his mortal wounds.

Can you see, Acilius, from this account, in how much constant danger we live? No slave owner should think himself secure from violence or derision, not even a gentle and lenient master. Slaves are influenced by wickedness not fairness.

Enough of this. I shall write at a later time on a more pleasant subject. Farewell. ■

# TEACHER IDEAS

## Discussion Questions

1. What does Valerius Paulinus's estate have to offer Zosinus?

2. How were Larcius Macedo's murderers punished?

3. Name Zosinus's talents.

4. Where was Larcius Macedo when he was attacked?

5. What is Zosinus's malady?

6. Who will pay for Zosinus's travel costs and living expenses?

7. What aroused Larcius Macedo after the attack?

8. Does Pliny consider himself safe from his slaves? Why or why not?

9. Pliny says, "Slaves are influenced by wickedness not fairness." Does your opinion differ from Pliny's? What do you think motivates the slaves to attack Larcius Macedo? What may have influenced Pliny to have such an opinion?

10. Who is truly enslaved—the slave or the master or both? Explain the reasons for your conclusion.

## History Lesson: Roman Citizenship

Many people lived under the auspices of the vast Roman Empire, but not everyone was a citizen with all the rights and privileges that status contained. To be a Roman citizen meant that you were protected by the laws of Rome and enjoyed certain privileges, including:

**ius suffragi:** the right to vote for magistrates;

**ius honorum:** the right to hold office;

**ius provocationis:** the right to appeal a sentence passed by the courts;

**ius conubii:** the right to a legal marriage; and

**ius commercii:** the right to own property in a Roman community.

Those without citizenship status did not enjoy these fundamental rights and privileges. No wonder that Roman citizenship was a coveted prize.

Originally, citizenship was granted only to patricians. The plebeians gained full rights in 337 B.C., but Rome continued to guard the gift of citizenship, granting it only to a chosen few. It took an actual conflict (Social War of 90 B.C.) for the cities of Italy to secure the privilege of *civitas* (citizenship) for themselves.

Prominent native leaders in the provinces were commonly endowed with coveted citizenship. Julius Caesar had given this to the influential Gauls he conquered. After he became dictator, he even extended the privilege to all doctors and teachers of liberal arts as an inducement for these professionals to settle in Rome.

As the Empire grew, a more liberal policy toward the inclusion of foreigners into Rome's elite group prevailed. Entire communities were granted citizenship. During the time of Claudius (A.D. 48), Gallic chieftains requested admission to the senate, and the Emperor championed their cause. Claudius extolled the granting of citizenship to these "barbarians" in the following speech cited by Tacitus:

> My ancestors, the most ancient of whom was the Sabine Clausus who was adopted into the Roman state, urge me to follow this example and to add to our state whatever is beneficial no matter from where it comes. After the short Gallic wars, there has been continual peace. These Gauls have mixed with our culture and now follow our customs. Let them bring their gold and wealth to us, as well. All customs, Senators, which now are thought to be very old, were once new. After the patricians came plebeian magistrates, then Latin ones, and then people from all over Italy served in these posts. This novelty of including the Gauls in the senate will soon seem natural and will one day be an example for others to follow.[3]

Other groups could become citizens. The increasing variety of those who were accorded citizenship status is reflected in the fact that the Emperors Trajan and Hadrian who were born in Spain were not considered foreigners.

To be a Roman citizen set one apart by placing him or her in the ranks of the privileged and making him or her a partner with the family of Rome. Finally, in A.D. 212, Emperor Caracalla granted citizenship to all free men of the Empire no matter where they might reside.

## SUGGESTED TOPICS FOR FURTHER RESEARCH

1. Caracalla

2. Marcus Aurelius

3. freedmen class of Roman Empire

4. Plato's *Republic* (especially treatment of slavery)

5. Tiro, Cicero's freedman

## Language Arts

### VOCABULARY BUILDING: Political Words Derived from Latin Sources

**Candidate:** A person who seeks an office or an honor. *Candidate* is derived from the Latin word *candidatus*, meaning "clothed in a white toga." Romans seeking political office would take their togas to a "fuller" who would clean the garments. Urine was used to remove stains and chalk to cover up spots. Dressed in this pure white toga the candidate would begin campaigning. Other words derived from the same base include *candid, incandescent, candor,* and *candle.*

**Constitution:** The system of fundamental laws that prescribes the nature of a government. *Constitution* is derived from the Latin verb *statuo/ere,* meaning "to set up, put, cause to start." A constitution is something that has been "set up." Other words from the same base include *statue, statutory,* and *statute.*

---

[3]Tacitus, *Annals* XI: 24.

**Fascism:** A system of government that advocates a dictatorship of the extreme right together with an ideology of belligerent nationalism. *Fascism* is derived from the Latin word *fasces*, meaning "a bundle of rods tied together and enclosing an axe." The fasces were originally the symbol of power for the Etruscan kings and later used by all Roman magistrates as their symbol of authority. The fasces appear on the back of older American dimes. The Italian dictator Benito Mussolini adopted them for his own use where it acquired its modern meaning.

**Governor:** A person who governs. In the United States, the Chief of State. *Governor* is derived from the Latin word *gubernator*, meaning the "helmsman of a ship." The governor is at the helm of the ship of state. Other words from the same base include *governs*, *governess*, and *governance*.

**Senate:** A council of citizens having a deliberative and legislative function of governing. In the United States, the upper house of Congress to which two members are elected from each of the 50 states. *Senate* is derived from the Latin word *senex*, meaning "an old man." The Roman senate traces its beginnings to the time of Romulus who appointed 100 men as his advisors. Other words from the same base include *senile*, *senior*, and *senator*.

**Fasces**

**Vote:** A formal expression of preference or opinion. *Vote* is derived from the Latin word *votum*, meaning "a vow or solemn promise, especially a promise to a god." By casting one's vote, a person is expressing his or her vow of allegiance to a particular candidate. Other words from the same base include *votive*, *votary*, and *voter*.

## WORD USE AND RECOGNITION

1. In groups of two or three use each of the previous words in a sentence.

2. Find four of these words used in newspaper articles and bring them to class.

## MINI-DEBATE

With a partner, discuss the issues of slavery. What are the historical reasons for slavery? What are the immoral aspects of slavery? Make a list of the pros and cons. From this list, choose one pro and one con only. Each partner must present his or her side of the debate to the class. Spend only five minutes per team. The class should grade the team on the following criteria: the validity of the argument presented, the manner of the presentation, and the uniqueness of the argument. Use a scale of 1 to 5 (5 being the best) to judge each team. Use the form in figure 16.1 to grade the debate.

**Team:** Susie and Tom

| | | | | | | |
|---|---|---|---|---|---|---|
| a. | validity | 1 | 2 | 3 | 4 | 5 |
| b. | manner | 1 | 2 | 3 | 4 | 5 |
| c. | uniqueness | 1 | 2 | 3 | 4 | 5 |

Fig. 16.1. Mini-debate Judging Form.

## CRITICAL THINKING

In the first century A.D., the philosopher Seneca wrote an essay (*Epistulae Morales* XLVII) discussing the human equality of all men. Study Seneca's arguments in the following excerpts and compare them with those presented by your class in the mini-debate above. Did you and Seneca plead a similar case? If so, in what way? If not, why do you think you had differing opinions? Whose reasoning was more valid? Whose argument was more persuasive? Use specific references to the text and individual speeches to support your answers.

Seneca to Lucilius[4]

I was happy to learn from my friends who visited your home recently that you live on equal terms with your slaves. This behavior befits your wisdom and intelligence. People might say, "They are slaves." I answer, "No, indeed, they are men." "They are slaves." "No, they are comrades." "They are slaves." "No, just humble friends." "They are slaves." "No, they are but our fellow slaves because the same fate might one day be ours."

...You should realize that the man whom you call your slave springs from the same seed as yourself. He enjoys the same sky, breathes like you, lives like you, and dies in the same way. Do not condemn that man who suffers the misfortune of slavery for you, too, might one day endure this fate. I will not discuss the issue of our treatment of slaves which is always most haughty, cruel, and insulting but rather to suggest this alternative: live with your inferior in the same way that you would wish a superior to live with you.

...Indeed, just as he is a stupid man who, when buying a horse looks at the saddle and reins and forgets to inspect the animal itself, thus he is a *very* stupid man who judges a man by his clothes or station in life. But people often say, "He is a slave." I reply, "Will this harm him?" Show me a man who is not a slave! One is a slave to desire, another to greed, another to ambition. We are all slaves to hope, all slaves to fear.

...Someone might ask me, "If slaves are to be equal, should I seat all of them at my dinner table?" The answer is, "No, of course not. No more than you'd have all free men at your meal!" You are wrong though if you think I would exclude certain slaves because of their involvement with menial labor. Whether he is a mule driver or a herder, I shall judge a man not by his profession but by his character. A man makes his own character, it is Fate that bequeaths him his occupation.

## Cultural Activity: Names

A freeborn Roman had three names, his *praenomen, nomen,* and *cognomen.* On the ninth day after a male's birth and the eighth day for a female, the first name (praenomen) was bestowed upon the child. There were actually only a few first or personal names (about 18) used by the patrician families for their sons. Marcus, Publius, Decimus, and Gaius were four popular ones. Girls often took the female form of their father's name, such as Gaia, Octavia, and Aemilia.

The nomen, or middle name, was the family name, most of which were derived from the place where the family patriarch had lived.

The cognomen designated the particular branch of the family to which the person belonged and often began as a nickname, e.g., Flaccus means "Floppy-eared" and Brutus means "Dull."

---

[4]Seneca, *Epistulae Morales* XLVII.

Occasionally, a fourth name, *agnomen*, was given to someone as an honor. For example, Africanus was added to Publius Cornelius Scipio's name after the Battle of Zama in 202 B.C. when he defeated the Carthaginian general Hannibal. The actual name of the Emperor Augustus was Gaius Julius Caesar Octavianus; the title *Augustus*, meaning "majestic," was conferred upon him by the Roman senate in 27 B.C.

In more modern times, around the tenth or eleventh century in Italy, surnames or family names were adopted. The custom spread throughout Europe, and by the fourteenth century, people in England used a last name. Almost all European family names originated in one of four ways:

1. From a man's place of residence, e.g., Redford, a town in Scotland.

2. From a man's occupation, e.g., Taylor or Baker.

3. From a father's name, e.g., Robertson, son of Robert.

4. From a descriptive nickname, e.g., Reed (red-haired).

Personal names come from many different countries. Angela in Greek means "angel or one who brings good news," and Daniel in Hebrew means "God is my judge."

## SPECIAL NAMES

1. Ask a family member how you received your name. Are you named after a relative? a famous person?

2. Go to the library and research your full name. Be able to tell the country of origin and meaning of all of your names.

# RESOURCES

*Ben Hur*. Culver City, Calif.: Metro Goldwyn Mayer/United Artists, 1987. Video (211 minutes).

Browder, Sue. *New Age Baby Book*. New York: Warner Books, 1974.

Seneca, Lucius A., *Letters from a Stoic*, ed., Robin Campbell. (Middlesex, England: Penguin Classics, 1969).

Smith, Elsdon C. *New Dictionary of American Family Names*. New York: Harper & Row, 1956.

*The Tormont Webster's Illustrated Encyclopedic Dictionary*. Montreal: Tormont Publications, 1990.

# XVII

# The Dolphin

## INTRODUCTION

From its founding in the eighth century B.C. until its fall in the fifth century A.D., Rome conquered the entire Mediterranean world and beyond. The greatest power the world had known, Rome subjugated and brought its civilization to all people. Britain, Spain, France, Greece, Egypt, Asia Minor, Palestine, and northern Africa were just a few territories dominated by Roman rule.

At the turn of the first century when Pliny the Younger wrote this story, Rome was at the height of its power and influence. Under Emperor Trajan, Rome's geographic domain reached its greatest extent. Rome had withstood the transition from a Republic to an Empire with relative ease despite the atrocious conduct of some of its leaders. The Roman Empire seemed invincible, but change was in the air. Christianity was spreading throughout the Mediterranean, bringing a new set of values to its converts. The enormous size and diversity of the Empire at its zenith contained the seeds of the problems Rome would later face. Its greatness, however, should not be judged by its military might but by its lasting cultural and intellectual legacy to the western world. Roman customs and ideas are indelibly marked upon all of us.

The following tale of the dolphin carries no political message. Instead, it is a simple but timeless story about the conflict between expediency and moral goodness. There are no easy answers, and the dilemma faced by the magistrates of Hippo admits of no easy solution.

### The Dolphin[1]

■ On the sun-baked shores of northern Africa lies a town called Hippo. Close by is a large navigable lake from which a river flows connecting the lake to the sea. Just like the ocean tides, this river ebbs and flows.

The people of Hippo, no matter what their ages, enjoy the benefits of the water. They can fish or sail or swim throughout the year, but the ones who relish these activities most are the young boys who engage in a perpetual game to test their courage and endurance. Whoever can swim the farthest becomes the winner of the contest.

It happened one day that a certain boy ventured boldly toward the opposite side of the lake, leaving his companions far behind. A friendly dolphin approached the lad and swam around him in circles. Then it dove beneath and lifted the boy upon his back. The two frolicked in the water as the dolphin carried the boy far from the shore. Finally, the dolphin turned around and returned the boy to the safety of the sands.

**Dolphin**

As one might expect, the story of this miracle spread quickly throughout the town, and many people came to meet the lucky boy and ask him about his adventure, listening with awe to his tale. The next day everyone waited on the shore to see this marvelous creature.

When the dolphin returned, the young boy who had ridden the beast was so frightened that he ran away. Undaunted, the dolphin jumped into the air and dove down into the water. Then it swam around in circles as if it were trying to summon the lad to join his game. The terrified boy remained steadfast on the shore, and the dolphin retired to the deep.

Every day, for the next three days, the dolphin returned and repeated its unusual dance. Finally, some of the spectators overcame their fears and approached the dolphin and even managed to touch the creature. The boy, too, gathered his courage and swam out to meet his awaiting friend. Without hesitation, he leaped upon the dolphin's back and was spirited on a wonderful ride. The lad loved his unusual comrade and in return was loved by the dolphin. Neither one was afraid, and as the trust of the boy and gentleness of the dolphin increased, the other children joined this curious pair, swimming alongside.

Incredible as it may seem, the dolphin was so tame that often it would drag itself onto the beach and bathe in the sun with the children. When it became too hot, it would allow its friends to roll it back into the water. Everyone thought the gods had sent this creature for some purpose. Octavius Avitus, the deputy governor, a perverse man, poured an ointment over the dolphin, claiming that it was his religious duty to do so. The pungent odor scared the dolphin who immediately sought escape in the water. It did not return for several days and when it did it seemed sad and somewhat sluggish. When its strength was finally restored, the dolphin once again played games with the young boys.

---

[1]Pliny the Younger, *Epistulae* IX: 33.

As the report of these events spread far and wide, many important dignitaries came to see this dolphin. The small town of Hippo was forced to entertain and house these officials. Soon, its resources were depleted, and the large numbers of visitors destroyed the serenity and solitude of this quiet village. The city magistrates soon took drastic measures to rid themselves of this financial burden. In secret, so no one would know their evil intent, these men captured and killed the delightful dolphin. The town's problems ceased, but no more was there enjoyable play between the boys of Hippo and the friendly creature from the deep. ■

# TEACHER IDEAS

## Discussion Questions

1.  What did Octavius Avitus pour on the dolphin? Why?

2.  What effect did Avitus's action have on the dolphin?

3.  What do the boys do to test their strength?

4.  Why did the dolphin roll into the water after sunbathing?

5.  How did the dolphin convince the boy to join him?

6.  Name the town in which the story takes place.

7.  Why did the magistrates resort to killing the dolphin?

8.  How did other children play with the boy and his dolphin?

9.  If Pliny had been the magistrate in charge at Hippo, how do you think he would have handled the situation? Remember Pliny's letter to Trajan regarding the Christians (see chapter 11).

10. The city officials of Hippo, driven by the instinct to survive, destroyed a creature of nature in order to rid the city of costly onlookers attracted by the magnificent dolphin. Do you believe their actions were justified? Why or why not?

## History Lesson: The Fall of the Roman Empire

After the stability established by the leadership of the "Five Good Emperors," the Roman State was once more thrown into chaos. Commodus, son of Marcus Aurelius, thought he was the greatest gladiator alive, and even after becoming emperor, he continued to spend most of his time in the arena. He was soon murdered by the Praetorian Guard and for the next 100 years, the Empire faltered under an ineffective government. Weak principates could not hold the vast structure of the Empire together. The German barbarians north of the Danube, who always coveted the wealth of Rome, began to break through the frontier defenses.

When the security of the Empire was at its most vulnerable, the arrival of Diocletian (A.D. 285-305) infused new vitality. Realizing that the military and administrative leadership of such a huge government could not be handled by one person, Diocletian divided the functions of the principate into four territorial districts, with four capitals and four leaders. He ruled as the main principate (now called an *Augustus*) in the East with a co-Augustus controlling the West. Beneath them were two prefects (called *Caesars*) who ruled other jurisdictions. The separation of power seemed more manageable and for a time, peace and prosperity returned to Rome.

With Diocletian's resignation, his heirs engaged in a bloody struggle for the supreme position. The victor was Constantine I who defeated his rival at the Battle of Milvian Bridge (A.D. 312). Legend says that during this engagement, Constantine saw a fiery cross, and this apparition caused him to embrace the Christian god as his protector. Christians were thus finally free to worship without fear of persecution. Later, Constantine made the colony of Byzantium the eastern capital and founded the city of Constantinople (modern Istanbul). In A.D. 379, Emperor Theodosius I decreed a complete separation of the east and west areas of the Empire. The once great Roman Empire, which stretched from Britain to the Persian Gulf, was no more.

While internal politics took a heavy toll on the stability of the Empire, its eventual demise was caused by external forces. Barbarian tribes held vast lands north of the Roman and Persian Empires. Mongolian Huns, driven by a desire for more land and wealth, began migrating in large numbers. They first headed east but were stopped by the powerful Chinese Empire. They then turned west and pushed into territory occupied by the German tribes who were unable to stop them. In turn, the Germans fled and invaded the land of the Romans.

In A.D. 375, the Visigoths took asylum within the eastern borders of Rome and soon attacked the Roman army. Aided by the stirrup, which gave their horsemen superior stability and created a fighting cavalry, the Goths defeated the Romans and penetrated further south. In A.D. 401, the Goths moved into Italy, and in A.D. 410 under the leadership of Alaric, these tribes entered the city of Rome itself. They occupied the city for three days, burned many buildings, and pillaged whatever goods they could transport. The Romans were forced to pay an enormous tribute to get them to leave.

Migrations continued and various other tribes moved into territory once controlled by Rome. The Visigoths settled western Gaul and Spain, the Angles and Jutes entered Britain, and the Franks settled northern and eastern Gaul. These tribes established their own kingdoms, and with this blend of Germanic and Roman cultures created the modern peoples of Western Europe.

On the eastern front, Attila and his Huns assaulted the frontiers and permanently occupied territory south of the Danube. Eastern Rome paid large tribute to the Huns, and Attila even managed to capture the western emperor's sister Honoria and claim her as his wife. Despite the fracture of the western half of the Empire, the eastern Byzantine Empire survived for another 1,000 years until the invasion of the Turks in 1453.

## SUGGESTED TOPICS FOR FURTHER RESEARCH

1. later emperors: Theodosius, Justinian, Diocletian, Septimus Severus

2. fall of the eastern Empire in 1453

3. Attila the Hun

4. Battle of Adrianople

5. Battle of Milvian Bridge

6. Honoria

7. Edict of Milan

## Language Arts

## VOCABULARY BUILDING

Negative prefixes:

- *de, in/ir/il, dis/di, non* (taken from same Latin prefixes)

1. Look up the meaning of the words in column A and then give the meaning for the antonyms in column B.

| A | B |
|---|---|
| audible | inaudible |
| militarize | demilitarize |
| sensitize | desensitize |
| rational | irrational |
| logical | illogical |
| enfranchise | disenfranchise |
| resistant | nonresistant |
| inclination | disinclination |
| solvable | insolvable |
| renewable | nonrenewable |
| interested | disinterested |
| scheduled | nonscheduled |

2. Select five words of your choice from either column above and use each in a sentence.

## ESSAY WRITING

You now know a great deal about the ancient Romans. You have learned about their conquests, customs, and political institutions. You have read what they themselves have written. For this exercise, choose one topic on which to write an essay (two-page minimum). Be certain to use specific examples from any of the chapters in this book and cite the particular reference. Suggestions:

1. In your opinion what made the Romans unique? What was their greatest strength? Their greatest weakness?

2. What are the similarities between their ancient civilization and our own? Are these two cultures alike in thought? in deed?

3. How have humans changed over the past 1,600 years? Do you think civilization has progressed?

4. Why do you think the Roman Empire lasted so long?

## CREATIVE WRITING: "An Ancient Diary"

Imagine you are an ancient Roman of either the Republican or the Imperial period. You may be any type of Roman you wish, male or female, senator or slave. Identify yourself and the date you select. Write a journal describing your daily activities. Be sure to include your thoughts as well.

## Cultural Lesson: Latin Abbreviations in English

| Abbreviation | Latin Word | English Translation |
|---|---|---|
| @ | ad | at or to |
| A.D. | anno domini | in the year of our Lord |
| a.m. | ante meridiem | before noon |
| c., cir. | circa | about |
| e.g. | exempli gratia | for example |
| et al. | et alia | and others |
| etc. | et cetera | and all other things |
| ibid. | ibidem | in the same place |
| i.e. | id est | that is |
| L.B. | Litterarum Baccalaureus | Bachelor of Letters |
| lb. | libra | pound |
| LL.B. | Legum Baccalaureus | Bachelor of Laws |
| M.D. | Medicinae Doctor | Doctor of Medicine |
| N.B., n.b. | nota bene | note well, take notice |
| Ph.D. | Philosophiae Doctor | Doctor of Philosophy |
| p.m. | post meridiem | after noon |
| pro tem | pro tempore | for the time being |
| P.S. | post scriptum | written afterward |
| Q.E.D. | quod erat demonstrandum | which was to be proven |
| $R_x$ | recipe | take |
| R.I.P. | requiescat in pace | rest in peace |
| S.P.Q.R. | senatus populusque Romanus | the Senate and People of Rome |
| vs. | versus | against |

## WORD RECOGNITION

Find five of the above words in books, newspapers, or magazines. Bring your findings to share with the class.

## Et Alia: Important Events in Roman History

## TIME LINE

This activity is for groups of two or more.

Throughout this book you have followed the 1,200-year history of Rome from its inception in 753 B.C. to the invasion by the Visigoths in A.D. 410. In this exercise, you must design a time line to cover the events that took place during these 1,200 years. Follow these directions:

1. Begin by designing your chart. You may use plain paper taped together or other appropriate materials. Be sure to make it long enough. 1,200 years is a long time!

2. Divide your line into B.C. and A.D. and mark this distinction clearly on your chart. Use different colors.

3. Divide your line into centuries marking these divisions with bold black ink.

4. Events that took place in each century should be marked in a color other than black. Indicate each date *plus* the particular event.

5. Decorate your chart with appropriate illustrations.

Refer to each chapter of *Classical Rome Comes Alive* for dates and important events. Both the stories themselves and the "History Lesson" in each chapter should help.

## ROMAN NUMERALS

Fill in the dates and identify the important events in Roman history. Refer to chapter 5 for help with Roman numerals. N.B.: All events are described in this book, use the table of contents for additional help.

| | Roman Numeral | Date | Event |
|---|---|---|---|
| 1. | DCCLIII | 753 B.C. | founding of Rome |
| 2. | XXXI | _____ B.C. | _____ |
| 3. | LXXIX | A.D. _____ | _____ |
| 4. | CXLVI | _____ B.C. | _____ |
| 5. | DIX | _____ B.C. | _____ |
| 6. | LXIV | A.D. _____ | _____ |
| 7. | XLIV | _____ B.C. | _____ |
| 8. | LXXIII | _____ B.C. | _____ |
| 9. | CDX | A.D. _____ | _____ |
| 10. | LXX | A.D. _____ | _____ |

# RESOURCES

Birley, Anthony, trans., *Lives of the Later Caesars*. Middlesex, England: Penguin Classics, 1976.

Perin, Patrick. *The Barbarian Invasions of Europe*. Morristown, N.J.: Silver Burchett Press, 1987.

# Glossary

**Adriatic Sea:** Sea that lies between Italy and Greece. (See chapter 1 map.)

**Aediles:** Roman magistrates in charge of the internal services of Rome, including sewers, streets, games, and public buildings.

**Alba Longa:** Most ancient town of Italy built, according to legend, by Ascanius, the son of Aeneas. In later times, it was the location of splendid villas owned by wealthy Romans.

**Alexander the Great:** Ruler of Macedonia at age 20, he went on to conquer Persia and Egypt
**(356-323 B.C.)** and marched as far as the Indian Ocean. He died at age 33 and was buried in Alexandria, Egypt. His general, Ptolemy, ruled Egypt after his death and was an ancestor of Cleopatra.

**Amphitheater:** Literally, *amphitheater* means "double theater." Amphitheaters were oval-shaped arenas with stone seats and a sand floor, the most famous of which is the Flavian amphitheater (nicknamed the Colosseum) and built in A.D. 80.

**Apollo:** Greek god of poetry, music, medicine, and athletics. The son of Zeus, Apollo was the embodiment of civilization, and his temple at Delphi contained the most important oracle in classical times.

**Atrium:** The central courtyard and entrance hall in a Roman house. It contained a hole in the roof (compluvium) to let in light and rain water and a small basin (impluvium) to catch the water that was then channeled to storage tanks below the floor.

**Augury:** A custom originated by the Etruscans of foretelling the future by observing the behavior of birds. Priests mostly interpreted the flight patterns of birds, but other aspects of bird behavior were also heeded (e.g., the way chickens ate grain).

**Bithynia:** District of northwest Asia Minor, south of the Black Sea. It became a proconsular province under Augustus.

**Black Sea:** Sea lying between Europe and Asia, connected to Mediterranean by the Bosporus. (See chapter 1 map.)

**Campania:** Fertile district of central Italy, including the Naples area. First colonized by Greeks and finally controlled by Rome. Used by Romans for summer vacation homes. (See chapter 4 map.)

**Campus Martius:** Large park built for exercise and other athletic amusements in Rome. It was dedicated to Mars, the god of war and the father of Romulus and Remus.

**Capri:** Small island at southern entrance of Gulf of Puteoli near Naples. Emperor Tiberius retired to his villa on Capri. (See chapter 13 map.)

| | |
|---|---|
| **Capua:** | A city founded by the Etruscans located due north of Mt. Vesuvius in Campania. Conquered by the Romans in 341 B.C., Capua gave sanctuary to Hannibal 100 years later during the Second Punic War. Rome retaliated by killing Capua's senators and selling all of its citizens into slavery. Known for its gladiator schools by first century B.C. |
| **Caspian Sea:** | Large saltwater lake in Asia; part of modern Russia. |
| **Censors:** | Persons holding office responsible for counting all Roman citizens every five years. Established in 444 B.C., it was held by two persons and disappeared under the Empire. |
| **Centurion:** | A professional military officer. The most junior centurion was in charge of one hundred men, but the senior centurion was second-in-command to the legion's commander. |
| **Cilicia:** | A country located in southeastern Asia Minor. The general Pompey made it a Roman province in 67-66 B.C., but the mountainous areas were not subdued until the reign of Emperor Vespasian (A.D. 70-79). |
| **Circus Maximus:** | Area used by the Romans for chariot races and other entertainments. It was originally a natural indentation between the Palatine and Aventine hills. Legend states that Tarquinius Priscus was the first person to build wood bleachers there. The Circus Maximus underwent many transformations. After a fire in A.D. 36, Emperor Claudius added marble seats so that 250,000 spectators could use the stands. Actual size is not certain, though it was approximately 2,000 feet long and 600 feet wide. |
| **Cisalpine Gaul:** | Northern part of modern Italy. Literally meant "Gaul this side of Alps" from a Roman's viewpoint. |
| **Clusium:** | Town in ancient Etruria. (See chapter 4 map.) |
| **Cohort:** | Military unit comprised of 500-600 soldiers, or one-tenth of a legion. See **Legion**. |
| **Comitia Centuria:** | Assembly of the entire population of Rome based on military participation. During the Republic this assembly elected the consuls, censors, and praetors and served as the court for capital crimes. |
| **Comitia Curiata:** | Assembly of patricians divided into 30 *curiae*. During regal period, this group confirmed or negated questions brought before them by the king. |
| **Comitia Tributa:** | Assembly of the entire population of Rome based on tribal association. This assembly elected minor magistrates including the aediles and tribunes. By 286 B.C., resolutions passed in the comitia tributa were binding on both patricians and plebeians. |
| **Comitium:** | The open area located at the end of the Forum in Rome that was used as a place for the assemblies and the courts to convene until the second century B.C. |

| | |
|---|---|
| **Consul:** | Highest of all Roman magistrates, elected yearly and numbered two. The consuls initiated all business in the senate and could command an army. |
| **Cumae:** | A city on the Bay of Naples founded by the Greeks around 900 B.C. Later, it became a popular resort. (See chapter 4 map.) |
| **Curiae:** | To facilitate vote counting, Romulus divided the population of early Rome into 30 groups called curiae. By first century B.C., they were obsolete. |
| **Dacia:** | Land that lies between the Danube River and Carpathian Mountains, west of the Black Sea. Emperor Trajan spent five years subduing the country, and afterward it was a Roman province. |
| **Delphi:** | City in central Greece. The Greeks believed it to be the center of the Earth and sacred to Apollo whose oracle resided in Delphi. |
| **Fasces:** | A bundle of rods tied together and enclosing an axe. Originally the symbol of power for the Etruscan kings, the fasces were later used by numerous Roman magistrates as their badge of office. |
| **Fates:** | From Greek mythology, three crones who held the threads of life: Clotho who spins the thread, Lachesis who determines its length, and Atropos who cuts the thread off, thereby determining the length of one's life. |
| **Forum:** | A large open area used by the Romans as a central meeting place. The Forum Romanum was located between the Palatine and Capitoline hills in Rome and contained important government buildings and temples. |
| **Freedmen:** | Former slaves who became Roman citizens after their manumission. Freedmen could vote but not hold political office or serve in the military. |
| **Gaul:** | Territory more extensive than present-day France, including parts of Belgium and Switzerland. Conquered by Julius Caesar. |
| **Haruspices:** | The custom of foretelling the future by inspecting the entrails of animals. Started by the Etruscans and continued by Roman priests. |
| **Hippocrates:** | Greek physician born circa 470 B.C. on the island of Cos. Traveled through Greece to practice his profession. He is known as the "Father of Medicine." |
| **Iberus River:** | River in northeastern Spain that starts in the present-day Cantabrian Mountains and flows into the Mediterranean. Now called the Ebro. (See chapter 5 map.) |
| **Interregnum:** | In the early days of Rome before the Republic, the five-day period of time between the death of one king and the appointment of another in which the senate was invested with regal power. |
| **Janiculum Hill:** | A hill of Rome, actually separated from the other seven and located on the western bank of the Tiber River. (See chapter 2 map.) |

**Janus:** Roman god of beginning and gates. Always portrayed with two heads because doors open both ways. The month of January is named for him, as well as the word *janitor* (door keeper).

**Knights:** Originally an elite division of the military. By the second century B.C. the *equites* (knights) had lost their military affiliation and were considered a social and economic class separate from the senators. Vied with the senate during the Republic over control of the courts. Knights gained wealth from commercial activities that were forbidden to the senate class.

**Lararium:** A shrine in an ancient Roman home dedicated to the good spirits of a family's deceased ancestors.

**Legion:** The central unit of the Roman army consisting of 5,000-6,000 men. By the first century B.C., a legion consisted mostly of Roman citizens from Italy. At this time, there were about 25-30 legions in existence, each with more than 5,000 soldiers. The remainder of the army consisted of auxiliary infantry, cavalry troops, and other forces.

**Lictors:** Attendants who accompanied Roman magistrates whenever they were in public. The lictors carried the fasces. Roman consuls had 12 lictors, and the praetor at Rome had two. These numbers varied throughout Roman history.

**Magistrates:** In the most inclusive sense, magistrate means all elected and appointed civil and military offices of the state. The term most often refers to elected officials and excludes military officials and lower-echelon elected city officials.

**Misenum:** Promontory located 20 miles from Mt. Vesuvius on the Bay of Naples forming an excellent harbor. (See chapter 13 map.)

**Nereids:** The 50 beautiful daughters of Nereus and Doris, sea nymphs. The most famous was Thetis, mother of Achilles.

**Nobles:** Aristocratic group of Rome formed from those families who held the office of consul. Both patricians and plebeians were part of the nobles.

**Nomen:** Latin word meaning "name." Each person actually had three names:

| | | |
|---|---|---|
| praenomen | personal name | Gaius |
| nomen | family name | Julius |
| cognomen | branch of family | Caesar |

**Numidia:** Ancient country located in northern Africa. Originally inhabited by Berbers. In 106 B.C., it became subject to Rome but retained its own monarchy. In 46 B.C., Julius Caesar ousted the local monarchy and turned Numidia into a Roman province. (See chapter 1 map.)

**Olympia:** Small city in western Greece where Olympic games were held in honor of Zeus.

**Optimate:** Title descriptive of first century B.C. political conservatives who were opposed to the popular party.

**Parthia:** Country southeast of the Caspian Sea in Asia. In 53 B.C., Crassus (First Triumvirate member) unsuccessfully attempted to conquer this country. In 39-38 B.C., Mark Antony's army managed to win several battles. Finally, the emperor Trajan (A.D. 115-117) invaded Parthia and managed to hold this country but only for a short time. This area includes modern Iran and Iraq.

**Patres:** The one hundred original members of the advisory senate established by Romulus. Their descendants became the patrician class of Rome.

**Patricians:** The wealthy land owners of early Rome, the upper crust of society.

**Picenum:** Region of central Italy on coast of Adriatic and once occupied by the Sabines. Conquered by Romans in 268 B.C.

**Plebeian:** A member of the Roman population that originated from the conquered Latin tribes. Lengthy struggle existed between the plebeians (or "plebs") and patricians until around 300 B.C. when the former gained almost all rights previously enjoyed only by the patricians. Later, plebeian generally referred to the lower class of society.

**Pontifex Maximus:** The official who headed the state religion and was elected by the assembly. The pontifex maximus was assisted by other priests during religious ceremonies. Originally only open to patricians, but finally some plebeians held this office. During the Empire, the emperor controlled this office.

**Pontus:** Northeastern district of Asia Minor located southeast of the Black Sea that became a Roman province in A.D. 62 during Nero's reign.

**Po Valley:** Land surrounding the Padus (now Po) River. This river begins in the Alps and flows through Cisalpine Gaul to the Adriatic. (See chapter 4 map.)

**Praetorian Guard:** Personal bodyguard of Roman emperors, started by Augustus. These troops enjoyed several privileges above ordinary soldiers. Disbanded by Constantine I.

**Praetors:** Roman magistrates who dealt with the administration of justice in Rome. Second most important office behind consul. Praetors proclaimed laws and supervised the courts. Originally only one praetor held office at a time, but by Julius Caesar's day there were sixteen. The position lost all importance during the Empire.

**Proconsul:** Roman official who oversaw a district outside the city. Appointed for usually one year, similar to a governor. Proconsuls controlled an army and the judicial matters of their province only.

**Procurator:** Under the Empire a fiscal administrator of equestrian rank in the imperial provinces. The procurator could serve with the proconsul or as the sole administrator of a province. Pontius Pilate was an independent procurator of Judaea.

| | |
|---|---|
| **Punic:** | Synonym for *Carthaginian*. |
| **Quaestor:** | Roman magistrate responsible for a variety of duties, including the prosecution of criminal cases, overseeing the state treasury, and acting as paymaster for the army. Their numbers varied throughout Roman history. |
| **Rhetoric:** | The art of speaking; forensic oratory. |
| **Rhodes:** | Island in the eastern Aegean that became dependent upon Rome under Emperor Claudius in the first century A.D. Famous for its school of oratory. (See chapter 1 map.) |
| **Sacred Way:** | The main street of central Rome that stretched from the Flavian amphitheater to the Forum Romanum, called the *Via Sacra* by the Romans. |
| **Saguntum:** | A town in Spain located south of the Iberus River near the Mediterranean coast, allied with Rome but seized by the Carthaginian general Hannibal in 219 B.C. This capture was the immediate cause of the Second Punic War. (See chapter 1 map.) |
| **Saturnalia:** | Annual Roman holiday in honor of the god Saturn that took place in late December. Characterized by revelry and feasting, it was especially enjoyed by the slaves of Rome who were relieved of all duties and could wear the badge of freedmen during the Saturnalia. Businesses and schools were closed, no war could be initiated, and no criminals punished during this holiday. |
| **Senate:** | The council of elders begun by Romulus who advised magistrates on all matters of state. Originally made up of just patrician members, but plebeians were admitted by the fourth century B.C. Only senators were allowed to wear a tunic with a broad purple stripe. |
| **Sesterces:** | Common monetary unit, usually a silver coin. Worth about 10 cents. |
| **Seven Hills:** | Rome is built on seven hills: Palatine, Aventine, Capitoline, Quirinal, Vimincal, Esquiline, and Caelian. (See chapter 2 map.) |
| **Stabiae:** | Small town south of Pompeii. (See chapter 13 map.) |
| **Stoicism:** | Philosophy founded by the Phoenician Zeno in the third century B.C. Embraced by educated Romans who identified with the basic tenet that virtue was the only good and that life must be controlled by virtue, and all other vagaries, whether painful or pleasurable, were equally unimportant. |
| **Syria:** | Country of western Asia conquered by Pompey in 64 B.C. |
| **Tarentum:** | Greek city on the eastern heel of Italy captured by the Romans in 272 B.C. During the Second Punic War, Tarentum sided with Hannibal but was retaken by Rome in 207 B.C. and made a Roman colony. (See chapter 4 map.) |
| **Thrace:** | A country located in northeastern Macedonia; roughly modern Bulgaria. |

**Tribune of the Plebs:** In the early Republic the magistrate who protected the rights of the plebeian class. The powers of this office increased over the years. By 149 B.C., there were ten tribunes who were automatically included in the ranks of the senate. Power lay in their veto, which could void the legislation of *all* magistrates including their fellow tribunes.

**Vercingetorix:** Chief of the Arverni tribe in Gaul who lost to Julius Caesar at the Battle of Alesia in 52 B.C. and was executed by order of Julius Caesar in 46 B.C.

**Vestal Virgins:** Six priestesses who served Vesta, goddess of the hearth. Maintained vigil over the eternal flame in Rome and kept public treaties and wills of influential citizens.

**Villa:** An elaborate country home for a wealthy ancient Roman.

# Answer Keys

## CHAPTER I

### Discussion Questions

1. To learn what is beneficial to humankind and what should be avoided.

2. Strong personages, both at home and while fighting.

3. It is divinely blessed.

4. Made her a Vestal Virgin.

5. Organized a group of young men to rid the countryside of brigands and robbers.

6. Faustulus.

7. River had overflowed.

8. Answers will vary.

### Language Arts

**VOCABULARY BUILDING**

1. regicide＝king      homocide＝person

   matricide＝mother      sororicide＝sister

   genocide＝group      patricide＝father

   fratricide＝brother      infanticide＝child

2. excise: to cut out

   incise: to carve

   incisor: a tooth used for cutting

3.   a. incisor(s)

     b. excised

     c. incise

## NAMES OF MODERN CITIES

1. Pierre, South Dakota:

   French word meaning "stone"; a man's proper name; named after Fort Pierre.

   Los Angeles, California:

   Spanish term meaning "the angels"; name given in 1769.

   Denver, Colorado:

   Named for J. W. Denver, governor of the Kansas territory in 1858.

   Bismarck, North Dakota:

   Name chosen in gratitude to the German stockholders who helped with the railroad building in North Dakota in the 1870s.

   Baton Rouge, Louisiana:

   French word meaning "red stick." Louisiana Indians used a red post or pole to mark the boundaries between tribes.

   Raleigh, North Carolina:

   Named for English colonist Sir Walter Raleigh.

   Phoenix, Arizona:

   Named for mythical bird that rises reborn from its own ashes.

   Albuquerque, New Mexico:

   Named for the viceroy of New Spain (1706), the Duke Albuquerque.

   St. Louis, Missouri:

   Named in 1764 for Louis IX of France.

   Memphis, Tennessee:

   Named after the ancient capital of Egypt.

   Chicago, Illinois:

   Altered spelling of Indian word *chigagou*, meaning "onion place."

2. Romulus:

   Michigan, New York; legendary founder of Rome.

   Carthage:

   New York, Arkansas, Illinois, Indiana, Kentucky, Maine, Mississippi, Missouri, New Mexico, North Carolina, South Carolina, Tennessee, Texas; Phoenician city of North Africa, enemy of Rome.

   Hannibal:

   Missouri, New York, Ohio, Wisconsin; Carthaginian general who was defeated at Battle of Zama, North Africa.

   Juno:

   Alabama, Florida, Texas; goddess of childbirth and marriage, and both sister and wife of Jupiter.

   Cincinnati:

   Iowa, Ohio; named for the Roman general Lucius Quinctius Cincinnatus.

   Rome:

   Georgia, Illinois, Indiana, Kansas, Kentucky, Massachusetts, Missouri, New York, Oregon, Pennsylvania, Texas; famous city in Italy.

   Cicero:

   Illinois, Indiana, Kansas, New York; named for Roman orator and statesman Marcus Tullius Cicero.

   Seneca:

   Illinois, Kansas, Maryland, Missouri, Nebraska, Ohio, Oregon, Pennsylvania, South Carolina, South Dakota, Wisconsin; named for Roman philosopher, playwright, and Nero's tutor.

   Augusta:

   Arkansas, Georgia, Illinois, Kansas, Kentucky, Maine, Michigan, Missouri, Montana, New Jersey, Ohio, West Virginia, Wisconsin, Virginia; title given to all female members of the imperial family of Augustus.

   Minerva:

   Kentucky, New York, Ohio, Texas; goddess of wisdom and handicrafts.

## CHAPTER II

### Discussion Questions

1. Free people and slaves.

2. Defense, religion, and laws.

3. 100; 100 was sufficient or there were only 100 men worthy of becoming senators.

4. The Sabine king; perfidy of Tarpeius's daughter.

5. At first they resented it, then they capitulated.

6. Named the 30 curiae after them.

7. "They killed her ... perhaps to set an example that a traitor should never be trusted."

8. Games in honor of Neptune to celebrate the founding of the new city.

## CHAPTER III

### Discussion Questions

1. He wished to enhance his private treasury and to lessen the hostility toward him of his over-taxed subjects.

2. To see whose wife was more virtuous by seeing what each was doing in her husband's absence.

3. To make fun of him.

4. He would shame her in the eyes of her husband.

5. His nephew.

6. The Earth.

7. Weaving.

8. To consult the oracle at Delphi.

### Language Arts

1&2.  acupuncture: Chinese practice of puncturing body with needles to cure disease (noun)
acrid: very bitter (adjective)
acrimony: a harsh manner (noun)
acute: sharp (adjective)
acumen: shrewdness (noun)

3.  a.  acute  b.  acrimony  c.  acrid  d.  acupuncture  e.  acumen

# CHAPTER IV

## Discussion Questions

1.  Father Tiber.

2.  Porsenna and Tarquin.

3.  Regulated salt prices and exempted plebeians from taxation.

4.  Horatius: statue and land.
    Mucius: land.
    Cloelia: statue.

5.  That there were 300 more Roman assassins eager to kill him.

6.  The king and his scribe were dressed alike.

7.  Left-handed.

8.  The young boys because they would suffer separation the most from their families.

## Language Arts

1&2.  circumlocution: evasion in speech (noun)
      circumnavigate: to sail or fly completely around (verb)
      circumspect: prudent (adjective)
      circumvent: to outwit (verb)
      circumstantial evidence: evidence not bearing directly on facts (noun)

3.  a.  yes  b.  yes  c.  no  d.  no  e.  yes

# CHAPTER V

## Discussion Questions

1.  24 years old.

2.  New Carthage.

3.  Celtberians.

4.  It was totally destroyed.

5.  Rome.

6.  Brought cavalry to aid in the war.

7.  476+.

8.  Oarsmen.

## Language Arts

1&2.  unit: an individual entity (noun)

unison: agreement of musical parts; at the same time (noun)

united: joined (adjective)

unique: being the only one of its kind (adjective)

universe: all existing things (noun)

3.    a.  universe    b.  unison    c.  unique    d.  united    e.  unit

## Cultural Lesson

1,492 = MCDXCII

844 = DCCCXLIV

73 = LXXIII

1,066 = MLXVI

210 = CCX

1,945 = MCMXLV

337 = CCCXXXVII

2,001 = MMI

# CHAPTER VI

## Discussion Questions

1. Killing every tenth person; used because the Roman soldiers retreated and abandoned their weapons.

2. Hoped to allow his men and their families to go home.

3. Crassus, he divided up his troops.

4. Thrace.

5. The armies of Clodius, Publius, Cossinius, Gellius, Cassius, and Mummius and the garrison at Capua.

6. They built a ditch 40 miles across the isthmus.

7. Died in battle.

8. A snake coiled around his head while he slept.

## Language Arts

1. biopsy: diagnostic study of tissue from a living being

   monocle: single corrective lens

   biodegradable: capable of decomposition by natural processes

   monogamy: having one spouse

   biography: account of a person's life

   monolith: a large pillar of stone

   biology: science of life

   bionic: having certain functions carried out by electronic equipment

# CHAPTER VII

## Discussion Questions

1. To keep their knowledge secret from commoners and because they believed memorization increased the power of the mind.

2. Exclusion from participating in sacrifices.

3. To appease the gods by giving a life for a life.

4. Exempt from taxation and military service.

5. Priests, judges, teachers to the young, administered sacrifices.

6. Dairy products and wild animal meat.

7. Hunting and making war.

8. Drinking cups at lavish banquets.

## Language Arts

1. benefactor: a good doer

   malefactor: an evil doer

   intermural sports: sports played between two schools

   intramural sports: sports played within the same school

2. An interstate highway connects two or more states, while an intrastate highway lies within the boundaries of one state.

3. benign

4. malady: a disease or ailment

   benefit: an advantage

   malaria: an infectious disease

   intermediary: one who acts as a mediator

   intermittent: stopping and starting at intervals

   intravenous: within a vein

## Cultural Lesson

**ROMAN DATES**

1. March 14
2. February 9
3. April 24
4. May 2
5. May 24

6. June 13
7. July 15
8. October 7
9. November 8
10. December 8

The day Julius Caesar was murdered on the Ides of March. Like Caesar, you should be on guard should someone utter this phrase to you.

# GRACCHI AND SCIPIO FAMILY TREE

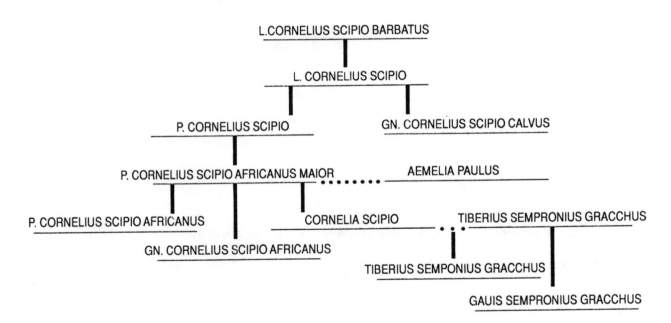

Family Tree (answer key) for Fig. 7.1.

# CHAPTER VIII

## Discussion Questions

1. The hill. Caesar brought reinforcements and attacked from the rear.

2. 23 towers, 20-foot trench, 15-foot ditches, 12-foot wall, small pits.

3. 30 days.

4. Gaius Reblius and Gaius Reginus.

5. 80,000 cavalry and 250,000 troops plus Gauls in Alesia.

6. The war would be determined in the day's battle.

7. 20-day holiday.

8. 4 cohorts and cavalry.

## Language Arts

| | | |
|---|---|---|
| aquiline: eagle | elephantine: elephant | piscine: fish |
| asinine: donkey | equine: horse | porcine: pig |
| bovine: cow | feline: cat | serpentine: snake |
| canine: dog | lionine: lion | ursine: bear |
| columbine: dove | lupine: wolf | vulpine: fox |

# CHAPTER IX

## Discussion Questions

1. To insure the food was always palatable.

2. Octavia, his sister.

3. To spy and laugh at commoners.

4. To use as a bribe.

5. Octavian's were small and fast, Antony's were tiered and armored.

6. Pretended she was near death.

7. Disaster, fought too soon.

8. Ptolemy, Alexander and Cleopatra (twins).

## Language Arts

1. telecast: to broadcast by television

   television: transmission of visual images

   telescope: instrument used to observe distant objects

   telephoto: lens used to create an image of a distant object

   telekinesis: movement of objects by inexplicable means

telephone: instrument used to transmit voice waves to distant locations

telegraph: communication of electric impulses

telemetry: automatic transmission of data by wire, radio, etc.

telethon: a long television program

telepathy: transference of thoughts

cast: from *broadcast*, to make known over a large area

vision: sight

scope: watcher

photo: an image

kinesis: motion

phone: sound/voice

graph: to write

metry: measure

thon: from *marathon*, a task of endurance

pathy: emotion/suffering

## Et Alia: Word Search

```
W I U F V E L Q K T W M U N H B N B I M F U B C
A T S D O F V W S Z P E C E E R G T D H Z S A A
X J U F X R W X P Y N A Y X S U S S R O P Q A G
Y X D U O N H P O M P E Y A M T N P M J J Q F E
N O I R A S E A C F G I A H S U T J M J G P B D
E Z P O S E V V I U L L I W T S S Y W U K L H C
O A E C K P O T A L P E H F K P H T X C I U I X
B I L T C O C D M V N O T N N F Y I B L L T O O
H D E L K C T U E I D T R P A C H G G C R A C B
E C E G S T E T S A M A A S Y R I A E R M R O A
F L L V U A S C T R R U D V O L M C F M C B C
L E W H I V H B T J O K E E G J F R P F N H G T
Z O I B S I C M E X M K J T E E L F O P T O U M
J P G N S A H O D I E L I N F T O G Y N O T N A
K A K A A D N T H M O Y N P J I R S M S H S G I
M T A N C E F G B L A U G U S T U S G U Q Q I A
O R F B D B R P N E E U Q H R Q D C U P I D O G
P A E C L C V L M N O E L D K N A V G J D T N G
```

Word Search (answer key) for Fig. 9.1.

# CHAPTER X

## Discussion Questions

1. Expressed concern, wailed with grief.

2. The sides of the couch held the roof up.

3. Too suspicious and Agrippina had become immune to poison.

4. She yelled she was the Emperor's mother.

5. Anicetus, Nero's ex-tutor.

6. Nero says he committed suicide.

7. Murdered by Nero's henchmen, buried at Misenum.

8. He expresses "sincere" devotion.

## Cultural Lesson

assassin: Arabic

nominate: Latin

trousers: Scottish Gaelic

policy: Latin Greek

pajama: Persian

vanquish: Middle English/Latin

dungaree: Indian

vivid: Latin

ranch: Mexican Spanish

catsup: Chinese

hamburger: German

mortal: Latin

lava: Latin

pretzel: German

crescent: Latin

cookie: Dutch

junction: Latin

bamboo: Malayan

spirit: Latin

tycoon: Chinese

audience: Latin

prairie: French

monarch: Latin/Greek

revolve: Latin

rat: German

tea: Chinese

# CHAPTER XI

## Discussion Questions

1. Use of stone walls, no common walls, more access to water.

2. 1 mile long, covered with jewels and gold, private zoo, 120-foot statue of Nero, surrounded by fields, wild animals in the parks.

3. In small shops near the Circus.

4. He opened the parks and public monuments to the homeless and lowered the price on grain.

5. He was on vacation.

6. Christians.

7. Mauled by beasts, used as human torches, crucified.

8. 10 districts, 3 totally, 7 partially.

## Language Arts

1. ingress: act of entering      transgress: to go beyond a limit, to sin

   egress: act of exiting      digress: to stray

   regress: to go backward

2. (Answers will vary)

3. (Answers will vary)

4. a. ingress, egress      b. regressed      c. digress      d. transgress

## Et Alia—Their Nicknames and Dates

| Full Name | Nickname | Dates |
| --- | --- | --- |
| 1. Gaius Julius Caesar Octavianus Augustus | Augustus | 27 B.C.-A.D. 14 |
| 2. Tiberius Claudius Nero Caesar | Tiberius | A.D. 14-37 |
| 3. Gaius Caesar Augustus Germanicus | Caligula | A.D. 37-41 |
| 4. Tiberius Claudius Drusus Nero Germanicus | Claudius | A.D. 41-84 |
| 5. Nero Claudius Caesar Drusus Germanicus | Nero | A.D. 54-68 |
| 6. Servius Sulpicius Galba | Galba | A.D. 68-69 |
| 7. Marcus Salvius Otho | Otho | A.D. 69-69 |
| 8. Aulus Vitellius | Vitellius | A.D. 69-69 |
| 9. Titus Flavius Savinus Vespianus | Vespasian | A.D. 69-79 |
| 10. Titus Flavius Sabinus Vespasianus | Titus | A.D. 79-81 |
| 11. Titus Flavius Domitianus Augustus | Domitian | A.D. 81-96 |
| 12. Marcus Cocceius Nerva | Nerva | A.D. 96-98 |
| 13. Marcus Ulpius Nerva Trajanus | Trajan | A.D. 98-117 |
| 14. Publius Aelius Hadrianus | Hadrian | A.D. 117-138 |
| 15. Titus Aurelius Fulvius Bionius Arrius Antonius Pius | Antonius Pius | A.D. 138-161 |
| 16. Marcus Aurelius Antonius | Marcus Aurelius | A.D. 161-180 |
| 17. Lucius Aurelius Commodus | Commodus | A.D. 180-193 |
| 18. Lucius Septimius Severus | Septimus Severus | A.D. 193-211 |
| 19. Marcus Aurelius Antonius Bassianus Caracalla | Caracalla | A.D. 211-217 |
| 20. Flavius Valerius Aurelius Constantine | Constantine the Great | A.D. 306-337 |

# CHAPTER XII

## Discussion Questions

1. Touching an elephant's trunk, seasickness.

2. Turnips, boar's bladder, drink of pig's marrow, testicles of a horse, mouse dung.

3. Pear.

4. Poppaea.

5. Headaches, chest and eye pains.

6. Salt lakes, evaporating salt water, salt mines, salt hills.

7. Turnip seed with wine, cooked pears, salt.

8. Mother's milk.

## Language Arts

### VOCABULARY BUILDING

1. acrophobia: fear of heights
   agoraphobia: fear of the market place (going out in public)
   claustrophobia: fear of confined spaces
   hydrophobia: fear of water
   necrophobia: fear of death
   monophobia: fear of solitude
   photophobia: fear of sunlight
   xenophobia: fear of strangers

# CHAPTER XIII

## Discussion Questions

1. August 24, A.D. 79

2. Herculaneum and Pompeii.

3. Asphyxiation.

4. Brave.

5. Sea receded and ferocious tremors.

6. Fabricated terrors.

7. A pillow bound with a piece of linen.

8. Pliny the Elder's Spanish friend.

## Language Arts

### VOCABULARY BUILDING

1&2.  spectacle: a public display (noun)

retrospect: a review (noun)

suspicion: a state of uncertainty (noun)

prospect: a possibility (noun)

conspicuous: obvious (adjective)

3.  a. spectacle    b. suspicion    c. prospect    d. retrospect    e. conspicuous

### Similes

"cloud looked like a pine tree"

"sky was ominous ... with flames similar to ... lightning"

"as if someone had turned off a light in a room"

"like during an eclipse"

"ash which looked like snow"

## Cultural Lesson

| Author | Occupation(s) | Work(s) |
| --- | --- | --- |
| Juvenal (c.57-67-c.128) | rhetorician, satirist | The Satires |
| Horace (65 B.C.-8 B.C.) | writer, poet laureate | Epodes, Odes, Satires, Ars Poetica, Epistles |
| J. Caesar (100 B.C.-44 B.C.) | statesman, general, author | On Civil War, On Gallic Wars |
| Seneca (3 B.C.-A.D. 65) | philosopher, statesman, Nero's tutor | Dialogues, Epistulae Morales, Tragedies, Apocolocyntosis, philosophical works, Naturales Questiones |
| Terence (c.195-185 B.C.-159 B.C.) | comic dramatist | Adelphi, Hecyra, Eunuchus, Andria, Phormio, Heauton, Timorumenos |
| Constantine (A.D. 272-337) | emperor | |
| Vergil (70 B.C.-19 B.C.) | poet | Eclogues, Georgics, Aeneid |
| Cicero (106 B.C.-43 B.C.) | orator, advocate, statesman | Orations (58 survive), Rhetorica, Philosophica, poems, letters |
| Hippocrates (460 B.C.) | physician | |
| Lucretius (c.95 B.C.-55 B.C.) | poet, philosopher | De Rerum Natura |

# CHAPTER XIV

## Discussion Questions

1. Philosopher.

2. Rattled chains above his head.

3. He lacked a proper burial.

4. A soldier.

5. The wound in his neck.

6. They turned to stone.

7. His body was black and blue.

8. They wanted the dead boy's body.

## Language Arts

### VOCABULARY BUILDING

1. readable: able to be read easily

   peaceable: disposed to peace

   enjoyable: capable of giving pleasure

   washable: capable of being laundered without damage

   perishable: liable to decay or spoil

   knowledgeable: possessing intelligence

   pitiable: deserving of compassion

   legible: capable of being deciphered

   audible: capable of being heard

   controllable: capable of being regulated

## Cultural Lessons

### MILEAGES

1. 701 miles

2. 2,125 miles

3. 1,370 miles

4. 2,794 miles

5. 547 miles

# CHAPTER XV

## Discussion Questions

1.  Dairy products.

2.  To persuade him to vacation there.

3.  Shrimp and sole.

4.  Hidden passageways.

5.  17.

6.  Because the sea spray does not harm them.

7.  In case his own were not heated if he arrived on short notice.

8.  Solar heat and furnaces.

## Language Arts

### VOCABULARY BUILDING

antemeridian: before noon

postmeridian: after noon

antedate: to give a date that is earlier than actual date

postdate: to give a date that is later than actual date

antebellum: period before war, especially American civil war

postpone: to delay until a future time

antecedent: an occurrence that precedes another

# CHAPTER XVI

## Discussion Questions

1.  Air and milk.

2.  Executed.

3.  Recites poetry, history, is a comic, plays the lyre.

4.  The bath house.

5.  Coughs and discharges blood.

6.  Pliny, Zosinus.

7.  Noise or the cool air.

8.  No, not even gentle and lenient masters are safe.

# CHAPTER XVII

## Discussion Questions

1. Ointment, claimed it was his religious duty.

2. Scared the dolphin.

3. Swim far distances.

4. It was too hot.

5. It swam in circles for three days.

6. Hippo.

7. The spectacle of the dolphin was depleting the town's resources.

8. Swam alongside.

## Language Arts

### VOCABULARY BUILDING

inaudible: unable to be heard

demilitarize: to replace military control with civilian

desensitize: to make less sensitive, especially to light or pain

irrational: not using reason

illogical: senseless

disenfranchise: to deprive of the right to vote

nonresistant: excessively obedient

disinclination: reluctance or aversion

insolvable: inanswerable

nonrenewable: unable to be extended

disinterested: impartial

nonscheduled: not according to plan

## Et Alia

2. 31 B.C., Battle of Actium

3. A.D. 79, eruption of Mt. Vesuvius

4. 146 B.C., destruction of Carthage

5. 509 B.C., establishment of the Republic

6. A.D. 64, Great Fire of Rome

7. 44 B.C., Julius Caesar's assassination

8. 73 B.C., Spartacus's revolt

9. A.D. 410, sack of Rome

10. A.D. 70, destruction of Jerusalem

# Appendix
## Schematic Teachers' Guide

|  | I | II | III | IV | V |
|---|---|---|---|---|---|
| **Story and Discussion Questions** | "Romulus and Remus" by Livy | "Sabine Women" by Livy | "Rape of Lucretia" by Livy | "Three Heroes" - Horatius, Mucius Scaevola, and Cloelia by Livy | "Scipio and the Virgin" by Livy |
| **History Lesson** | Kings of Rome | Patricians and Plebeians | Magistracies of Republican Rome | Etruscan Power in Italy | Life of Hannibal |
| **Language Arts** | A. Vocabulary - "cide/cise" B. Etiological myths Creative Writing Research City Names | A. Vocabulary from Greek and Roman mythology B. Creative Writing C. Movie Watching | A. Vocabulary - "ac (u) /acr" B. Creative Writing | A. Vocabulary - "circum" B. Legends C. Creative Writing | A. Vocabulary -"uni" and other numbers B. Essay Writing - Dido's Curse |
| **Cultural Lesson** | Guardians of the Roman House-Vesta and the Lares and Penates | Development of Romance Languages | Oracles | The modern calendar, a Roman creation | Roman numerals |
| **ET ALIA** | Mottoes of the 50 United States |  | Geography |  | Map making |

|  | VI | VII | VIII | IX | X |
|---|---|---|---|---|---|
| **Story and Discussion Questions** | "Spartacus" by Plutarch | "Druids of Gaul" by Julius Caesar | "Siege of Alesia" by Julius Caesar | "Anthony and Cleopatra" by Plutarch | "Nero and Agrippina" by Tacitus |
| **History Lesson** | Great Generals of the First Century B.C. | Optimates and Populares | Conquest of Britain | Principate of Augustus | Three Emperors, Tiberius, Caligula, and Claudius |
| **Language Arts** | A. Vocabulary - "bio and mon" B. Critical Thinking C. Movie Watching | A. Vocabulary -"inter/ intra and bene /male" B. Critical Thinking | A. Vocabulary - "ine" B. Creative Writing C. Dramatic Reading | A. Vocabulary -"tele" B. Poetry Writing C. Movie Watching | A. Vocabulary - from Greek mythology B. Essay Writing C. Movie Watching |
| **Cultural Lesson** | Roman Theater | Dates of the Roman Calendar | Archaeology | Roman Weddings | Influence of Latin on the development of the English Language |
| **ET ALIA** |  | The Gracchi and Scipio Family Tree |  | Word Search Puzzle |  |

|  | **XI** | **XII** | **XIII** | **XIV** | **XV** |
|---|---|---|---|---|---|
| **Story and Discussion Questions** | "Great Fire of 64 AD" by Tacitus | "Panaceas" by Pliny the Elder | "Eruption of Vesuvius" by Pliny the Younger | "Three Eerie Tales" by Pliny the Younger and Petronius | "Pliny's Villa" by Pliny the Younger |
| **History Lesson** | The Jewish War and the Siege of Masada | Flavian Dynasty | Praetorian Gaurd | Trajan | Hadrian |
| **Language Arts** | A. Vocabulary - "grad/gress" <br> B. Creative Writing and Critical Thinking | A. Vocabulary - "phobia" <br> B. Satire | A. Vocabulary -"spec/ spic/spect" <br> B. Similes ; <br> C. Creative Writing <br> D. Etymology of Words | A. Vocabulary -"able /ible" <br> B. Dramatic Presentation <br> C. Creative Writing | A. Vocabulary - "ante and post" <br> B. Critical Thinking |
| **Cultural Lesson** | Common Latin Phrases used in English | Roman Meals | Familiar Latin Quotations | Roman Roads | Roman Baths |
| **ET ALIA** | Emperors and their Nicknames | | Science of Volcanoes | | Art - making a "Villa" |

|  | **XVI** | **XVII** | **EXTRAS** 1 illustration per chapter |
|---|---|---|---|
| **Story and Discussion Questions** | "Slavery" by Pliny the Younger | "The Dolphin" by Pliny the Younger | each story preceded by introduction <br> each story followed by discussion questions - A.B.C. - graduating in difficulty |
| **History Lesson** | Roman Citizenship | Fall of Rome | each History Lesson followed by a list of suggested topics for further study |
| **Language Arts** | A. Vocabulary - modern political words from Latin <br> B. Mini-Debate <br> C. Critical Thinking | A. Vocabulary - negative prefixes <br> B. Essay Writing <br> C. Creative Writing | all answers to all questions found in back of book <br> glossary of Latin terms |
| **Cultural Lesson** | Roman Names | Latin abbreviations used in English | each Cultural Lesson includes activities for students |
| **ET ALIA** | | Time Line Roman Numbers | each chapter has its own bibliography |

# Index

# About the Author

Hildegarde Wulfing Roberts received her B.A. in Latin from Wellesley College and her M.A. in Latin from the University of Colorado. She has taught for ten years at the secondary school level and continues to extend her classical education.